DOMESTIC ARCHITECTURE
OF THE AMERICAN COLONIES AND
OF THE EARLY REPUBLIC

DOMESTIC ARCHITECTURE
OF THE AMERICAN COLONIES AND
OF THE EARLY REPUBLIC

BY

FISKE KIMBALL

ILLUSTRATED

NEW YORK
DOVER PUBLICATIONS, INC.

Published in Canada by General Publishing Company, Ltd., 30 Lesmill Road, Don Mills, Toronto, Ontario.
Published in the United Kingdom by Constable and Company, Ltd., 10 Orange Street, London WC 2.

This Dover edition, first published in 1966, is an unabridged and corrected republication of the work originally published by Charles Scribner's Sons in 1922.
This edition is published by special arrangement with the Philadelphia Museum of Art.

Standard Book Number: 486-21743-4

Library of Congress Catalog Card Number: 66-29154

Manufactured in the United States of America
Dover Publications, Inc.
180 Varick Street
New York, N. Y. 10014

THIS BOOK EMBODIES THE SUBSTANCE OF A COURSE OF LECTURES DELIVERED BY PROFESSOR FISKE KIMBALL AT THE METROPOLITAN MUSEUM OF ART IN 1920, AND IS PUBLISHED UNDER THE AUSPICES OF ITS COMMITTEE ON EDUCATIONAL WORK

PREFACE

In this book, lectures delivered at the Metropolitan Museum during February and March, 1920, have been elaborated in an effort to present a comprehensive and accurate view of the evolution of the early American house.

A work with aspirations to completeness, even within a limited field, involves obligation to many. Indebtedness to published works is acknowledged individually in the notes and in the legends. My thanks are here tendered to those who have generously helped me by the gift or loan of photographs or by calling attention to special points: to William Sumner Appleton, Henry W. Belknap, Edward Biddle, Charles Knowles Bolton, George Francis Dow, William C. Endicott, C. F. Innocent, Henry W. Kent, Robert A. Lancaster, Jefferson M. Levy, George C. Mason, Jr., Lawrence Park, Pleasants Pennington, Ulrich B. Phillips, and Edward Robinson, Miss N. D. Tupper, Mrs. Austin Gallagher, Mrs. George F. Lord, Mrs. J. M. Arms Sheldon, and Mrs. Annie Leakin Sioussat—to two friends above all, Ogden Codman for his constant and disinterested assistance and for the freedom of his unrivalled collection of photographs, measured drawings, and early architectural books; Donald Millar for the use of his drawings and for many important suggestions unselfishly given.

The Boston Athenæum, the Boston Public Library, the Essex Institute, the Harvard College Library, the Historical Society of Pennsylvania, the Library of Congress, the Library Company of Philadelphia, the Maryland Historical Society, the Massachusetts Historical Society, the Massachusetts Institute of Technology, the New York Historical Society, the Pocumtuck Valley Memorial Association, and the University of Virginia, as well as Ferdinand C. Latrobe, R. Clipston Sturgis, and John Collins Warren have, now or in the past, kindly permitted the photographing of original material in their possession.

William N. Bates, Philip Alexander Bruce, W. G. Collingwood, Harold Donaldson Eberlein, Fairfax Harrison, John H. Hooper, John H. Latané, Robert M. Lawrence, Malcolm Lloyd, Jr., Moses Whitcher Mann, George Dudley Seymour, D. E. Huger Smith, William G. Stanard, Charles Stearns, Julius Herbert Tuttle,

PREFACE

Edward V. Valentine, and Walter Kendall Watkins, Miss Gertrude Ehrhardt, Mrs. Alice Waters Dow, and Mrs. Mary Owen Steinmetz, as well as the owners of many of the houses discussed, have courteously answered inquiries, often involving much trouble.

The following authors and owners of copyright have been generous enough to give permission for reproduction of illustrations not available otherwise: Miss Alice R. Huger Smith, Mrs. Clara Amory Coolidge, Messrs. H. S. Cowper, F.S.A., Norman Morrison Isham, George H. Polley, William K. Semple, Samuel H. Yonge, The American Institute of Architects, The Association for the Preservation of Virginia Antiquities, The Cumberland and Westmoreland Antiquarian Society, The Essex Institute, The Medford Historical Society, The Topsfield Historical Society, The Architectural Book Publishing Company, J. B. Lippincott Company, Preston and Rounds Company.

The staff of the Metropolitan Museum has given unfailing courtesy and help. Particularly to Miss Winifred E. Howe, who has seen the book through the press, I owe much skilled and willing assistance.

F. K.

University of Virginia,
August 24, 1922.

TABLE OF CONTENTS

ILLUSTRATIONS

ILLUSTRATIONS

ILLUSTRATIONS

ILLUSTRATIONS

xiv

ILLUSTRATIONS

XV

ILLUSTRATIONS

INTRODUCTION

For fifty years and more admiration and study of Colonial architecture have grown, stimulating each other, until to-day a vast literature and a wide-spread revival testify to the high appreciation of this phase of American art.

It is hard for us to realize that this must not always have been the case, and that, like other styles, the Colonial had to pass through its day of contumely and neglect at the hands of the generations immediately following its creators. To them, eager to substitute something more monumental or romantic, it was merely crude and old-fashioned. Jefferson was the first to voice this judgment of pre-Revolutionary structures, when, in 1784, he characterized the college buildings at William and Mary as "rude misshapen piles, which, but that they have roofs, would be taken for brick kilns," and when, writing from abroad in 1786, he says, à propos of English buildings, "Their architecture is in the most wretched style I ever saw, not meaning to except America, where it is bad, or even Virginia, where it is worse than in any other part of America, that I have seen." In an interesting sketch of the art in this country published by the North American Review in 1836, H. W. S. Cleveland speaks with great condescension of any work previous to the Greek and Gothic revivals. The first historical account of American buildings, included by Mrs. Tuthill of Philadelphia in her now almost forgotten "History of Architecture"(1848), speaks of the old New England meeting-houses as "outrageous deformities to the eye of taste," and of the houses as "wooden enormities"!

By the middle of the century, however, Colonial buildings began to attract affection and respect, though more for their halo of age and Revolutionary association than for intrinsic artistic reasons. Hawthorne's "House of the Seven Gables" of 1851 and Longfellow's "Wayside Inn" of 1863 at once marked and strengthened popular appreciation. The effort to preserve Mount Vernon, culminating in its purchase in 1859, was a significant episode. The attempt to save the Hancock house the same year, although unsuccessful, occasioned the making by John Sturgis of a set of measured drawings of it, one of the earliest instances of such record of our old buildings. By 1869 professional interest had risen sufficiently to call forth a paper by Richard Upjohn at the third annual meeting of the American Institute of Architects, on "The Colonial Architecture of New York and the New England States." At the Centennial Exposition the State buildings of Massachusetts and Connecticut were reproductions of local Colonial houses, and the Queen Anne movement, stimulated by the Centennial, had for its avowed object the reintroduction of the vernacular style of the time of Anne and the Georges. Such a revival, after constant gains in knowledge and strength, constitutes to-day perhaps the most powerful force in American domestic architecture.

Like every modern artistic revival it has demanded and has produced a great body of publications, supplying the needful material for imitation in the form of sketches, photographs, and measured drawings. For the requirements of the artist the exactness, or even the presence, of an accompanying text has been a secondary matter, and it is but natural that in most of the publications intended for professional use the standard of historical accuracy has been extremely low. For instance, photographs of the Bergen house on Long Island, which owes its exterior form chiefly to 1819, with additions as late as 1824,[1] have been several times published to illustrate the early Dutch type, and dated 1655. Attempts, with such assumptions, to fix the date of other buildings by analogy of style have inevitably resulted in still worse confusion. Even where the main course of development has been too obvious to be mistaken, the causes and the instruments of change in many cases have not been understood. None the less, works of the character described— most notable of them "The Georgian Period," published in three volumes from 1899 to 1902—have done great historical service in making accessible for study and comparison graphic reproductions of a very considerable part of our wealth of early buildings.

Simultaneously, but in most cases wholly apart from this activity in drawing and photographing, the documents relative to buildings of historic interest have been sought out by local antiquaries. Papers on a great number of these have gradually been published in local historical "Collections," providing the material for an exact knowledge of the dates and circumstances of their erection. It is but rarely that the attempt has been made to employ both instruments of study, so that internal and documentary evidences might supplement and confirm each other. Such thorough studies of individual buildings are even now few enough, and works on a larger scale in which several are combined as the material for a discussion of relationships and development are fewer still. To the pioneer examples, the "Early Rhode Island Houses" and the "Early Connecticut Houses,"

---

[1] C. A. Ditmas, "Homesteads of Kings County" (1909), pp. 31–34.

INTRODUCTION

by Norman M. Isham and Albert F. Brown, has recently been added the "Dwelling Houses of Charleston," by Miss Alice Huger Smith and her collaborators. In the volume "Thomas Jefferson, Architect" (1916), we have ourselves attempted to cover the chief houses of the Piedmont region of Virginia, and in a forthcoming work for the Essex Institute have undertaken a similar task for the later buildings of Salem.

Efforts have not been wanting, also, to write a comprehensive account of our early domestic architecture, and to outline its development. In no case, however, have these involved adequate study of the documentary evidence, nor of the special literature of individual buildings and localities. What is needed is a synthesis of the individual results so far won—a synthesis every hour of which, as Fustel de Coulanges has said, presupposes a year of analysis.

For such an account of development the necessary basis is a series of examples authentically dated by documents. In domestic architecture this requirement is hard to supply. Documentary evidence is relatively scarce in comparison with that bearing on public buildings and churches. Will and deed records, the largest group, often leave much latitude owing to long lives and long tenures. Several different houses, even, may succeed one another on the same site without any suggestion of a change appearing in such records. The constant remodelling of occupied dwellings makes it sometimes uncertain what material belongs to the period of building or to any given period of rebuilding. In spite of this, it has been possible by the aid of building contracts and accounts, inscriptions, and original designs, as well as inventories, wills, deeds, and other documents in favorable cases, to determine with sufficient and in most cases with absolute exactness the dates and original form of nearly two hundred houses between the time of settlement and 1835. These houses, listed in order in the Chronological Chart, are discussed individually in notes at the end of the book. It is on these houses exclusively that the conclusions of the present study are based, although others are cited as illustrating specific points or indicating the diffusion of types.

The work covered—limited to the colonies under English rule—extends in time from the coming of the European colonists to the triumph of romanticism in the second quarter of the nineteenth century. The terminus is selected not as marking any supposed death of traditional art, but merely as being the end of one chapter in the evolution of style. All told, we have to cover three such chapters, two falling before the Revolution, in the seventeenth and eighteenth centuries respectively, the third after the Revolution in the days of the early Republic. To guard against misunderstanding we will use the term "Colonial architecture" neither in

INTRODUCTION

the sense in which it has been stretched to apply to the whole period from 1620 to 1820, nor in the one in which it has been restricted to the time before the advent of the so-called "Georgian," about 1700, but only in its original and natural sense of architecture before the Revolution.[1] The Revolution, as we shall see, brought a far more fundamental change in American domestic architecture than is generally appreciated. A change within the Colonial period, equally significant as regards style, took place at the close of the seventeenth century.

[1] For the evolution of the nomenclature and of the division into periods see "The Study of Colonial Architecture" in the *Architectural Review*, n. s., vol. 6 (1918), pp. 29 and 37.

AMERICAN
DOMESTIC ARCHITECTURE

THE SEVENTEENTH CENTURY

PRIMITIVE SHELTERS

IN all the European settlements in North America, more primitive shelters—
the very types of which have long since been swept away—preceded dwellings of frame or of masonry, and continued for a greater or less time to
subsist beside them. It is currently supposed that this was uniquely the
result of pioneer conditions in a new world, forcing the adoption of existing
native types or the spontaneous creation of others adapted to the environment.
It has also been generally assumed, even by careful students, that the first
houses of the colonists were log houses of the general scheme of the "log cabins"
of later frontier settlements, built of logs laid horizontally and chinked with
clay.

An attentive study of the documents regarding the earliest dwellings in the
colonies and of the ordinary houses of England at the same period leads us, however, to very different conclusions. The earliest records of the English colonies
nowhere indicate the use of the construction just described, although they reveal
the employment of many other primitive modes of building. These, it appears,
represent neither invention of necessity nor borrowing from the Indians, but
transplantation and perpetuation of types current in England, still characteristic
then of the great body of minor dwellings in the country districts.

It is little realized that few of the old cottages now standing in England ante-
date the seventeenth century, and that they represent a general rise in the "culture stage" of the English yeomanry which took place at that time, bringing to
them, as of right, things which had before appertained only to the gentry, and
involving the destruction and replacement of the cruder dwellings which had been
usual hitherto.[1] In his recent and fundamental study, Innocent has shown that
the usual dwellings of agricultural laborers in England down to this period, and
in remote districts long afterward, sometimes nearly to the present day, were

[1] C. F. Innocent, "The Development of English Building Construction" (1916), esp. pp. 4, 150.

3

not of stone or brick, or even of frame, but of much more rudimentary construction—of branches, rushes, and turf, of palings and hurdles, of wattle, clay, and mud.

All these modes of building were practised by the American colonists—at first often in cases which involved a great retrogression from English standards of the time, as well as in the many which did not. Thus, although to the gentlemen who were the leaders and chroniclers, their first abodes in the new world were mean enough compared with those to which they were accustomed, to many farm servants and poor people the rude shelters meant no more than a perpetuation of conditions at home.

Figure 1. Charcoal burners' hut
South Yorkshire
Courtesy of C. F. Innocent

The simplest of the primitive dwellings of the colonists were conical huts of branches, rushes, and turf; Lieutenant-Governor Dudley, of Massachusetts Bay, speaks in 1631 of "some English wigwams which have taken fire in the roofs covered with thatch or boughs."[1] Such conical huts were employed in England as late as fifty years ago by goatherds and shepherds, as well as by agricultural laborers during harvest, and are still in wide-spread use there by charcoal burners[2] (figure 1).

A step in advance was the elongation of such a hut by the adoption of a ridge-piece supported on forked poles. This was the case in the earliest church in Jamestown, the account of which by Smith is our most specific description of the first shelters in Virginia: "In foule weather we shifted into an old rotten tent; for we had few better. . . . This was our Church, till we built a homely thing, like a barne, set upon Cratchets, covered with rafts, sedge, and earth, so was also the walls: the best part of our houses (were) of the like curiosity; but the most part farre much worse workmanship, that could neither well defend wind nor raine."[3] This corresponds almost precisely with more developed English huts, having low

[1] Letter to the Countess of Lincoln, reprinted in P. Force's *Tracts*, vol. 2 (1838), IV, p. 19. For other allusions to early English huts as "wigwams" see "Memoirs of Captain Roger Clap" in A. Young's "Chronicles . . . of Massachusetts" (1846), p. 351; J. Winthrop's "History of New England" (1825 ed.), p. 36; and two quotations from Edward Johnson, below, one, to be sure, in a different sense.

[2] Innocent, "English Building Construction," pp. 8-11, figs. 1 and 2.

[3] "Works," ed. by E. Arber (1886), p. 957.

walls of branches and earth, and the ridge-pole lashed to vertical, forked poles, with intermediate poles covered with sods[1] (figure 2). The "Cratchets" which Smith alludes to, otherwise "crotchets," were the posts with a forked top—characteristic elements of primitive house construction in England.[2]

Another very rudimentary type is mentioned by Edward Johnson, himself one of the first comers to Massachusetts Bay, who says of the New England settlers, "They burrow themselves in the Earth for their first shelter under some Hill side,

Figure 2. Bark-peeler's hut, High Furness
From *Transactions of the Cumberland and Westmoreland Antiquarian Society*, vol. 16 (1901)
Courtesy of W. G. Collingwood and H. S. Cowper

casting the Earth aloft upon Timber; they make a smoky fire against the Earth at its highest side . . . yet in these poor *Wigwames* (they sing Psalms pray, and praise their God) till they can provide them houses."[3] At the founding of Philadelphia in 1682 similar shelters "were formed by digging into the ground, near the verge of the river-front bank, about three feet in depth; thus making half their chamber underground, and the remaining half above ground was formed of sods

[1] H. S. Cowper, in *Transactions of the Cumberland and Westmoreland Antiquarian Society*, vol. 16 (1901).
[2] "English Building Construction," esp. pp. 14–16, and supplementary letter from the author.
[3] "Wonder Working Providence," 1654 (reprint of 1867), p. 83.

of earth, or earth and brush combined.   The roofs were formed of layers of limbs, or split pieces of trees overlaid with sod or bark, river rushes, etc."[1]   Although efforts to put an end to these "caves" were made in 1685, some persisted, and one was still in existence as late as 1760.

Many of the early cottages were of wattle, with or without a daubing of clay. In Plymouth Colony, Bradford and Winslow report that in 1621 a storm "caused much daubing of our houses to fall downe,"[2] and Bradford, speaking of the burning of the houses of Robert Gorges's colonists in 1623, says: "This fire . . . broke out of yᵉ chimney into yᵉ thatch . . .   And shortly after, when yᵉ vehemence of yᵉ fire was over, smoke was seen to arise within a shed yᵗ was joined to yᵉ end of yᵉ storehouse, which was wattled up with bowes, in yᵉ withered leaves whereof yᵉ fire was kindled."[3]   Since, as we shall see, framed houses were not in use at Plymouth even several years later, we must conclude that this wattle did not form the filling of a frame, but was on stakes or posts driven into the ground, as in the ordinary houses of the mediaeval period in England, which lingered in remote districts.[4]

The first buildings of timber in the colonies seem to have been of trunks or planks stood vertically, like palisades, as in the earliest timber construction in England.[5]   In 1629, when Ralph Sprague and his companions came to Charlestown, "they found there but one English palisadoed and thatched house."[6]   Of similar type would seem to have been the houses at Plymouth, seven years after its settlement, described by Isaack de Rasières as "constructed of hewn planks, with gardens also enclosed behind and at the sides with hewn planks."[7]   The phrase "*hewn* planks" excludes the possibility that the planks formed the covering of a frame, for in that case they would certainly have been sawn, like the "thick sawn plank" which formed the roof of the meeting-house.   The use of an identical phrase in referring to the garden enclosures suggests that the planks were set vertically, and indeed Bradford and Winslow speak of the allotments in December, 1620, "for houses and gardens to impale them round."[8]   At a later day the same methods were employed by the first British settlers in East Jersey. Gawen Lawrie writes in 1684: "The poor sort set up a house of two or three

[1] J. F. Watson, "Annals of Philadelphia" (1830), pp. 65, 159–160.
[2] "Relation or Iournall" (1622), reprinted by H. M. Dexter (1865), p. 79.
[3] "Of Plimoth Plantation" (1898 ed.), pp. 182–183.
[4] Innocent, "English Building Construction," pp. 126–129.
[5] Innocent, "English Building Construction," pp. 109–111, 128–129.
[6] "Early Records of Charlestown," in Young, "Chronicles of Massachusetts," p. 374.
[7] Translation in *Collections of the New York Historical Society*, 2d ser., vol. 2 (1849), pp. 351–352.   Dutch text in *Nederlandsch Archief voor Kerkgeschiedenis*, n. s., vol. 15 (1919), p. 274.
[8] Young, "Chronicles of the Pilgrim Fathers" (1841), p. 170.

rooms themselves, after this manner; the walls are of cloven timber about eight or ten inches broad, like planks set one end to the ground, and the other nailed to the raising, which they plaster within."[1]

The suggestion that the earliest English settlers probably lived in log houses of the familiar type was first made by Alexander Young in 1841, as an inference from the mention of daubing in Plymouth.[2] John Gorham Palfrey in 1860 drew a similar inference from the same passage,[3] although he continued in later writings to qualify the belief as probable but not certain.[4] Subsequent writers, even the very best, have been less cautious and have generally accepted the view without qualification.[5] So far as the argument from "daubing" is concerned, the word nowhere appears in connection with log houses until the nineteenth century; its true bearing in the colonies has already been discussed. None of the earliest records of the English colonies suggests a structure of horizontal logs. This is the more significant since it seems that this form of construction was totally unknown in England, and thus would certainly have called forth a word of description. Innocent states: "There is no satisfactory evidence that this form of building was ever in use in England in any of its forms";[6] and the "New English Dictionary" reveals no reference to it there. It is not until 1669 and 1680 that allusions to log houses in the colonies appear.[7] Only in Georgia, founded 1733, were log houses occasionally used from the start as a superior form of construction,[8] and even here the first dwellings were "Clap-board Huts," not framed.[9]

A derivation of the log house from the Indians has been tempting to those who have wished to emphasize the mastering of the colonist's inherited traditions by the wilderness: "It puts him in the log cabin of the Cherokee and Iroquois and runs an Indian palisade around him."[10] Unfortunately for this belief, none of the tribes with whom the early settlers came in contact lived in log houses.

[1] S. Smith, "History of New-Jersey" (1765), p. 180.

[2] Young, "Chronicles of the Pilgrim Fathers," p. 179, note.

[3] "History of New England," vol. 2, p. 62.

[4] "Compendious History of New England," 2d ed. (1872), vol. 1, p. 296.

[5] W. B. Weeden, "Economic and Social History of New England" (1890), vol. 1, pp. 213–214; Isham and Brown, "Early Rhode Island Houses" (1895), p. 16; P. A. Bruce, "Economic History of Virginia" (1896), vol. 2, p. 147; T. F. Waters, "The Early Homes of the Puritans," *Essex Institute Historical Collections*, vol. 32 (1897), p. 49; S. H. Yonge, "James Towne" (1907), pp. 36 ff.

[6] "English Building Construction," pp. 109–111.

[7] *Archives of Maryland*, vol. 2 (1884), p. 224; *Colonial Records of North Carolina*, vol. 1 (1886), p. 300.

[8] "True and Historical Narrative of Georgia" (1741), in Force, *Tracts*, vol. 1 (1836), IV, p. 70; "Account Shewing the Progress . . . of Georgia" (1741), *ib.*, V, p. 20.

[9] "Brief Account of . . . Georgia" (1733), *ib.*, II, p. 10; "State of the Province of Georgia" (1740), *ib.*, III, pp. 5, 8, 17.

[10] F. J. Turner, "The Significance of the Frontier in American History," *Annual Report of the American Historical Association* (1893), p. 201.

The Indian huts described in contemporary narratives, including the long-house of the Iroquois, are all of radically different construction. Even in the case of the Creek, who sometimes did employ the log house in the later eighteenth century, all evidence agrees that it was unknown to them until after the founding of Georgia.[1] It was one thing among many others adopted by this exceptionally gifted tribe from the colonists.

A more reasonable supposition is that the log house was brought to America by the people in whose native land at that time it was the customary form of dwelling—the Swedes and Finns who settled on the Delaware in 1638 and the years following. Peter Kalm, writing in 1749 and quoting a settler ninety-one years old, describes the first houses as of round logs chinked with clay,[2] and contemporary accounts describe the fort built at New Gothenburg in 1643 as "made of hemlock beams, laid one upon the other."[3] From the very beginnings of New Sweden there was trade with both Virginia and New England, and the interchange of ideas which resulted, with time, in the building of an "English house" at Fort Elfsborg,[4] seems ultimately to have taught the English colonists a method of construction so obviously suited to pioneer conditions in the new, heavily forested continent.

How late the primitive types of English origin persisted cannot be exactly determined, but even in the regions first settled it was much later than is generally recognized. In Virginia they must still have been characteristic of the isolated plantations in 1623, for George Sandys wrote of possible advantages of the massacre in the previous year, "in drawing ourselves into a narrower circuite, whereby the people might have been better governed . . . framed houses erected," and so on.[5] Sir John Harvey speaks as if they were still not uncommon even in 1639.[6] In relation to the remoter agricultural districts of the British Isles, as we have seen, however, the elimination of crude shelters was rapid. Johnson could write of Massachusetts Bay by 1654: "The Lord hath been pleased to turn all the wigwams, huts, and hovels the English dwelt in at their first coming into orderly, fair and well built houses."[7] It must not be forgotten

---

[1] Early descriptions quoted in C. C. Jones, "History of Georgia," vol. 1 (1883), pp. 7–8, 41. Benjamin Hawkins's detailed "Sketch of the Creek Country in the Years 1798 and 1799," *Collections of the Georgia Historical Society*, vol. 3 (1848), speaks of "a dwelling house and kitchen built of logs" as exceptional (p. 30), and describes the typical buildings as having vertical posts covered with slabs and clayed (p. 69).

[2] "Resa" (1753), vol. 3, p. 70; English translation (1771), vol. 2, p. 121.

[3] A. Johnson, "The Swedish Settlements on the Delaware" (1911), vol. 1, p. 306.

[4] *Ib.*, p. 347.

[5] Quoted in Neill's "Virginia Vetusta" (1885), p. 124.

[6] Letter of January 18, 1639, *British State Papers, Colonial*, vol. 10, no. 5.

[7] "Wonder Working Providence" (reprint of 1867), p. 174.

that economic conditions in the colonies, with their free grant of wooded land, were far more favorable than in England at that time to the common man, and that their equalizing tendency levelled up as well as down.

FRAME HOUSES

Long before the last primitive shelters disappeared in the colonies many better houses had been built. The large majority of them were framed structures of wood. With the natural focussing of attention on the more pretentious buildings abroad, it has been little realized that this was but in accordance with the ordinary character of the more prosperous yeomen's houses in England up to this time. S. O. Addy, a pioneer student of humbler English dwellings, writes: "In historic times the houses of the English peasantry were mostly built of wood, stone being only used where wood could not be obtained. . . . Houses were built of wood even in places where stone was most abundant, and this kind of building continued to the close of the 16th century."[1] Innocent fixes the seventeenth century, with the drain on the oak forests made by the creation of the navy, and with the profound impression made by the Great Fire in 1666, as the time during which other materials tended to supplant wood.[2] The use of wood by the colonists was thus not the adoption of an inferior material due to local conditions, but the perpetuation of English custom where the need for abandoning it was lacking. For the poorer men, indeed, it was even a step forward.

The first framed houses in the English colonies were erected following the arrival in Virginia in August, 1611, of Sir Thomas Dale and his company. Ralph Hamor, secretary of state from 1611 to 1614, wrote of Jamestown on his return to England: "The Towne itself by the care and Providence of Sir Thomas Gates is reduced into a hansome forme, and hath in it two fair rowes of houses all of Framed timber (two stories, and an upper garret, or corne loft, high)," and of the newly founded town of Henrico: "There is in this town three streets of well framed houses" near which "hath Mr. Whitacres . . . a fair framed parsonage house . . . called Rock Hall."[3] None the less, there remained but five or six houses at Jamestown in 1617, on the arrival of Deputy-Governor Argall, who wrote: "We were constrained every yeare to build and repaire our old Cottages,

[1] "The Evolution of the English House" (1898), pp. 107–108; Innocent, "English Building Construction," p. 119.
[2] *Ib.*, pp. 76, 123, 150. *Cf.* also J. E. Thorold Rogers, "Agriculture and Prices in England," vol. 5 (1887), p. 529.
[3] "True discourse of the Present Estate of Virginia" (1615), quoted in A. Brown, "First Republic in America" (1897), pp. 208–209, 210.

which were alwaies decaying."[1]   Decay in the damp climate, and neglect accompanying the abandonment of old frame cottages to use as negro quarters, have continued to work a havoc unequalled in New England, for, although further special study may bring discoveries, we know of no wooden house in Virginia for which a date within the seventeenth century is established or even claimed.   For those mentioned in court records of the last quarter of the century, the dimensions range from twenty to forty feet in length by fifteen to twenty in breadth, the longer houses having chimneys at either end.[2]   The number of rooms ranged from two or three to as many as twelve or thirteen.   Three rooms on each of two floors were not uncommon, the position of the chimneys making possible an "inner room," a "little room opposite the stairs," or "porch chamber."[3]

In the New England colonies framed houses were erected very much sooner after their settlement than was the case in Virginia.   The salt-maker sent to the Plymouth colonists in 1624, regarded as very extravagant in his projects, "caused them to send carpenters to rear a great frame for a large house."[4]   Higginson speaks of finding in Salem in 1629 "about half a score houses and a fayre house newly built for the Governor."[5]   In Charlestown Thomas Graves, the engineer of the Massachusetts Bay Company, "built the great house this year for such of the company as are shortly to come over, which afterwards became the meeting house."[6]   From the special terms by which they are distinguished it seems reasonable to suppose that the "fayre house" and the "great house" were framed buildings, and almost equally certain that they were unique in this.[7]   Winthrop almost immediately on his arrival in 1630 "ordered his house to be cut and framed" in Charlestown,[8] but shortly removed to Boston, "whither also the frame of the Governor's house . . . was also carried."[9]   Another house begun by Winthrop at Cambridge was of similar character, for Dudley complained in August, 1632, "that the governour had removed the frame of his house, which he had set up at Newtown."[10]   The house built for Winthrop in 1643, which he described as "more convenient,"[11] was, according to his inventory, 1649, of two

[1] Quoted by John Smith, "Works," pp. 535–536.
[2] Bruce, "Economic History of Virginia," vol. 2, pp. 151–153.   [3] *Ib.*, pp. 153–157.
[4] William Bradford, "Of Plimoth Plantation" (1898), p. 203.
[5] Francis Higginson, "New England's Plantation" (1630), reprinted in Young's "Chronicles of Massachusetts," p. 258.
[6] Early Records of Charlestown in Young's "Chronicles of Massachusetts," pp. 375–376 and note, 378.
[7] Roger Clap in May, 1630, found in Charlestown, "Some wigwams and one house," *ib.*, p. 349.   The "great house" is believed to have stood until 1775.   *Ib.*, p. 375, note.
[8] Town Records quoted from Young's "Chronicles of Massachusetts," p. 379.
[9] *Ib.*, p. 381.   [10] Winthrop, "History of New England" (1825 ed.), vol. 1, p. 32.
[11] *Proceedings of the Massachusetts Historical Society*, 2d ser., vol. 11 (1897), p. 186.

stories and a half, two rooms on a floor besides the kitchen, entry, and porch chamber over it.[1]

Although we are ignorant of the precise form of these first governors' houses, we are so fortunate as to have in 1638 most detailed prescriptions for the house of another official, Deputy-Governor Samuel Symonds, at Ipswich, in a letter to John Winthrop the younger. If we read this without merely fitting it to our preconceptions, we will find every sentence full of illumination on unfamiliar points:

From a photograph by The Halliday Historic Photograph Co.

Figure 3. "Scotch House" (Boardman house), Saugus, Massachusetts. 1651

"Concerning the frame of the house . . . I am indiferent whether it be 30 foote or 35 foote longe; 16 or 18 foote broade. I would have wood chimnyes at each end, the frames of the chimnyes to be stronger than ordinary, to beare good heavy load of clay for security against fire. You may let the chimnyes by all the breadth of the howse if you thinke good; the 2 lower dores to be in the middle of the howse, one opposite the other. Be sure that all the dorewaies in every place be soe high that any man may goe vpright vnder. The staiers I think had best be placed close by the dore. It makes noe great matter though there be noe particion vpon the first flore; if there be, make one biger then the other. For windowes let them not be over large in any roome, & as few as conveniently may be; let all have current shutting draw-windowes, haveing respect both to

[1] A. M. Earle, "Margaret Winthrop" (1903), pp. 174–180.

present & future vse.   I thinke to make it a girt howse will make it more chargeable than neede; however the side bearers for the second story, being to be loaden with corne &c. must not be pinned on, but rather eyther lett in to the studds or borne vp with false studds, & soe tenented in at the ends.   I leave it to you & the carpenters.   In this story over the first, I would have a particion, whether in the middest or over the particion vnder, I leave it.   In the garrett noe particion, but let there be one or two lucome windowes, if two, both on one side.   I desire to have the sparrs reach downe pretty deep at the eves to preserve the walls the better from the wether, I would have it sellered all over and soe the frame of the howse accordengly from the bottom.   I would have the howse stronge in timber, though plaine & well brased.   I would have it covered with very good oake-hart inch board, *for the present*, to be tacked on onely for the present, as you tould me.   Let the frame begin from the bottom of the cellar & soe in the ordinary way vpright, for I can hereafter (to save the timber within grounde) run vp a thin brick worke without.   I think it best to have the walls without to be all clapboarded besides the clay walls. . ."[1]

The house, it will be observed, was one room deep but was two stories and a half in height besides a cellar, which was framed like the rest instead of having masonry walls.   It is interesting to note that it had chimneys at both ends, and thus furnishes an early example of a type usual in Virginia, but not reputed to have been common in New England until a later time.   We may surmise that the reason lay in the use of the wooden chimneys, and that the practice continued in New England during their persistence.

The New Haven Colony was noted for the mansions erected by wealthy men among the first settlers.[2]   William Hubbard wrote before 1682: "They laid out too much of their stocks and estates in building of fine and stately houses, wherein they at first outdid the rest of the country."[3]   The fragmentary and sometimes inconsistent data concerning these houses, however, do not permit reliable conclusions regarding their form.[4]   Nothing in the inventories requires more than lower additions at the ends and rear of the simple two-story type.

All these, of course, were the houses of people of quality.   Before 1640, however, framed houses began to be built in Massachusetts more generally.   Bradford records that in 1639 "Thomas Starr . . . hath sould unto Andrew Hellot one frame of a house, with a chimney, to be set up and thacked in Yarmouth."   The first description we have of a framed house for an artisan is that of one to be

---

[1] *Collections of the Massachusetts Historical Society*, 4th ser., vol. 7 (1865), pp. 118–120.

[2] Governor Theophilus Eaton, Reverend John Davenport, Isaac Allerton, and Thomas Gregson.   Stiles, "History of . . . the Judges of Charles I" (1794), p. 64, cited and discussed by Isham and Brown, "Connecticut Houses," pp. 110–111.

[3] "History of New England," *Collections of the Mass. Hist. Soc.*, 2d ser., vol. 6 (1815), p. 334.

[4] See the individual discussion of the Eaton house below.

built by John Davys, joiner, for William Rix, a weaver, in 1640—for which Thomas Lechford preserved the contract in his "Note Book":

"One framed house 16 foot long & 14 foote wyde, wth a chamber floare finisht, summer & ioysts, a cellar floare wth ioysts finisht, the roofe and walles Clapboarded on the outsyde, the Chimney framed without dawbing to be done with hewen timber."[1]   In other words this was a story-and-a-half house with a single

Figure 4.   Whipple house, Ipswich, Massachusetts.   Western part before 1669, eastern part before 1682
Courtesy of the White Pine Bureau

room in each story.   The contract price was £21.   Such were the great majority of the oldest existing houses of Providence Plantation, as well as some of those of Newport and Narragansett.[2]   Such too were the initial portions of some still standing in Massachusetts, for instance the John Balch house in Beverly.[3]   In Connecticut, where few examples are preserved—even in Hartford where there are

[1] *Transactions of the American Antiquarian Society*, vol. 7 (1885), p. 302.
[2] Isham and Brown, "Rhode Island Houses," *passim*.
[3] *Cf.* the drawing by Isham in *Bulletin of the Society for the Preservation of New England Antiquities*, no. 15 (1916), p. 10.

none—Norman Isham recognizes the type as one which appeared as an inferior or temporary dwelling. The Ipswich records show that houses of this type and size were commonly erected in Massachusetts in 1665 and 1670.[1]

By 1650 better houses were generally built for ministers and the wealthier members of the community. Witness the parsonage at Beverly, Massachusetts, contracted for by John Norman, March 23, 1656-7, which was thirty-eight feet by seventeen, and eleven feet stud, having three fireplaces;[2] or the minister's house at New London, 1666, thirty-six feet long and twenty-five broad, "thirteen foote stud between yᵉ joints."[3] The latter was apparently of two full stories, and the same may perhaps be inferred of the house of John Whittingham of Ipswich (died 1648), from the presence of hangings in the chamber over the parlor.[4]

For the frame houses of the second half of the century in New England, however, we have no longer merely the evidence of written documents; we reach authentically dated buildings which are still preserved—much modified, rebuilt, and restored though they are—or which have been perpetuated by drawings, engravings, or early photographs. We thus secure an idea not only of accommodations and materials, but henceforth also of architectural style. From them it appears that the Colonial style of the seventeenth century is still essentially mediaeval: its significant element is structure; form and details continue traditions of the Middle Ages.

If we demand rigorously established dating as a foundation for the study of development in others, we are limited as yet to some ten houses, all in Essex County, Massachusetts, where preservation of Colonial buildings, as well as documentary research in regard to them, has been carried further than elsewhere:[5]

1651   "Scotch House" (Boardman house), Saugus (figure 3)

Between 1651 and 1660   Eastern part of Pickering house, Salem

Before 1669   Western part of Whipple house, Ipswich (figure 4)

Between 1661 and 1671   Narbonne house, Salem

About 1671   Western part of Pickering house, Salem

[1] Waters, "Homes of the Puritans," *Historical Collections of the Essex Institute*, vol. 33 (1897), pp. 50–51.
[2] Quoted in full, *ib.*, pp. 52–53.   [3] Isham and Brown, "Connecticut Houses," pp. 159–160.
[4] Waters, *op. cit.*, pp. 49, 62.
[5] The documentary evidence accepted by Isham and Brown as establishing the dates of those seventeenth-century Rhode Island and Connecticut houses on which their dating of others is based cannot be regarded as really conclusive. Thus, in the fundamental case of the "John Clark house" in Farmington, the deed of 1657 (p. 19), on the basis of which they regard it as having been "the oldest house in the colony," does not establish more than that there was a dwelling-house on the lot in that year, and the belief that the house which stood in 1880 was identical with this and was not a successor, is based on details merely postulated as early. It is to be noted that Julius Gay, who unearthed the documents, himself dates the house 1700! "Farmington" (1906), p. 7.

Figure 5. Capen house, Topsfield, Massachusetts. 1683

Finished 1675   Jonathan Corwin ("Witch") house, Salem

Before 1680   Main body of Turner house ("House of the Seven Gables"), Salem

Before 1682   Eastern part of Whipple house, Ipswich

1683   Capen house, Topsfield (figures 5, 8)

Between 1682 and 1693   Benjamin Hooper house ("Old Bakery"), Salem

After 1684   John Ward house, Salem (figure 6)

Before 1692   South wing of Turner house ("House of the Seven Gables"), Salem

After 1695   Benaiah Titcomb house, Newburyport

These are supplemented, so far as the exterior aspect is concerned, by old views of two dated houses in Boston and four others in Salem now long destroyed.

1670   Henry Bridgham house ("Julien's"), Boston (figure 7)

Between 1673 and 1682   Deliverance Parkman house, Salem

After 1679   Daniel Epes house, Salem

1680   "Old Feather Store," Boston

Between 1683 and 1692   Philip English house, Salem

After 1698   Hunt house, Salem

All these were originally simple rectangular houses of one or two rooms in plan: a hall, serving also as kitchen, and, if possible, also a "parlour," containing one of the beds.   Each house had a steep gable roof, a single great chimney (central in the houses of two rooms), and stairs winding up in front of this in a space which constituted an interior entrance "porch."   The main frame was of heavy timbers with elaborate jointing.   The interiors were of the simplest, deriving their character from the direct revelation of the functional elements, especially from the huge fireplace spanned by a great beam, and from the framing of the ceiling.

Without repeating descriptions of the individual houses, we may seek to determine the course of evolution in different elements, not merely enumerating the variations of a given motive, but noting the duration of its use and seeing whether there were any transformations with the nature of a development.

In the matter of accommodations, as should really be expected, differences were less a matter of chronological sequence than of means.   Thus, the initial portions of the Pickering, Whipple, Narbonne, Hooper, and Ward houses, ranging in date from about 1651 to after 1684, were of a single room in each of two full stories; the "Scotch House," the Corwin and Capen houses, 1651 to 1683, were of two rooms in a story. Many houses originally of one-room plan were subsequently lengthened beyond the chimney: the Pickering house about 1671, the Whipple house before 1682, the Hooper house not until well into the eighteenth century. Whether the second room belonged to the original construction or not, functional considerations took precedence over symmetry in determining the relative size of

Figure 6.   John Ward house, Salem.   After 1684
Courtesy of the Essex Institute

the two.   Symonds wrote in 1638, "make one biger than the other."   In the Turner, Whipple, Capen, Ward, and Hunt houses, at least, this is the case.   Such mediaeval tolerance of asymmetry persisted long after the abandonment of mediaeval details.

Even with two rooms to a floor the houses were so small that it was natural they should be enlarged in the course of time.   A characteristic form of addition was the lean-to at the rear, roofed by an extension of the rear slope of the main roof.   Some of these additions were made very early.   Thomas Lechford records a document stating that one Brackenbury, in Boston, "shall have . . . liberty to make a leanto unto the end of the parlor."[1]   Before the close of the century houses were built with a lean-to from the start.   The agreement of the town of Deerfield, Massachusetts, in calling John Williams as its minister in 1686, states: "That they will build him a hous: 42 foot long, 20 foot wide, with a lento of the back side of the house."[2]   The lean-to was ordinarily of only one full story, but in the Pickering and Whipple houses as they now stand it is of two stories.   The raising of the rear roof of the Pickering house to this height did not occur until 1751.[3]   Because of the central chimney the rear rooms of such houses could ordinarily be reached only by traversing those in front—economical considerations taking precedence over those of privacy.

Another accessory not uncommon was a projecting porch with a "porch chamber" over it, and a gable to the front.   A "porch of eight foote square" was to form part of the minister's house at Cape Ann in 1657.[4]   A porch chamber is mentioned in Governor Winthrop's inventory of 1649, as we have seen, and it appears in other inventories such as that of James Richards in Hartford, 1680.[5]   Mention of a porch chamber, to be sure, may perhaps not always imply that the porch projected, for one occurs in the inventory of Richard Smith, Jr., of Narragansett in 1692, yet the plan of his house shows only the interior porch or entry.[6]   The form and appearance of the projecting porches we learn from the old views of the Bridgham, Parkman, and Corwin houses, all from the 'seventies, and from the Turner house—some with the second story of the porch overhanging in a way soon to be discussed.

Many of these houses had one or more "lucome windows," already mentioned by Symonds.   The word, with many variants, is derived from the French *lucarne*, dormer; but gabled dormers of the Middle Ages and the Renaissance rose over the face of the wall below, and thus the term was applied to a gable also.[7]   In the form of subsidiary gables on the main mass, at right angles to the principal ridge, these occurred throughout the half century covered in the "Scotch House," the Pickering, Bridgham, Corwin, Parkman, Epes, Turner, Hooper, English, Ward, and Hunt houses, and the "Old Feather Store."   They were lacking, however, in houses precisely contemporary with these: the Capen house and others, so that

[1] "Note Book" (1885), p. 54.
[2] G. Sheldon, "History of Deerfield," vol. 1 (1895), p. 197.
[3] See the individual discussion of this house, *infra*.
[4] Waters, "Homes of the Puritans," *Historical Collections of the Essex Institute*, vol. 33 (1897), p. 53.
[5] Isham and Brown, "Connecticut Houses," p. 52, note, quoting *Hartford Probate Records*, vol. 4.
[6] *Ib.*, "Rhode Island Houses," p. 63 and plate 52.
[7] E. Moore, "Suffolk Words" (1823), p. 212, quoted in "New English Dictionary."

we are not in a position to say whether use at this time represented a decrease or an increase in proportion relative to the earlier decades of the colony. In general they corresponded in number to the number of rooms on a floor—a single one in the houses with end chimney, two in houses with central chimney, but, if we may trust old views,[1] in certain instances there were three: the Corwin house and the undated Governor Bradstreet house.

A feature which has been thought to undergo a definite evolution with time, and thus incidentally to furnish an indication of date, is the projection of the second story over the first, common also in England, which appears in many

Figure 7. The Bridgham house ("Julien's"), Boston
From C. Shaw: *Description of Boston* (1817)

houses in the colonies, more usually as a framed overhang. It was not uncommon for the lower ends of the second-story posts to be carved into pendants or drops. The minister's house at Cape Ann in 1657 was to be "Jotted ouer one foote ech way."[2] Another reference, which reveals the terms then used, occurs in Boston records for 1663:

"Upon complaint of sundry inhabitants, of hurt done and further danger by the lownes of Jetties ouer the towne land it is therefore ordered that noe Jettie nor pendill yt shall be erected but shall be full 8 foot in height from the ground. . . ."[3]

It is not to be assumed from this protest that jetties were then first coming into use—a sufficient reason for it would be the closer upbuilding of the town.

Among the houses we have been studying, the Narbonne house, like the west-

---

[1] See note, p. 29.
[2] Waters, "Homes of the Puritans," *Historical Collections of the Essex Institute*, vol. 33 (1897), p. 53.
[3] "Boston Town Records, 1660–1701" (1881), p. 17.

ern end of the Whipple house, has no overhang. The "Scotch House," the Corwin, Hooper, and Capen houses, covering the years from 1651 to 1683, had each such a framed overhang along the front only. The Ward house and the Hunt house have one on one end also. The Bridgham house seems to have had one, and the Epes house, the Old Feather Store, and the Philip English house likewise had an overhang on one end if not on both, so that the end overhang was used at

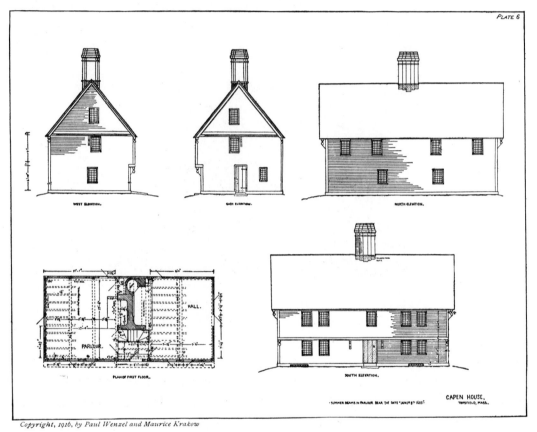

Figure 8. Capen house, Topsfield, Massachusetts. Plan and elevations
From Donald Millar: *Measured Drawings of Some Colonial and Georgian Houses*

least from 1670 to 1698. The single dated instance of a hewn overhang, on the east end of the Whipple house, Ipswich (figure 4), between 1669 and 1682, is also contemporary with these. None of the original drops or pendills preserved occurs in the accurately dated examples.

Messrs. Isham and Brown, believing in a progressive abandonment of imported features, supposed with very inadequate documentary evidence that houses with end overhangs in the Connecticut Colony were older than those with overhangs on the front only, and that the framed overhang as a whole disappeared after

1675.[1] Joseph Everett Chandler, on the other hand, considers that the overhangs "were not usually of the earliest date, but came along after the buildings with a straight front had been constructed for some time."[2] Our group of Massachusetts houses indicates that there at least the framed overhang appeared in houses as early as any now remaining, that it persisted until the end of the century, and that the end overhang is no sign of priority. The insecure dating of houses elsewhere makes it possible that these conclusions apply more widely, and that the course of development in the Connecticut Colony has been misconceived.

Gable-ends framed to overhang the second story appear in the Bridgham house, the Feather Store, the Capen house—thus 1670 to 1684; and the east gable of the Whipple house, from the same period, has a hewn overhang. In the Capen house an original sawn bracket remains in the centre of the gable, and similar ones appear in the views of the Feather Store, likewise from the 'eighties.

The frame itself, in its methods of jointing and of treatment by bracketing and chamfering, offers rich material for the study of development. The great diversity existing in examples preserved in Rhode Island and Connecticut has been admirably shown by Messrs. Isham and Brown. Unfortunately, the dates of the houses there cannot be well enough established to demonstrate the evolution which governs this variety. The chamfers in dated houses elsewhere do not indicate that the variations of this feature represent successive stages of evolution. For instance, there is a marked difference between those in the hall and in the parlor of the Capen house, built all at once. Those of the notable Tufts house, of brick, 1677 to 1680, are much more elaborate than those of the Ward house, after 1684. Difference of means would seem to have had an important influence in the matter.

The filling and covering of the frame present interesting problems. In England the most primitive form of filling, still common in many districts, was of wattle daubed on one side or both with clay, usually mixed with hay or straw, and finished with a thin coat of lime plaster for greater resistance to rain.[3] In work of superior quality laths were often used instead of wattle, still usually coated with clay, which was regarded in England as having its own advantages.[4] Sometimes the clay was used alone as a filling.[5] In "cat and daub" the cats were pieces of "straw and clay worked together into pretty large rolls and laid between the wooden posts."[6] Closely allied to this was the use of sun-dried bricks, lumps of clay pressed in moulds of any convenient size, the predecessors of burnt brick for

---

[1] "Connecticut Houses," pp. 32, 233.   [2] "The Colonial House" (1916), p. 120.
[3] Innocent, "English Building Construction," pp. 126–134, 142.
[4] *Ib.*, pp. 138–142.   [5] *Ib.*, p. 133.
[6] "New English Dictionary," article *Cat-and-Clay*.

this purpose.[1] Different districts, as is well known, show characteristic preferences; it is less well known that great variety may be found in a single English district. Thus, in villages near Cambridge showing characteristics of East Anglia, Innocent found, besides walls of chalk and burnt brick, others of sun-dried brick, of stud-work with lath and plaster, of wattle work, and of horizontal weather-boarding.[2]

A similar variety in wall fillings, among which all the methods enumerated occur, is found in early New England. Donald Millar informs us that a section of daubed wattle is still in place in the Fairbanks house in Dedham.[3] Clay and hay alone as a filling formerly persisted in part of the back wall of the Corwin house in Salem, finished 1675.[4] The filling of the walls of the old Stoughton house at Windsor, destroyed in 1809, was described in 1802 as "built of mud and stones built in on the outside between the joists or timbers."[5] When bricks were used, many of them, as Mr. Isham remarked,[6] were little better than sun-dried. Such bricks appear in what was once an outside wall of the Ward house, Salem, after 1684 (figure 9).

Figure 9. Brick filling from the Ward house, Salem

Courtesy of the Essex Institute

In all these cases the filling of the frame was found covered on the exterior with some form of wooden boarding. That such a covering was commonly used within a few years of the settlement cannot be doubted. Symonds's house in 1638 was, as we have seen, to be "covered with very good oak-hart inch board," and was "to have the walls without to be all clapboarded beside the clay walls." The contract for the building of the church at Salem in 1639 called for it "to be covered with 1½ plank and with board upon that to meet close," as well as "to be sufficientlie finished with

[1] "English Building Construction," p. 154.   [2] *Ib.*, p. 156.
[3] For comparison we may cite the description of the early houses at Germantown, Pennsylvania, by J. F. Watson, "Annals of Philadelphia," 2d ed. (1844), vol. 2, p. 19: "Some old houses seem to be made with log frames and the interstices filled with wattles, river rushes, and clay intermixed."
[4] Isham and Brown, "Connecticut Houses," p. 198, where the house is spoken of as the Roger Williams house.
[5] *Ib.*, p. 248, quoting Oliver Ellsworth, Jr., from Stiles, "Ancient Windsor," vol. 1, p. 142.
[6] *Ib.*, p. 181.

daubings."[1] Jasper Dankers wrote in 1679, "Houses in Boston are made of thin small cedar shingles, nailed against frames and then filled with brick and other stuff."[2] No instance is definitely known of a framed building erected by the English colonists in which the filling of the frame was exposed on the exterior as "half timber." Nevertheless, as Messrs. Isham and Brown have recognized, we do not need to assume that every house was clapboarded (or boarded) here during the first four or five years. A Moravian schoolhouse of exposed half-

From a photograph by H. Winslow Fegley

Figure 10. Moravian schoolhouse, Oley Township, Pennsylvania. 1743 to 1745

timber, built 1743 to 1745,[3] still stands in Oley Township, Berks County, Pennsylvania (figure 10), and other buildings of the Pennsylvania Germans show the same construction.[4] One should not overlook that Symonds told Winthrop the inch board were "to be tacked on only for the present *as you tould me*," which might suggest that this covering was an addition recommended by experience during the first eight years of the colony. A reason for such an addition, besides

[1] J. B. Felt, "Annals of Salem" (1827), p. 119.
[2] *Collections of the Long Island Historical Society*, vol. 1 (1867), p. 394.
[3] Daniel Miller, "The Early Moravian Settlements in Berks County," in *Transactions of the Historical Society of Berks County*, vol. 2 (1910), p. 318.
[4] A. L. Kocher, "Early Architecture of Pennsylvania," *Architectural Record*, vol. 49 (1921), pp. 31–47.

the greater severity of American climate, may well have lain in the great difficulty, which we shall note in Massachusetts and in the Connecticut Colony, of
securing lime for the finishing coat of the filling. On the other hand, the suggestion of Isham and Brown that "the idea . . . of covering the filling of the timber
frame with overlapping boards may not have been a new thing to our ancestors"
receives support from recent study of English building. Whereas Ralph Nevill
doubted whether the covering of frames by tiles and apparently also by weather-
boards, as in Kent, was ever prior to 1730,[1] Innocent points out very early examples of the use of weather-boards, in some cases even without any filling.[2]

Instead of weather-boards or clapboards, plaster worked in relief was later
occasionally used as a covering for frame and filling, as was the case at the same
time in some parts of England, especially in East Anglia.[3] Speaking in 1795 of
the various modes of building at successive periods in Boston, Jeremy Belknap
says: "The houses and warehouses near the town dock, which were rebuilt after
the great fire of 1679, were either constructed of brick, or plastered on the outside
with a strong cement, intermixed with gravel and glass and slated on the top.
Several of these plastered houses are yet remaining in Ann-street, in their original
form; others have been altered and repaired."[4] One of these houses in Ann Street
was the "Old Feather Store," of which we may quote from the earliest and fullest
description. "The outside is covered with plastering or what is commonly called
rough-cast. But instead of pebbles . . . broken glass was used. The glass appears like that of common junk bottles, broken into pieces of about half an inch
in diameter, the sharp corners of which penetrate the cement in such a manner,
that this great lapse of years has made no perceptible effect upon them. The
figures 1680 were impressed into the rough-cast to show the year of its erection,
and are now perfectly legible. The surface was also variegated with ornamental
squares, diamonds and flower-de-luce."[5] A large section of the plaster gable from
the house of Colonel William Browne in Salem, after 1664,[6] showing a similar ornament (figure 11), is preserved at the Essex Institute, and is likewise rough-cast,
with broken glass of a brownish green.

Not only in the first rude shelters, but in the frame houses of many years fol-

---

[1] "Old Cottage and Domestic Architecture in South West Surrey" (2d ed., 1889), pp. 21–22.
[2] "English Building Construction," pp. 116–118. He writes us, coupling with his opinion that of J. Ken-
worthy: "We feel sure that such boarding was in use here long before the settlement of America."
[3] B. Oliver, "Old Houses and Village Buildings in East Anglia" (1912), pp. 56, 58, cites houses dated 1685
and 1692.
[4] *Collections of the Massachusetts Historical Society*, 1st ser., vol. 4, pp. 189–190.
[5] C. H. Snow, "History of Boston" (2d ed., 1828), p. 167.
[6] Browne acquired the lot August 3, 1664, *Essex Antiquarian*, vol. 8 (1904), p. 114.

lowing, the roofs were frequently covered with thatch. References to thatch abound in Winthrop's journal and other early records. Mr. Isham cites a court order in New Haven in 1640 regulating the wages of "a skilfull thatcher, working diligently," and a mention of thatch by Increase Mather in Northampton in 1664.[1] A house with a roof of thatch was built in Ipswich, Massachusetts, in 1657,[2] and thatching tools are mentioned at Lancaster in an inventory of 1662.[3] In 1671 the records speak of the burning of a thatched house in Haverhill.[4] Whereas in England, however, thatch continued to be the usual roofing for humbler dwellings of many districts until the later eighteenth century, and still remains in use there, in America the dates given constitute approximately the final limits of its use and persistence. That this was true was due not merely to greater severity of climate than in England, but to greater availability of a better material. Many years before this, wooden shingles had been adopted as the usual material for roofing in the colonies. Shingles had been common in England down through the fourteenth century, and even to-day

Figure 11. Rough-cast ornament from the Browne house, Salem. After 1664

Courtesy of the Essex Institute

remain in use for church spires in the southeastern counties,[5] although now generally superseded by slate and tile. Shingles in lengths varying from fourteen inches to three feet are familiarly mentioned in court orders in New Haven in 1640 and 1641, immediately after the settlement. Whereas the town barn in Windsor, Connecticut, in 1659, was to be "repaired and thatched," the meeting-house there in the following year was to be shingled.[6] Winthrop wrote in 1646 as if roofs other than thatch were by that time not uncommon in Boston.[7] The "Perfect Description of Virginia" in 1649 speaks of houses "covered with Shingell for Tyle."[8]

In the early houses of frame, and in many long afterward, the chimneys were constructed of wood and clay. In Massachusetts, although Dudley wrote in 1631, "in our new towne intended to be builded, we haue ordered that noe man there shall build his chimney with wood . . .,"[9] Symonds proposed wood for his chim-

---

[1] "Connecticut Houses," p. 230, notes.
[2] Waters, "Homes of the Puritans," *Historical Collections of the Essex Institute*, vol. 33 (1897), p. 51.
[3] Weeden, "Economic History of New England," p. 214, note.
[4] G. W. Chase, "Haverhill" (1861), p. 115.
[5] Innocent, "English Building Construction," pp. 184–185; also W. Leyburn, "A Compendium of the Art of Building" (1734), which speaks of them as "very chargeable."
[6] "Connecticut Houses," pp. 249–251.
[7] "History of New England" (1825 ed.), vol. 2, p. 264.
[8] Force, *Tracts*, vol. 2 (1838), VIII, p. 7.
[9] *Collections of the Massachusetts Historical Society*, 1st ser., vol. 8, p. 46.

neys in 1638, as we have seen; William Rix's chimney in 1640 was to be "framed without dawbing to be done with hewen timber"; and George Norton's new house in 1656, otherwise like a certain house with brick chimneys, was to have instead, "sufficiently catted chimneys."[1] In Connecticut chimneys of wood and clay were in use in 1639, and may have persisted until 1706 when the last chimney-viewer of Hartford was elected.[2] That they still commonly existed outside of New England even after the Revolution may be inferred from reiterated observations by Washington during his tour of the eastern states in 1789, after leaving New York, that "no dwelling house is seen without a Stone or Brick Chimney."[3] Isham recognized that they were not "so much a makeshift of the frontier as many imagine,"[4] and Innocent multiplies instances in which they have remained in use in England in the nineteenth century.[5] It should be noted concerning chimneys, as was remarked of the houses as a whole, that there is no mention of logs laid cob fashion, according to the supposition of most writers. In every case they seem to have been supported by upright posts. Symonds wished "the frames of the chimnyes to be stronger than ordinary." The assumption sometimes made that "catted" meant cobbed, we have seen to be a misconception.

By the middle of the seventeenth century chimneys of masonry were used in houses of frame. The "Perfect Description of Virginia" (1649) states that chimneys were constructed of brick.[6] William Fitzhugh wrote in 1686 that all the dwellings on his plantation were furnished with chimneys of brick,[7] but, although the same was doubtless true of planters of equal prominence, the implication is that it was still by no means universal. Brick chimneys are mentioned in the records of Hartford in 1639.[8] They existed in the Corwin house in Salem before its remodelling in 1675, when the contract called for their rebuilding, the central one with five fireplaces.[9] Where conditions favored, as in Connecticut and Rhode Island, chimneys were built of stone at a very early date, and this remained characteristic throughout the seventeenth century. The minister's house at New London in 1661 was to have "a stack of stone chimneys in the midst."[10] In form the chimneys, as they appear above the roof of framed houses, often show nar-

[1] J. B. Felt, "Annals of Salem," 2d ed. (1845), p. 401.
[2] Isham and Brown, "Connecticut Houses," pp. 188–190.
[3] "Diary of George Washington, 1789–1791" (1860), p. 20, also p. 29.
[4] "Connecticut Houses," p. 189.
[5] "English Building Construction," p. 269. See also S. O. Addy, "Evolution of the English House" (1898), p. 115, and J. L. Bishop, "History of American Manufactures" (1861), vol. 1, p. 219.
[6] Reprinted by P. Force, *Tracts*, vol. 2, VIII, p. 7.
[7] Bruce, "Economic History of Virginia," vol. 2, p. 143.
[8] Isham and Brown, "Connecticut Houses," p. 188.
[9] *Essex Antiquarian*, vol. 7 (1903), p. 169.   [10] "Connecticut Houses," p. 159.

row pilaster-like strips on the face, or a series of planes receding either way from the centre. Among dated houses the former scheme occurs in the "Scotch House," 1651, and the Corwin house, 1675; the latter in the Pickering, Bridgham, Parkman, and Hunt houses, spanning the half-century. As we know in the case of the Corwin house, even brick chimneys were sometimes rebuilt, so that one can scarcely be certain, in any event, of priority or development.

In the seventeenth century, in the colonies and even in England, glass windows were by no means so universal as may be supposed. The "current shutting draw windows" of Symonds's house in 1638, "having respect both to present and future use," were doubtless sliding panels of board, closing windows which were later to be provided with glass. In "Leah and Rachel" (1656), Virginia buildings are spoken of as having "if not glazed windows, shutters which are made very pritty and convenient."[1] Shutters taking the place of sash were common in the seventeenth century in England.[2] John Aubrey, born 1626, writes of glass windows, "In my own time, before the Civil Wars, copyholders and poor people had none in Hertfordshire, Monmouthshire, and Salop; it is so still."[3] Edward Winslow, writing from Plymouth in 1621, says: "Bring paper and linseed oil for your windows."[4] In 1629, however, Francis Higginson, in counselling emigrants to Massachusetts Bay, writes: "Be sure to furnish yourselves with . . . glass for windows."[5] The suggestion for supplies needed by a colonist in Maryland, 1635, include "Glasse and Leade for his windowes,"[6] and by an adventurer in New Albion, on the Delaware, 1648, "glasse casements for his house."[7]

These, which were universal in the better houses after 1650, were hinged casement sash with leaded panes, either diamond or oblong in shape, a considerable number of which are preserved, although I know no case of one remaining in its original position.[8] Sash windows, which Samuel Sewall mentions in Boston in 1714, did not become common in England, even for houses of the better sort, until the reign of William III, and their introduction into the provinces was very gradual.[9] In some retired districts and villages they did not appear until 1725

---

[1] Reprinted by P. Force, *Tracts*, vol. 3 (1844), XIV, p. 18.
[2] Innocent, "English Building Construction," pp. 253–255.
[3] Quoted by Addy, "Evolution of the English House," p. 121.
[4] "Relation or Iournall" (1622), reprinted in A. Young, "Chronicles of the Pilgrim Fathers" (1841), p. 237, with a note giving further references as to the rarity of glass in England.
[5] Young, "Chronicles of Massachusetts," p. 264.
[6] "A Relation of Maryland," in C. C. Hall, "Narratives of Early Maryland" (1910), p. 98.
[7] Force, *Tracts*, vol. 2, VII, p. 32.
[8] *Cf.* the discussion of early sash by G. F. Dow in "Old-time New England," vol. 12 (1921), pp. 8–9, supplemented on p. 32.
[9] Innocent, "English Building Construction," p. 262.

or even 1750. Many English examples of mullioned casements are certainly as late as 1730; they appear in an elevation for a farmhouse, in a work otherwise purely Georgian, in 1787![1] Colonel Timothy Pickering, of Salem, furnishes the

From a photograph by Frances and Mary Allen

Figure 12. Door of the Sheldon house, Deerfield, Massachusetts. Before 1704

latest instance known to me of the renewal of leaded casements in America in 1751.[2] William Bentley writes of seeing them still in place in old Salem houses in 1794 and 1796;[3] some remained in Boston as late as 1817,[4] and in Philadelphia even in 1830.[5] Normally two or more of these sash were grouped, except in the upper entry, the garret, and perhaps the end, where single sash were common. If we accept the conscientiousness of the restorations in following the old mortises, we find banks of three sash in the principal rooms of the Whipple and Hooper houses, a few years apart. Only for the Capen and "Scotch" houses is it believed—on the high authority of Messrs. Dow and Millar—that single casements were employed throughout from the start.

Only two original doors of the seventeenth century have come down to us, the more important being that of the John Sheldon house in Deerfield, preserved by the Pocumtuck Valley Memorial Association for its rôle in the Indian attack of 1704 (figure 12). It is of wide boards, in two thicknesses, vertical outside, horizontal inside, studded with wrought nails in diagonal lines, as was common in England.[6] Part of a similar door was found in restoring the Turner house, Salem. Doorheads with an ogee curve are shown

[1] W. Pain, "Builder's Golden Rule," 3d ed. (1787), plate 91.
[2] Quoted in F. L. Lee's "Scrap Book I," p. 191, at the Essex Institute.
[3] "Diary," vol. 2 (1907), pp. 115 and 172.   [4] C. Shaw, "Description of Boston" (1817), p. 291.
[5] J. F. Watson, "Annals of Philadelphia" (1830), p. 198.
[6] R. Nevill, "Old Cottage and Domestic Architecture," p. 41; Innocent, "English Building Construction," figs. 63, 64.

in old views of the Parkman house, built between 1673 and 1682, and the Governor Bradstreet house[1] there, from the same general period.

The interior face of the frame walls during the seventeenth century, in most of the New England colonies, was frequently sheathed with wide boards, grooved together and often chamfered or moulded at the joints, and similar sheathing was used for partitions (figure 13). In England such boarding, generally vertical, was

Figure 13. Parlor of the Capen house, Topsfield

common in partitions of mediaeval and Renaissance buildings.[2] On outer walls it was horizontal, on partition walls, generally vertical; and the differences seem to have been matters of local variety rather than of developmental sequence. The earliest record occurs in the well-known passage of Winthrop's journal regarding Thomas Dudley's house at Cambridge: "The governor having formerly told him, that he did not well to bestow such care about wainscoting and adorning his house,

[1] Water-color painting at the Essex Institute, "probably painted by Barthole in 1819." The house was demolished by 1755. See the discussion by R. S. Rantoul in *Historical Collections of the Essex Institute*, vol. 24 (1887), pp. 247–248.
[2] Innocent, "English Building Construction," pp. 114–115, fig. 44.

in the beginning of a plantation . . . his answer now was, that it was for the warmth of his house, and the charge was but little, being but clapboards nailed to the wall in the form of wainscot."[1] Messrs. Isham and Brown state that wainscot sheathing remained in use in Connecticut houses until about 1735–40.[2] Just at the close of the century began the transition to panelling. Thus the house built by Benaiah Titcomb in Newburyport, after 1695, has strips fastened over the sheathing to constitute panels.

Interior plastering in the form of clay daub antedated even the building of houses of frame, and must have been visible in the inside of wattle filling in those earliest frame houses in which Dudley's extravagance of wainscot had not been indulged. Clay continued in use long after the adoption of laths and brick filling for the frame. Records of the New Haven Colony in 1641 mention clay and hay as well as lime and hair.[3] In praising Virginia buildings as superior to ordinary houses in England the author of "Leah and Rachel" (1656) speaks of the rooms as "daubed and white-limed."[4] In Massachusetts Bay, where lime was scarce, the town of Dedham voted in 1657 to "have the meeting house lathed upon the inside and so daubed and whited over, workmanlike."[5] As late as 1675, in the Corwin house in Salem, clay plaster was left exposed in the walls of the garret, and was used as a first coat in all the rooms. We must infer from the terms of the contract with Daniel Andrews that a finishing coat of lime was by no means regarded as universal:

"As for lathing and plaistering he is to lath and siele the 4 rooms of the house betwixt the joists overhead with a coat of lime and haire upon the clay, also to fill the gable ends of the house with brick and plaister them with clay. . . . To lath and plaister the partitions of the house with clay and lime, and to fill, lath and plaister with bricks and clay the porch and porch chamber and to plaister with lime and hair besides; and to siele and lath them overhead with lime; also to fill, lath and plaister the kitchen up to the wall plate on every side."[6]

In the German houses of Pennsylvania the use of clay persisted much later still.[7]

The staircases in those seventeenth-century houses where they are preserved uniformly had winders at either end, with at most a short straight run between. Along this in the more elaborate examples, between the newel posts at the turns, was a short range of balusters. Stair "banisters" in the house of Colonel Daniel

---

[1] "History of New England" (1825 ed.). vol. I, p. 32. [2] "Connecticut Houses," p. 257.
[3] Isham and Brown, "Connecticut Houses," p. 198. [4] Force, *Tracts*, vol. 3, XIV, p. 18.
[5] Quoted by Palfrey, "History of New England," vol. 2 (1860), p. 59, note.
[6] *Essex Antiquarian*, vol. 7 (1903), p. 169.
[7] Watson, "Annals of Philadelphia," 2d ed. (1844), vol. 2, p. 18.

Figure 14.   Stairs of the Capen house, Topsfield

Parke are mentioned in a Virginia deposition of 1665.[1] Although in Rhode Island they were often sawn to a profile,[2] and sawn balusters appear as late as 1749 in the attic stairs of the Van Cortlandt house in New York City, they were usually turned in a lathe. Messrs. Isham and Brown state that "a judgment as to the age of the stair can be made by noting the turning of these balusters. The stumpy forms, with short curves, are the older." This is true of the seventeenth-century forms as a whole, as against the eighteenth. Whether the nature of any evolution within the seventeenth century can be established is very questionable, however, owing to the small number of really dated examples of original stairs. Of these the Corwin house, before 1775, has banisters with the turned part ten inches by two and one-half inches; the Capen house, 1683 (figure 14), thirteen and one-half inches by one and three-quarter inches; but the Titcomb house, Newburyport, after 1695, has heavier proportions once more, with the form of a double baluster. The forms of newels and rails likewise vary without positive tendency.

By analogy with the authentically dated houses it is easy to recognize a great number of frame houses in New England, with a few elsewhere, as belonging generally to the seventeenth century, and to note regional variations. Messrs. Isham and Brown have done this superlatively well for the houses of Rhode Island and Connecticut, and have pointed out the main types of New England as a whole (figure 15). The Connecticut plan (*A*) is similar to that of the Massachusetts houses we have been studying, but characteristically with the summer running at right angles to the fireplace instead of parallel to it (*G*). This was the scheme in the Plymouth Colony also. The one-room Rhode Island houses (*F*) had the chimney showing on the exterior, constituting the "stone-end" type, whereas the houses of similar plan in Massachusetts (*E*) had an end wall of wood, which we may suggest was employed in the dearth there of lime mortar. Supplementary gables or "lucome windows" were found in Rhode Island but not in Connecticut. When rear rooms were incorporated from the start (*B*), the lean-to form (*B1*) was not always retained, but later, perhaps after the end of the century, houses were carried up two full stories over their entire width (*B2*). The chimney tended to be removed from its central position in favor of a central entry.

In Maryland such a house as Bond Castle (figure 16) suggests interesting material for further study.[3]

---

[1] Quoted in Bruce, "Economic History," vol. 2, p. 158, note. Turned balusters in a bridge at Hartford are spoken of as early as 1639. Isham and Brown, "Connecticut Houses," p. 266.

[2] Isham and Brown, *ib.*

[3] A useful guide is furnished by Mrs. Annie Leakin Sioussat's "Old Manors in the Colony of Maryland," 1st and 2d series (1911 and 1913), from which our figure is reproduced by her kind permission.

It will have been noticed that the frame houses preserved show no feature of the academic style introduced into England by Inigo Jones: the subordination of structural considerations to those of form — space or mass, the abandonment of aspiring mediaeval lines in favor of peaceful horizontals, the employment of the classic orders and of related form for all details. This is not surprising when we

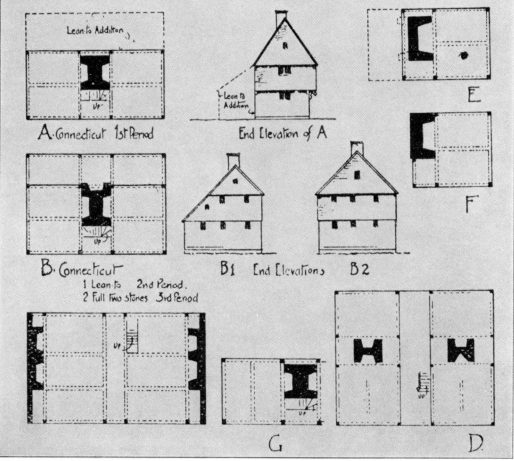

Figure 15. Types of New England houses
From Isham and Brown: *Early Connecticut Houses*

recall how few and isolated were works in that style down to the time of the Great Fire. Although the Banqueting House at Whitehall was built in 1619 to 1622, the number of country houses in the new manner before the Restoration may almost be counted on the fingers of one hand. There are no authentic country houses by Wren; the great period of aristocratic house-building lay ahead in the eighteenth century. The infiltration of the academic forms in the architecture of the provincial towns and small manor-houses had just begun. The earlier Renaissance in England had passed over the minor buildings almost without affecting their style, so that it was inevitable that the early framed houses of America should be survivals fundamentally mediaeval.

For a generalization regarding the course of development within the type, our study of the chronological evolution of single elements gives us a wealth of authentic material hitherto unavailable. The only students who have seriously discussed the question, Messrs. Isham and Brown, advanced the theory—chiefly *a priori*—of a gradually "diluted" tradition, a progressive abandonment of imported tradi-

Figure 16.   Bond Castle on Chesapeake Bay
Courtesy of Mrs. Annie Leakin Sioussat

tional features.[1] The overhang, regarded by them as a conspicuous example of this, we have seen, in rigorously dated Massachusetts examples, to give no justification for such a view. Other specific features of the houses preserved are scarcely more conclusive in their testimony. Wooden chimneys, window-panes of oiled paper, roofs of thatch, and other unmistakable signs of early origin have long ago disappeared, through replacement, like the frail shelters of the first generation as a whole. For the points of difference remaining, the variety of traditions derived from the several districts of England, even the variety existing here, as there, at a given time in a single district, is responsible for more than are due to chronological development. Only in wealth and accommodations can we trace any consistent tendency. To New England, where the existing frame houses of the seventeenth

[1] "Connecticut Houses," esp. pp. 31-32.

century stand, emigration practically stopped with the outbreak of the Civil Wars in England in 1648, and the forces which eventually brought about a fundamental change of style were not felt by the dwellings of humbler material before the close of the century. It should not be surprising, then, that these houses, ranging, so far as we can prove, only from 1650 to 1700, represent a homogeneous style in which there was little evolution.

For houses where documents are lacking, dates assigned in this period must have regard always to the social and financial standing of the owner, and to the relative advancement of the community. Even then there will remain a wide margin of doubt. Any dates prior to 1650, obviously, must be advanced with extreme caution. Thus in the case of the Fairbanks house at Dedham, Massachusetts, two stories high, with central chimney, it is rash to maintain the very year of Jonathan Fairbanks's admission as a townsman, 1636–7, as the date of the building of the central part of the existing house.[1]

HOUSES OF MASONRY

Not only during the seventeenth century but throughout the Colonial period, as to this day, the vast majority of houses in America remained of wood. The primary reason was, of course, economic; for in the densely forested new continent where timber had to be felled before the ground could be tilled, masonry was at a disadvantage in cost unknown in England after the sixteenth century. The very early introduction of sawmills and their wide use long before they became established in England,[2] was a corollary which reinforced this condition.

A serious obstacle to the adoption of masonry construction in many regions was the difficulty of securing lime for mortar. As early as 1631 Governor Winthrop had "erected a building of stone at Mistick," but "there came so violent a storm of rain . . . (it not being finished, and laid with clay for want of lime) two sides of it were washed down to the ground."[3] Lime was equally lacking, to be sure, in some regions of England before the day of modern communications, and clay mortar was common there,[4] but in the colonies a more severe climate was to be withstood. In spite of the optimistic reports of John Smith,[5] Higginson,[6] and

---

[1] *Cf.* the discussion by E. Worthington in the Dedham *Historical Register*, vol. 9 (1898), p. 4.

[2] Bishop, "American Manufactures," vol. 1, pp. 93–115; Weeden, "Economic and Social History of New England," vol. 1, pp. 168, 172, 198, 200, 201.

[3] Winthrop, "History of New England" (1825 ed.), vol. 1, p. 63.

[4] Innocent, "English Building Construction," pp. 121, 142.

[5] "A Description of New England" (1616) in Force's *Tracts*, vol. 2 (1838), I, pp. 5–6.

[6] "New England's Plantation," Young's "Chronicles of Massachusetts," p. 244 and note.

Morton,[1] limestone was not abundant in the eastern part of Massachusetts. As late as 1697 the discovery of limestone at Newbury was thought worth reporting to a meeting of the Governor and Council.[2] It was almost wholly absent in the Connecticut Colony and in tidewater Virginia. Only Rhode Island was well supplied with deposits near Providence, worked from 1662.[3] Elsewhere they were dependent on importation (especially from Rhode Island),[4] or on the use of the inferior lime from oyster shells, and these resources together were really inadequate. In Massachusetts Johnson wrote that the fort on Castle Island had to be rebuilt in 1644, "by reason the country affords no Lime, but what is burnt of Oyster-shels,"[5] and John Josselyn in 1663 alludes to the absence of "stones . . . that will run to lime, of which they have great want."[6] As late as 1724 shell lime was in common use, and the inroads made were such that it was "ordered that muscles shall not be used for making lime or anything else, except for food or bait."[7] In the Connecticut River towns there was no lime before 1679, and its use long remained restricted.[8] In Virginia the situation cannot have been greatly unlike that in Massachusetts, although in a sanguine description of 1649 lime is spoken of as abundant, and Bullock wrote that the colonists preferred the shell lime to chalky lime sometimes met with in England.[9]

Even when the difficulty of securing lime was overcome there remained another obstacle, later recorded by Jefferson in his "Notes on Virginia" (1784), and doubtless also intensified by American climate: "the unhappy prejudice . . . that houses of brick and stone are less healthy than those of wood," due to damp.[10] It is reported that the first brick house in Salem, built 1707, was soon pulled down as a result of this supposition, and in consequence of this the building of others was long postponed.[11] Notwithstanding such conditions, the desire for more permanent and dignified dwellings led the Colonial governments and especially prominent citizens, from an early period, to erect masonry structures.

Stone was totally lacking in the Virginia peninsula. In Massachusetts, where rounded glacial field stones were readily obtainable, experiment with these in the

---

[1] "New English Canaan," in Force's *Tracts*, vol. 2, V, p. 57. [2] S. Sewall, "Diary," vol. 1 (1878), p. 458.
[3] W. R. Staples, "Annals of Providence" (1843), pp. 513, 514.
[4] Isham and Brown, "Connecticut Houses," pp. 183–184.
[5] "Wonder Working Providence" (1867 reprint), p. 194.
[6] "An Account of Two Voyages to New England" (1674, reprint of 1865), p. 39.
[7] J. B. Felt, "Annals of Salem," 2d ed. (1845), p. 406. [8] "Connecticut Houses," pp. 182–186.
[9] "Perfect Description of Virginia" in Force's *Tracts*, vol. 2, VIII, p. 7; W. Bullock, "Virginia" (1649), p. 3.
[10] "Writings," edited by P. L. Ford, vol. 3 (1894), p. 258. *Cf.* also the "Diary of George Washington" (1860), p. 45, Nov. 3, 1789, which shows that this idea was unfamiliar to Washington until his visit to New England at that time.
[11] J. B. Felt, "Annals of Salem," 2d ed. (1845), pp. 414–415; also W. Bentley, "Diary," vol. 2 (1907), p. 268, under date of May 10, 1798.

absence of lime, as we have seen, was not encouraging. In the New Haven Colony and in Rhode Island lime and suitable ledge stone were both available. John Winthrop, Jr., who removed from New London in 1657, alludes to "the Stone-house, formerly my dwelling in New London."[1] The Whitfield house at Guilford, of which the first documentary mention is in 1659, is of stone. In Pennsylvania the abundant stone began to be used very soon after Penn's arrival, if we may accept the date of 1689 scratched in a wide joint of the older gable at Wynnestay.[2]

Brick was far more widely used than stone in the colonies generally. No

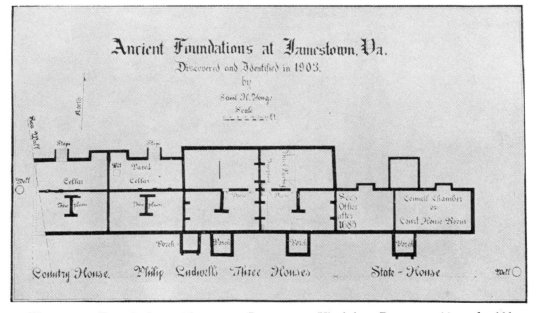

Figure 17. Foundations of houses at Jamestown, Virginia. Between 1662 and 1666
From S. H. Yonge: *The Site of Old James Towne*

phase of Colonial building has received such thorough investigation.[3] Bricklayers were included among the first settlers at Jamestown in 1607,[4] and brickmaking, begun certainly by 1611, increased continuously in Virginia.[5] In the Massachusetts Bay Colony, Higginson noted the setting of a kiln in 1629;[6] at Plymouth the first mention of brick is stated to be in 1643.[7] At Hartford and New Haven brick and brickmaking are spoken of in the earliest records.[8] In Maryland "we find a

[1] F. M. Calkins, "History of New London" (1852), p. 90.
[2] H. D. Eberlein and H. M. Lippincott, "The Colonial Homes of Philadelphia" (1912), p. 155.
[3] The pioneer discussion, still unequalled in fulness, is in Bishop, "American Manufactures," vol. 1, ch. 9.
[4] Smith, "Works," p. 94.
[5] Bruce, "Economic History of Virginia," vol. 2, pp. 134–143.
[6] "New England's Plantation" (1630), reprinted in Young's "Chronicles of Massachusetts," p. 244.
[7] *Collections of the Massachusetts Historical Society*, ser. 2, vol. 3, p. 183.
[8] Isham and Brown, "Connecticut Houses," pp. 178–180.

contract for making brick as early as 1653, and still earlier mention of brick-makers."[1] At Philadelphia a brickmaker was in the neighborhood before the city was laid out, and within three years many makers were at work.[2] Only in Rhode Island was brickmaking long delayed.[3]

Contradicting the oft-repeated assertion about old houses, that the bricks were brought from England or from Holland, is the universal consensus of students of the records that importation of brick in the English colonies was negligible where it was not completely unknown. Bruce states: "It would appear that all bricks used in Virginia in this century were manufactured there."[4] Of Maryland,

From a photograph by H. P. Cook

Figure 18.   Warren house, Smith's Fort, Virginia, as it stands
to-day.   1651 or 1652

Browne says: "It is doubtful whether a single house was built of imported brick."[5] A single case in New Haven, itself perhaps questionable, is, according to Isham, "the only instance we know in New England, except for the ten thousand brick recorded as to be shipped to Massachusetts Bay in 1628."[6] Several shipments, though amounting to but a few thousand brick altogether, were made to New Sweden.[7] Only in New Netherlands do brick seem to have been imported to any

[1] W. H. Browne, "Maryland" (1899), p. 166.
[2] T. Westcott, "The Historic Mansions and Buildings of Philadelphia" (1877), pp. 15–16; and H. C. Wise and H. F. Beidleman, "Colonial Architecture . . . in Pennsylvania . . ." (1913), pp. 16–17.
[3] Isham and Brown, "Rhode Island Houses," pp. 45–46.
[4] "Economic History," p. 134; likewise L. G. Tyler: "Were Colonial Bricks Imported from England?" *Century Magazine*, vol. 51 (1896), pp. 636–637, though he cites a cargo of 100,000 brick from New England later, between 1736 and 1739.
[5] "Maryland," p. 166.   [6] "Connecticut Houses," p. 181.
[7] Johnson, "Swedish Settlements," vol. 1, pp. 170, 193, 242.

considerable extent, coming from Holland as ballast as early as 1633, and continuing to be mentioned down to the Revolution, although bricks were burned in the colony as early as 1628.[1] The imported brick were superior in quality to those of New Amsterdam. In general, the traditional statements regarding brick from England or from Holland seem to rest initially on popular misinterpretation of the phrases English and Flemish bond.[2]

Efforts have been made to see whether the size of bricks used might furnish an index to the date of houses,[3] but the data adduced have been fragmentary and the results inconclusive. It is very questionable whether an exhaustive study would be more fruitful, for all the evidence points to wide variation in size even

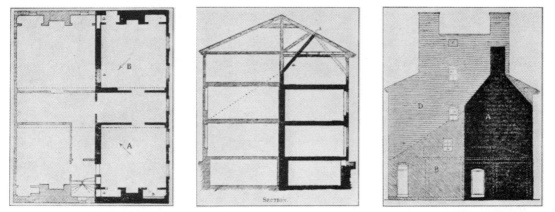

Figure 19. Usher (Royall) house, Medford, Massachusetts. Plan, section, and elevation of south end

From the *Medford Historical Register*, vol. 3 (1900)

Courtesy of John H. Hooper and Moses Whitcher Mann

in a given building, and complete freedom at any given time irrespective of the numerous statutes intended to secure standardization.

The first use of brick was for chimneys, and houses wholly of brick were some time in making their appearance, in spite of demands for them on the part of the home government in the case of Virginia. According to "The New Life of Virginia," 1612, the houses at Henrico had "the first storie all of bricks,"[4] although, as we have seen, Hamor spoke of them as "well framed houses." In 1638 Richard

---

[1] E. H. Hall, "Philipse Manor Hall" (1912), pp. 211–212.

[2] L. G. Tyler, in the article cited above, and D. Millar: "Some Colonial and Georgian Houses," vol. 1 (1916), introduction, alike suggest that the phrases "English brick" and "Dutch brick" had reference to the kind or size of brick, Tyler supposing the Dutch brick to be the larger of the two, Millar the smaller, which is borne out by the article *Brick* in the "Builder's Dictionary" (1734).

[3] Innocent, "English Building Construction," pp. 152–153; Hall, "Philipse Manor Hall," pp. 211–213; M. T. Reynolds, "The Colonial Buildings of Rensselaerwyck," *Architectural Record*, vol. 4 (1895), p. 420, note; and Isham and Brown, "Connecticut Houses," p. 181.

[4] Reprinted by Force, *Tracts*, vol. 1, VII, p. 14.

Kemp, secretary of the colony, constructed a residence entirely of brick in Jamestown, "the fairest that ever was known in this country for substance and importance."[1] As to New England, it has often been repeated that William Coddington

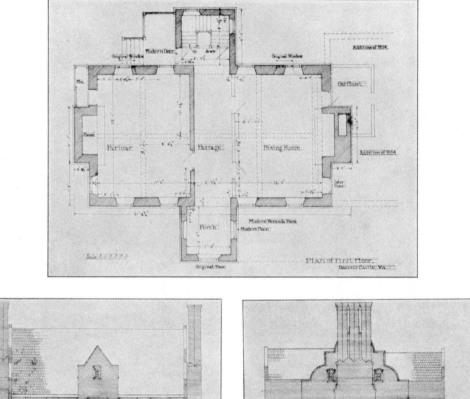

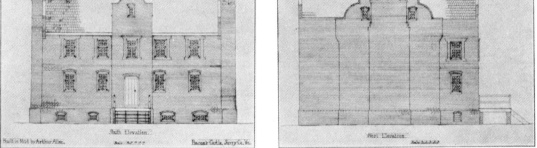

Figure 20. Bacon's Castle, Surry County, Virginia. Plan and elevation, restored. Before 1676
From measured drawings by Donald Millar

built the first brick house in Boston, prior to 1638, but this is an error.[2] Just when the first brick house was built is uncertain, but by 1654 Johnson could speak sanguinely of "some fairly set forth with Brick, Tile, Stone and Slate."

[1] Letter of Sir John Harvey, already cited.
[2] First made by John Callender in his "Historical Discourse on . . . Rhode Island" (1739), p. 50, misinterpreting a statement of Coddington in his "Demonstration of True Love . . ." (1674), which actually runs: "Before Boston was named (i. e., 1630) . . . I built the first good house. . . ." Quoted in Palfrey, "History of New England," vol. 1, p. 328, note 4.

Existing brick houses of the seventeenth century are few and scattered, as well as much modified and insufficiently investigated, but it is possible, nevertheless, to trace their evolution to some extent. The following can be dated authentically:

Begun 1651 or 1652 Warren house, Smith's Fort, Gray's Creek, Surry County, Virginia (figure 18)

Before 1676 Bacon's Castle, Surry County, Virginia (figures 20, 21)

Figure 21. Bacon's Castle
From an old woodcut in *Frank Leslie's Illustrated Weekly*

Between 1677 and 1680 Peter Tufts ("Cradock") house, Medford, Massachusetts (figure 25)

1682 to 1683 William Penn ("Letitia") house, Philadelphia (figure 27)

Before 1697 Usher house (nucleus of Royall house), Medford, Massachusetts (figure 19)

To these may be added several now destroyed, yet known through old views, photographs, or excavation:

Between 1662 and 1666 "Country House" and Philip Ludwell houses, Jamestown (figure 17)

1676 to 1679 Peter Sergeant house ("Province House"), Boston (figure 24)

Between 1681 and 1691 John Foster (Hutchinson) house, Boston, in its original form

1692 Fairfield (Carter's Creek), Gloucester County, Virginia (figure 22)

Before 1700 "The Slate House," Philadelphia (figure 23)

The choice of bond for the brickwork has been thought to be a matter of chronological evolution, and the idea has been advanced that English bond—

Figure 22. Fairfield (Carter's Creek), Gloucester County, Virginia
Courtesy of R. A. Lancaster

courses of headers alternating with courses of stretchers—was the one employed in Virginia before 1710; and that Flemish bond—a header and a stretcher alternating in each course—became popular after that date.[1] In England at the time, however, these two bonds were both used by Inigo Jones, and "their use in the seventeenth century seems to have depended on the use of special bricks for facing"[2]—the Flemish bond being preferred in this case because of its greater proportion of stretchers. In Jamestown English bond is found in the tower of the church,

[1] *William and Mary College Quarterly*, vol. 15 (1907), p. 212.
[2] Innocent, "English Building Construction," p. 151.

built 1639–1647, and in the walls of the houses excavated there, 1662–1666; but in the Warren house at Smith's Fort, built in 1651 or 1652, Flemish bond is used, and it appears in the chimney at Fairfield, 1692. In New England the Usher-Royall house, throughout its brick ends, has three courses of stretchers followed by one of headers. In Philadelphia Flemish bond was used from the establishment of the city, at least in the best houses such as the Penn house and the "Slate House."

In form, although some of the simpler brick houses did not differ essentially from the better ones of wood, other types appeared as pretensions increased. As

Figure 23. "The Slate House," Philadelphia
From the original drawing for Watson's *Annals of Philadelphia*, 1830
Courtesy of the Library Company of Philadelphia

in wooden houses, an elongated rectangular mass with a steep gable roof was usual. It was not uncommon to have but two rooms on a floor, as in the houses at Jamestown (figure 17), the Warren house (figure 18), and, originally, the Usher-Royall house (figure 19). Of these the Warren house had one full story, the Usher house two. While two-story houses presumably grew more numerous as time went on and means increased, others of a single story continued to be built. A basement partly above ground appears in the Warren and Sergeant houses and in Bacon's Castle.

An elaboration of such a plan as that of the Usher house appears in Bacon's Castle, surely before 1676 (figures 20, 21). There is a projecting entrance with a porch chamber, and a corresponding projection on the rear for the stairs, making a cruciform mass.

All these houses in their general scheme represent rather developments of the English cottage than derivatives of the great mansions. There were, however, two instances of a more pretentious scheme, the E or H plan common in the great houses of Elizabethan and Jacobean England, and not unusual there in the better farmhouses.[1] The American examples are Fairfield, 1692 (figure 22), and the "Slate House" (figure 23), just before 1700—both already showing in certain other respects characteristics of the age to follow.

Toward 1680 there appeared for the first time certain brick houses built from the start with a depth of two rooms in each story: the Sergeant house (figure 24), the Tufts house (figure 25), and the Penn house (figure 27), all built within a period of five or six years. The Penn house is even deeper than it is wide. In it the door opens directly into the chief apartment, which must be traversed to reach the rear rooms; but in the other two a central hallway for the first time gives privacy of access. This doubling of rooms and introduction of passages which marked the post-Renaissance dwellings of the continent and of England in the seventeenth century, was, in America also, a symptom of the onset of a new style.

The roofs in houses of masonry were sometimes of more permanent materials than those of wooden houses. We have seen that Johnson speaks of slate at Boston in 1654. In British settlements in East Jersey, according to a document of 1684, "there are some houses covered after the Dutch manner, with panticles."[2] By the houses of 1662 to 1666 at Jamestown were found fragments of slate and tile,[3] and in the storm of 1684, it is said, a large portion of the damage inflicted was in the destruction of the tile roofs by hail.[4] The "Account of Pennsylvania," published by Gabriel Thomas in 1698, speaks of "tile-stone, with which . . . Governor Penn covered his great and stately pile, which he called Pennsbury House."[5] In Philadelphia the "Slate House" took its name from its unusual roofing material.

The roof form characteristic of the time as a whole—the steep mediaeval gable —appears in the Warren house, in Bacon's Castle, and in the Usher (Royall) house,

[1] Gervase Markham, "The English Husbandman" (1613, often reprinted), figures and recommends this plan, pp. 23 and 24.
[2] S. Smith, "History of New Jersey" (1765), p. 184. [3] Yonge, "James Towne," p. 95.
[4] Bruce, "Economic History of Virginia," vol. 2, p. 159.
[5] Quoted in Westcott, "Historic Mansions of Philadelphia," p. 38.

spanning at least from 1650 to 1680. In Bacon's Castle, unique in America, the gables have the steps and cuspings of Jacobean England.[1] In several of the houses, however, forms prophetic of a coming day make their first appearance. Thus, in the Tufts house the main slopes of fifty-one degrees are sharply truncated at the top—producing our earliest example of the so-called "gambrel" or curb roof (figure 26). Much time has been wasted in seeking the origin of the gambrel roof of the English colonies elsewhere, for instance among the Dutch about New

Figure 24. The Province House. Boston. 1676 to 1679
From S. A. Drake: *Old Landmarks of Boston* (1873)

York.[2] This example should demonstrate, to all who know the history of European architecture, that the form originated in the desire to reduce the height of the mediaeval roof, especially over buildings of a double file of rooms. Although known, when used on all four slopes with a level cornice, by the name of the French architect, Mansart, it was by no means confined to France, many examples appearing in England in the later seventeenth and eighteenth centuries. The use of the curb roof while retaining the gable was a compromise, which we see in an early English example over the great hall at Hampton Court, and which re-

[1] A late English example, dated 1678, is in a building at Carleton St. Peters, Norfolk. B. Oliver, "Old Houses in East Anglia," pl. 73. Medway in South Carolina, Landgrave Smith's house, has a stepped gable, rebuilt.
[2] An early discussion in the *American Architect*, vol. 5 (1879), p. 153.

mained frequent in the colonies as nowhere else. The forms most significant of the future were the hip-roof and the pediment-gable. Horizontal members transforming the gable, necessarily flatter, into a rudimentary pediment, appeared in the Sergeant and Penn houses. The hip-roof is used in both the houses of E plan, and in both is of lower slope—at Fairfield with the eaves of the main house higher than those of the wings; at the "Slate House" with the eaves everywhere on a level. Both, like the Sergeant house, also show, for the first time in America,

Figure 25. Peter Tufts house, Medford, Massachusetts. Between 1677 and 1680
Courtesy of the Society for the Preservation of New England Antiquities

enrichment by blocks or modillions. Thus, as the century draws to a close, the staccato of the mediaeval gable gives way gradually to the legato of the classic cornice.

In the Sergeant and Penn houses the "lucome windows" over the plane of the wall gave way to dormers of the type first used in England in such academic houses as Coleshill, and defined in 1703 as "a window made in the Roof of a House, it standing upon the Rafters."[1]

The chimney in brick houses differed significantly in its position from that of

[1] T. Neve, "City and Countrey Purchaser and Builder's Dictionary" (1703).

the typical wooden house. In some of the houses at Jamestown there was a central chimney, but the same motives of economy which in wooden houses of two-room plan with a masonry chimney led to its placing in the centre, in houses of masonry made chimneys in the end wall preferred. Thus it was characteristic of the brick house with gables, whether North or South, to have them terminate in tall chimney-stacks. This was the case in the Warren house, Bacon's Castle, the Tufts and Usher houses. The chimney itself in two houses shows the separate clustered flues of Elizabethan England—Bacon's Castle and Fairfield—the latter

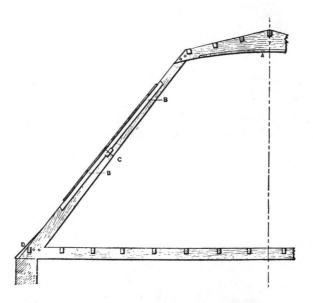

Figure 26.   Roof framing of the Tufts house
From *Carpentry and Building*, vol. 6 (1884)

as late as 1692, and in some ways more advanced in style. In the "Slate House" the chimneys were L-shaped. Aside from these the chimneys in the dated brick houses are merely rectangular, and do not show features of special note. Some have perhaps been rebuilt, but in others the absence of such treatment as is common in the chimneys of wooden houses may be due to the approach of the style to come.

The doorways of the brick houses in general do not show much elaboration. Those of Bacon's Castle and of the Tufts house have segmental arched heads, whereas that of the Penn house, somewhat later, has a flat arch. The Warren house, Carter's Creek, and the "Slate House" had light gabled porches, but it is impossible to tell whether they date from the time of the original construction. In the Peter Sergeant house there appeared for the first time a small portico with columns and entablature—a feature first used in England at Thorpe Hall, during the Commonwealth—which seems always to have belonged to the house, since it was precisely in its iron balcony rail that occurred the first owner's initials and the date 1679.

Figure 27.   William Penn ("Letitia") house, on its original site.   1682–1683
From an old photograph in the possession of the Historical Society of Pennsylvania

The windows of many of the brick houses have been enlarged, and there is not such good evidence for their size and proportion as that furnished by the mortises of a wooden house.   In the Tufts house there were apparently banks of case-

48

ments beneath a segmental relieving arch. At Bacon's Castle the chief openings, also segmental in the lower story, were larger, and Mr. Millar is doubtless correct in restoring them with a transom—a feature which appears in the old view of the Bradstreet house in Salem. The large rectangular openings must also have made transoms necessary with the original casement sash mentioned in the early description of the "Slate House." As this finest house in Philadelphia, recommended by

Figure 28. Interior of Penn house
Courtesy of Ogden Codman

Logan for the proprietor's residence, would scarcely have fallen behind the more modest residence built by Penn fifteen years earlier, we may reasonably assume that this also originally had transomed casements beneath its broad flat arches. It is extremely doubtful if double-hung sash windows were used in any Colonial house during the seventeenth century.

Most of the windows lack any enframement, but in Bacon's Castle those of the upper story have one of brick, suggestive of an architrave with ears—the sole feature of the house which suggests classic influence, and the only example of this element in houses of the seventeenth century.

The interior treatment of the brick houses generally does not show characteristic differences of style from that of wooden houses. Plastered wall surfaces seem to have been the rule during the seventeenth century; the panelling found, for instance, in the Warren house and in Bacon's Castle being of a style to indicate later insertion. A unique anticipation of the coming style appears in the chimneypiece of the great room of the William Penn house, which is framed by an architrave of heavy bolection moulding, with frieze and cornice (figure 28).

We thus find, as might well be expected, that the houses of brick, the most pretentious of early Colonial dwellings, show advances in the same direction in which architectural style was progressing in England. Few of them are without some minor phrase of the academic language of form: a window architrave in one case, a level cornice with modillions in others, a hip-roof, or a gambrel. Two at least, the Sergeant and Penn houses, by the strength of the new spirit in arrangement, mass, and detail may justly be regarded as works of transition.

The early appearance of such transitional features in the finest brick houses, coupled with the survival of mediaeval features in minor houses of a later day, makes it necessary to leave a wide margin of latitude in assigning dates to early brick houses for which no documents are preserved. Dates before 1650 must obviously be put forward with special caution. So, for instance, it is very doubtful if the Thoroughgood house in Princess Anne County, Virginia, was built by Adam Thoroughgood, who died in 1640, only two years after the building of the first brick house in Jamestown.

In many instances the mediaeval methods of the seventeenth century were continued long after 1700, as indeed they have been perpetuated to this day in obscure corners of Europe. The log house became the typical pioneer dwelling. The wooden chimney and the leaded casement, as we have seen, long persisted in country districts, as did the lean-to and the overhang. The Williams house in Deerfield, as originally rebuilt in 1707, was untouched by any breath of innovation. Mr. Isham has suggested that in Connecticut the fundamentally mediaeval methods of framing, and even a vestige of the overhanging stories, were retained until 1730 or even 1750. The most notable instances of such survivals occur in the buildings of the German sectarians of Pennsylvania, especially the monastic buildings at Ephrata (figure 29). The "Saal" or Prayer House here was completed in 1741; "Bethania," the Brother Hall, in 1746.[1] The construction is of hewn beams, put

[1] J. F. Sachse, "The German Sectarians of Pennsylvania," vol. 1 (1889), *passim*.

From a photograph by Lewis L. Emmert

Figure 29.   Porch of the Sister House, Ephrata, Pennsylvania

together without iron for ritual reasons, and filled with stones and clay, beneath the boarding or stucco. The steep roofs and small windows, the illuminated texts of the interior, the picturesque porches, have an old-world air which is unique on this side of the ocean.

Thus, in the midst of the eighteenth century, faded the last afterglow of the art of the Middle Ages in America.

THE EIGHTEENTH CENTURY

WITH the opening of the eighteenth century the academic spirit and the academic architectural forms, which had hitherto just begun to appear here in a few transitional houses, won the upper hand in Colonial architecture at large, as in the architecture of England. The academic style involved much more than merely a general symmetry and an application of the classic orders, already introduced into the great houses of England by the Renaissance. It involved a transference of the emphasis from functional considerations to those of pure form. Tall gables and chimneys, bay windows and mullioned casements, exposed beams and other functional elements with which the northern Renaissance, following mediaeval traditions, had built up such picturesque arrangements, gave way to more abstract compositions of space, mass, and surface.

The tinge which this universal style of the post-Renaissance period took on in the colonies was primarily dependent on its character in England. As received from Jones, its great English protagonist, this is well suggested in his own demand that architecture should be "solid, proportionable according to rule, masculine and unaffected." He followed Palladio in a puristic treatment of the orders and openings, with less dissolution of the individual parts into the general unity. The simplest cubical mass dominated by a "pavilion" or a loggia; superposed orders or, more characteristically, a single order, either above a basement or embracing the whole height of the building; a foil of broad masonry surfaces, either plain or grooved, with scarcely a leaf of carved ornament—such were the characteristic elements of his monumental style, well suited for the dwellings of the monarch or of a great aristocracy.

In the hands of Wren the style became less austere and more intimate. Something of baroque surprise and movement appeared. Baroque elements, like the broken and scroll pediments, were admitted, consoles were more freely used, rusticated quoins penetrated the enframements, more exuberant carving enriched the interiors. Under Dutch influence brick became the favored material. In the ser-

53

vice of the Universities, the London parishes, and the City Companies, the new style was adapted to a wider domestic use, for which the rebuilding of London after the Great Fire gave the first occasion.

A fresh initiative of international importance was taken in the years after 1715 by Lord Burlington, who, championing the style of Palladio and of Jones, outdid them in purism and in classical ardor. Already, just before this, William Benson

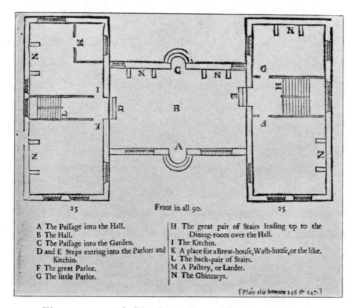

A The Paſſage into the Hall.
B The Hall.
C The Paſſage into the Garden.
D and E Steps entring into the Parlors and Kitchin.
F The great Parlor.
G The little Parlor.

H The great pair of Stairs leading up to the Dining-room over the Hall.
I The Kitchin.
K A place for a Brew-houſe, Waſh-houſe, or the like.
L The back-pair of Stairs.
M A Paſtery, or Larder.
N The Chimneys.

[Place this between 146 & 147.]

Figure 30.   "A Platform for a Mansion-house"
From Stephen Primatt: *City and Country Purchaser and Builder* (1667)

had built perhaps the first house in England with a great projecting portico: Wilbury House in Wiltshire,[1] soon followed by many others.

Provincial England first saw academic forms in a few houses ascribed to Jones and Webb, built about 1650, the most notable being Coleshill and Thorpe Hall, characterized by simple rectangular masses with double files of rooms, level cornice lines, hip-roofs, and uniform ranges of classic windows. Wide diffusion of the style among minor buildings outside of London came only with the reigns of Queen Anne (1702–1714) and the Georges,[2] as the name "Georgian" applied to this vernacular work suggests. In such buildings the traits significant of style are less accentuated: general regularity, the use of the hip-roof with level eaves and mo-

[1] Vol. 1 of the "Vitruvius Britannicus," in which it is figured on pls. 51 and 52, appeared in 1717. Benson seems to have settled in Wiltshire about 1712.
[2] J. A. Gotch, "The English House from Charles I to George IV" (1918), pp. 99 ff.; H. Field and M. Bunney, "English Domestic Architecture of the XVII and XVIII Centuries" (1905), pp. 2, 9–10.

dillion cornice, of sash windows with wooden bars, of a framed pedimented doorway, of quoins or some simple pilaster treatment.

The means of transmission to the colonies of the new gospel, in its successive
English versions, were several. In the younger settlements, like Pennsylvania or,
later, Georgia, it may have been brought partly by immigration; laymen and craftsmen alike having finally absorbed the new
fashions and traditions at home. In such
colonies as Virginia and New England,
where there was no special influx of fresh
colonists during the eighteenth century,
there were still instances of new arrivals
of importance. Thus among the constant
succession of royal governors there were
men of cultivation who demanded dwellings of more modern style, and set a conspicuous example. Sir Francis Bernard
and a few other new-comers, such as John
Smibert and Peter Harrison, were gifted
amateurs, who exercised their talents
chiefly on public works. Cases are recorded where a master workman was
brought specially from England for a given
house, as David Minitree was brought in
1751 to take charge of the erection of Carter's Grove in Virginia,[1] or John Hawks
in 1765 for the building of Governor
Tryon's "Palace,"[2] but these were very

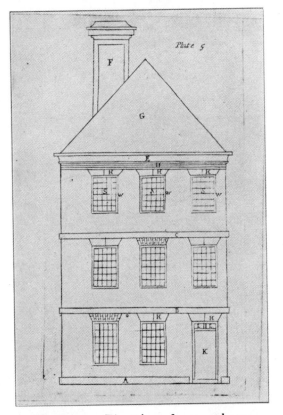

Figure 31. Elevation of a town house
From Joseph Moxon: *Mechanick Exercises* (1700)

exceptional. Among professional architects of reputation, then few enough even
in England, only one is known to have been in America: John James, " of Green-
wich," who was in Boston in the late seventeen thirties. Despite traditional
statements that a given house was designed by some famous English architect, or
was copied from some English building, no authentic instance is known of a house
in the Colonial period for which the designs were brought specially from England.

In reality the adoption of the new style came about in America in the same
way in which it did, as any general or wide-spread matter, in England: through the

[1] R. A. Lancaster, "Historic Virginia Homes" (1915), p. 54.
[2] Tryon to the Earl of Shelburne, January 31, 1767, in *Colonial Records of North Carolina*, vol. 7 (1890), p. 431.

making of its forms universally accessible to intelligent workmen, or even laymen, by means of books. It has been little appreciated that this was scarcely accomplished in England before 1700, and that its successful issue, in creating an extremely high standard of formal knowledge among all builders, constitutes one of the great artistic accomplishments of the eighteenth century. The books in foreign

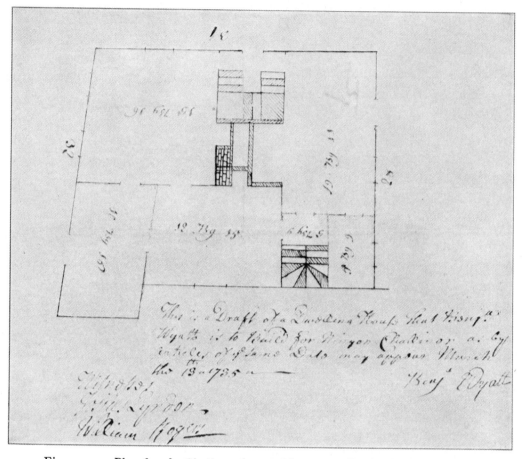

Figure 32. Plan for the Challoner house, Newport. Benjamin Wyatt, 1735
From the original drawing in the possession of George C. Mason

languages which had long been published were available and useful only to a small number; works on architecture in England were rare prior to the Restoration. Of those which then began to pour forth, few issued before 1700 provided suitable material for the adoption of the classic style in ordinary domestic buildings. Most of them showed only the forms of the five orders, suitable ornaments for a nobleman's seat like Hatfield but not the things most needed for an ordinary dwelling.

Sir Henry Wotton's suggestive work, "The Elements of Architecture," published in 1624, is without illustrations, and in so far as it does not deal with practical matters common to all styles, consists of rather erudite discussion of Vitruvian doctrine. Sir Balthazar Gerbier's two books (1662 and 1663) are likewise composed mainly of text, which urges the employment of an architect, then a luxury possible only for the great.

Only the orders were shown in John Shute's "First and Chiefe Groundes of Architecture" (1563), the earliest English book on academic architecture,[1] and in Evelyn's translation of Fréart de Chambray's "Parallèle" (1664).[2] Little more

From a photograph by Frank Cousins

Figure 33. Cliveden, Germantown, Pennsylvania. After 1763

was included in the translations of Bluom's "Quinque columnarum . . ." (1600 and 1608),[3] of Vignola (1665),[4] and of Mauclerc (1676). The folio translations of Lomazzo (1598) and of Serlio (1611) contained, in addition, drawings of ancient buildings, Venetian palace fronts, and some ancient doorways, and that of Francini's "Livre d'Architecture" (1669) had "gates and arches triumphant." Even the translation (1670) of Le Muet's "Manière de bien bastir pour touttes sortes de personnes," which had first furnished models for houses in France, had little

[1] New editions 1579, 1584.   [2] New editions 1680, 1723, 1733.   [3] The latter reissued in 1660.
[4] Third edition 1673, fourth 1694, fifth 1702, others 1703, 1729. Another translation, in folio, 1666.

that was relevant in England. All these books were far less useful to house builders than the pocket versions of Palladio's Book I (1663) and of Scamozzi (1669).[1] One had an appendix from Le Muet—here was its great appeal—"touching Doors and Windows," with a chimneypiece, showing a broken scroll pediment; the other, "two manteltrees" and "The Ornament for a Corinthian Doore or Window." An idea of the special demand for the Palladio may be gathered from its having flashed through twelve editions between 1663 and 1733.

Designs for ordinary dwellings were first shown in Stephen Primatt's "City and Country Purchaser and Builder" (1667), and Joseph Moxon's "Mechanick Exercises." Primatt shows only plans, the majority of them not dissimilar to the ordinary two-room plan of the seventeenth century in America—one an H plan (figure 30). Moxon, whose primary purpose was instruction in handicraft, shows in "The Art of House Carpentry" (1694), a city house front of frame, with banks of mullioned casements and a gable to the street; but in "The Art of Bricklayers-Work" (1700), a vernacular classic front with large sash windows, a hip-roof, and cove cornice (figure 31). Another plate shows a cornice of full classic profile.

Really academic suggestions for contemporary dwellings were not available in print until 1715, when, under the patronage of Lord Burlington, the great apostle of Palladianism, a complete edition of Palladio in two folio volumes was issued by Giacomo Leoni.[2] Further versions were made by Isaac Ware (1738) and others. The designs of Inigo Jones, likewise championed by Burlington, were published with his support in 1727 under the editorship of William Kent, who included also some of the designs of his patron. Additional designs ascribed to Jones were published by Ware (1735) and Vardy (1744). Colin Campbell, another protégé of Burlington, began in 1717 the issue of a great corpus of English academic buildings, the "Vitruvius Britannicus," not hesitating to exploit designs of his own. From this it was but a step to the frank publication—like Palladio's—of one's own designs, executed and unexecuted, as was sumptuously done by James Gibbs in 1728. Gibbs explicitly suggested in his Introduction that his book "would be of assistance to such Gentlemen as might be concerned in building, especially in remote parts of the Country, where little assistance in design is to be secured," and in this his hopes were amply justified, as we shall see. Ware's "Complete Body of Architecture" (1756) was filled with model designs showing the application of academic elements.

Such great folios of magnificent country-seats, however, were surpassed many

---

[1] Third edition 1676, fourth 1700, seventh 1774. Another translation was published in folio in 1676.
[2] Twice reissued, in 1721 and 1742.

Figure 34. Hancock house, Boston. 1737 to 1740
Courtesy of the Society for the Preservation of New England Antiquities

fold in accessibility and relevance by the less ambitious publications of men devoting themselves specifically to supplying builders and owners with suggestive designs and details of smaller houses. Notable among them were the works of Robert Morris (from 1728), Abraham Swan (from 1745), and especially William Halfpenny (from 1724), Batty Langley (from 1729), and William Pain (from 1758), each responsible for a small shelf-full of books, of which Halfpenny's "Modern Builder's Assistant" (1747) was perhaps the first to give general designs. A unique collection of these works, unrivalled in richness even in England, is deposited in the Metropolitan Museum as a loan by Ogden Codman. Such books, not excepting those of the same author at different periods, differ markedly among themselves in the precise phase of style illustrated, following, with their dates, the evolution which brought the ornament of the rococo to England, and then replaced it by the ever-cooling chasteness of pseudo-classic decoration. An analogous evolution took place in the plans, where the initial rectangularity was diversified by octagonal and oval rooms.

Copies of all these works found their way to America, often within a very few years of their issue, and nowhere were they more needed or more avidly welcomed. We have elsewhere,[1] by the aid of sales catalogues, library catalogues, and inventories of the time, brought out the surprising numbers, both of monumental folios and of pocket handbooks, which were available here. General and detailed comparisons of the engraved plates of these works with plans and details of executed American buildings, will demonstrate that they were actually used as sources in a great number of cases. Every new English fashion had thus its reflection in the colonies.

The degree of success and rapidity with which these fashions were assimilated in Colonial America was not substantially less than in provincial England, for buildings representing the same social grade. Many Colonial buildings have an application of the classic orders in an isolated and ungrammatical way, but English buildings from the same period showing similar traits may readily be instanced. On the other hand, as we shall see, American houses like Mount Airy, 1758, stand on the same artistic level with their true congeners, the best houses of the smaller English gentry of the day.

It is scarcely necessary to refute the suggestion of a reverse influence of Colonial architecture on that of England, recently put forward by an English writer.[2] The similarity of the small houses of the later Georgian period in England with contemporary buildings in America, which he remarks, is sufficiently explained by

[1] "Thomas Jefferson, Architect" (1916), pp. 20, note, 34–35, 90–101.
[2] S. C. Ramsay, "Small Houses of the Late Georgian Period" (1919), p. 7.

the derivation of both from English handbooks. Such a theory arises merely because appreciation of these smaller English houses, which have been eclipsed by their great neighbors, has only come after the Colonial work has been long familiar.

Armed with books, a cultivated owner or an ambitious mechanic was often able to erect buildings which would have honored an architect by profession, and to deserve honor as an architect, although not a professional either in training or

From a photograph by H. P. Cook

Figure 35.   Mount Airy, Richmond County, Virginia.   1758

in practice. The drawings made, with rare exceptions, were few and crude. Even in England, in 1700, conditions were similar, and the desirability of drawings for ordinary buildings had still to be argued.

'Tis usual, and also very convenient, for any person before he begins to erect a Building, to have Designs or Draughts made upon Paper or Vellum . . . the Ground Plat or Ichnography of each Floor or Story. . . . As also the fashion and form of each Front, together with the Windows, Doors and Ornaments. . . . The drawing of Draughts is most commonly the work of a Surveyor, although their may be Master Workmen that will contrive a building, and draw the Designs thereof, as well and as curiously, as most Surveyors: Yea, some of them will do it better than some Surveyors; especially those Workmen who understand the Theorick part of Building, as well as the Practick."[1]

[1] J. Moxon, "Mechanick Exercises . . . the Art of Bricklayers-Work" (1700), p. 15.

The plans used by Benjamin Wyatt and Richard Munday of Newport, among the ablest of the early builders—the oldest domestic designs preserved, now first published (figures 32 and 45)—are incredibly elementary. Only Peter Harrison and Sir Francis Bernard, who are not known to have designed any dwellings, with Hawks and Jefferson in their designs for Tryon's Palace and for Monticello, are known to have made better drawings here before the Revolution. That such poor

Figure 36. Hutchinson house, Boston
From the *American Magazine of Useful Knowledge* (1836)

diagrams sufficed was due less to "traditional" knowledge on the part of the craftsmen—for they had constantly to assimilate new gospel from London—than to the admirable designs and details in books, consistent in style and clear in presentation, available for selection and adaptation.

The dependence on books tended to give the leading houses a style common to all the colonies. Differing economic and social conditions influenced their arrangement but did not greatly affect the character of their forms. Minor houses were more subject to local influences, materials, and traditions, so that among them sharply distinguished local types grew up, like those representative of Germantown or of the Connecticut Valley. Characteristics personal to individual designers are more difficult to trace, for artistic personalities were not often highly and consistently developed. Where designs or details were taken from books they scarcely embody a personal quality. Indeed, it is possible to find identical details in different buildings, signifying identity, not in the hand that fashioned them, but in the plate from which they were derived. Nevertheless, internal evidence may possibly suffice in a few exceptional cases for the attribution of buildings to individual designers, either men, such as Munday and Harrison, known from documents to have designed other buildings, or men whose names are still unknown.

Figure 37. Capital from the Hutchinson house, Boston

In the possession of the Massachusetts Historical Society

The development of the academic style in America was a process the reverse of that in England, not beginning with a great personality and great monuments embodying the really fundamental ideas of form, but with adoption of the more superficial forms and gradual infusion of more thoroughgoing academic character. The evolution between 1700 and the War of Independence will be found to consist less in the employment, at successive periods, of this or that special type of plan or of detail, than in the increasing permeation of the designs by the academic spirit of formal organization. This evolution naturally proceeded faster in the more important houses. In minor buildings or in outlying regions earlier types persisted long after the first introduction of new forms. As we trace the progress of development shown by the most advanced examples, we must understand that many houses lagged a generation behind in this or that respect, or even as a whole.

Of the established materials of construction, masonry became more usual in the eighteenth century for houses of importance. Wood continued to be the common material for ordinary Colonial dwellings, while in England its increasing cost rendered frame houses a rarity soon after the adoption of the academic style. In the colonies the objection to masonry on the score of dampness continued, and this must have been especially felt in the North, where the trouble from condensation was greater. In any case, whereas in the Middle Colonies and the South scarcely a house of the first distinction was built of wood, in New England wood remained in use for many of the very finest dwellings until long after the Revolution. In both regions, however, there were exceptions to the rule, such as the splendid

From a photograph by H. P. Cook

Figure 38. Stratford, Westmoreland County, Virginia. Between 1725 and 1730

wooden house built by Colonel John Stuart in Charleston about 1772, so that one cannot regard the general choice of material as any sure index of development.

Among the houses of masonry, local conditions, rather than any chronological change, influenced whether brick or stone should be used, fine houses of stone being really common only in Pennsylvania. In the type of stone masonry employed, however, an evolution is clearly traceable. At Wynnestay in 1689 rubble was used throughout; at Graeme Park, 1721, although the rear and ends are of rubble, the front is of ashlar, very irregular in the height of its courses; in the Daniel Pastorius house, 1748, and at Whitby, 1754, the ashlar is more regular, although with courses still differing somewhat; at Cliveden (figure 33), after 1763, and in the later portion of the Bartram house, 1770, there is almost perfect regularity in the height and length of the blocks. This did not prevent the more modest houses from lagging behind: Mill Grove, 1762, and the Johnson house in Germantown, 1768, both have rubble in parts. In Massachusetts ashlar appeared earlier, in the remarkable house built by Thomas Hancock in 1737, where the walls were of granite in courses of uniform height, with trim of Connecticut sandstone (figure 34). In New York, the Van Cortlandt house at Lower Yonkers was built of rubble in 1748; in Vir-

From a photograph by Frank Cousins

Figure 39.   Mount Pleasant, Philadelphia.   After 1761

ginia, Mount Airy, perhaps the most ambitious house in the colony, 1758, had coursed ashlar of somewhat varying height, with the central pavilion and trim of lighter stone in regular courses (figure 35).

Little moulded or carved detail was executed in stone, for skilful stone-cutters were few. Nevertheless, there are notable instances, such as the pilasters of the Hutchinson house in Boston (figures 36 and 37). Although they were built two inches into the wall, it is almost inconceivable that these excellently understood Ionic capitals can date from the original erection of the house, between 1681 and 1691. Possibly they were added after the fire which destroyed the cupola in 1748. The Marston house, the first brick dwelling in Salem, ascribed to 1707, as we have seen, certainly had "stone Corinthian capitals."[1] At Drayton Hall, before 1758,

[1] Bentley saw one in 1798. "Diary," vol. 2, p. 268.

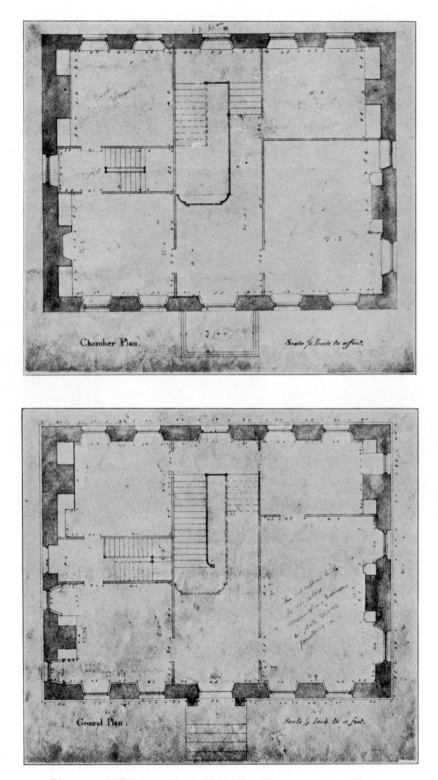

Figure 40.   Plans of Hancock house, Boston.   1737 to 1740
From measured drawings by John Sturgis
Courtesy of R. Clipston Sturgis

the columns are of stone. The Miles Brewton house in Charleston, finished 1769, has stone columns for its fine portico; and the Bartram house in Philadelphia has not only engaged columns of stone two stories in height but moulded stone window architraves added in 1770.

Brick was usually laid in Flemish bond, but this was not an absolute rule, and little conclusion can be drawn from the deviations from it, or from the employment of dark headers. Dressings in harder brick of slightly contrasting color about the windows, not infrequent in England, are found in several early houses—the Mul-

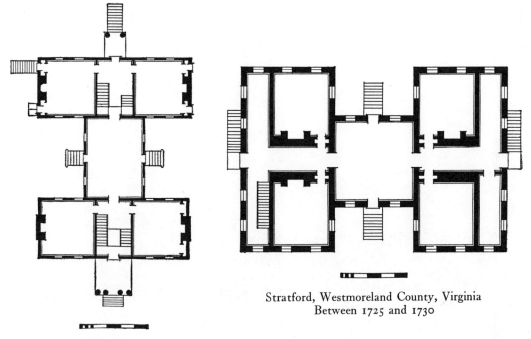

Tuckahoe, Goochland County, Virginia
Before 1730

Stratford, Westmoreland County, Virginia
Between 1725 and 1730

Figure 41. Examples of houses with the H plan

berry, Rosewell, and Stratford (figure 38)—and they reappear later in paint at Whitehall in the 'sixties. Moulded bricks were used for the water table in a building as early as the Mulberry, and they found application in chimney-caps, and even in cornices, after the manner figured by Moxon in 1700.[1] Colonel Robert Brewton's house in Charleston, built before 1733, has a brick cornice. In a few Virginia buildings of the first half of the century classic doorways were executed in brick: Stratford, 1725–1730; Christ Church, Lancaster County, 1732; the Nelson house, Yorktown; Carter's Grove, 1751.

[1] "Mechanick Exercises . . . the Art of Bricklayers-Work," p. 28.

Stucco was occasionally used from an early date, especially in Charleston and near Philadelphia, as a covering for both brick and rubble. Increased warmth and weatherproofness seem to have been the principal reasons for its employment rather than a desire to imitate stone. Even at Mount Pleasant (figure 39), after 1761, where joints are ruled to resemble ashlar, the brick is revealed in quoins. No artistic objection to brickwork arises until after the Revolution.

Although the general tendency, even in the North, was toward the more permanent materials, the desire for richer academic detail worked in the opposite

From a photograph by H. P. Cook

Figure 42. Tuckahoe

direction. Cornices, window and door enframements, in masonry houses, with the few exceptions noted, were ordinarily of wood, as was also the case in minor houses in England. Wood might be used for the whole fronts, to which the openings were chiefly confined, when the gable-ends of the house were of brick: in the Usher (Royall) house before 1700; in Tuckahoe; in the Dummer house, Byfield, Massachusetts. Later, the same forces even led to the casing of brick walls with wood, in which elaborate door and window treatments could be executed, as was done with the east façade of the Royall house between 1733 and 1737, or with the Pickman house on Washington Street in Salem, built of brick in 1764 and faced with wood about 1790.

In the matter of accommodations the houses of the new century reflected the greater accumulation of wealth and higher standards of comfort and convenience. The ordinary number both of living-rooms and of bedrooms was increased. Kitchen and hall, parlor and bedroom, were no longer combined in houses of any pretensions. Beyond this, however, differentiation in the functions of rooms was slow, as it had been abroad. It is difficult to arrive at the original functions of the rooms in the eighteenth-century houses of the colonies, since the elaborate inventories of an earlier time tended to be discontinued, but documents preserved in a

Figure 43. The Mulberry, Goose Creek, South Carolina. Between 1708 and 1725
Courtesy of Ulrich B. Phillips

few cases show that the uses were somewhat indeterminate. Thus the contract for the Ayrault house in Newport, 1739, speaks of "the Front Rooms . . . with a Boffet in the biggest of them."[1] Specifications regarding the Charles Pinckney house in Colleton Square, Charleston, 1746, mention best parlor, back parlor, study and office, with a dining-room on the second floor.[2] In Charleston it was usual for the principal rooms to be above the ground story, even where this was not regarded as a basement. Examples occasionally occur further north, as in the Corbit house, Odessa, Delaware, built 1772 to 1774. The arrangement was not uncommon in

[1] Published in full by G. C. Mason, Jr., in *American Architect*, vol. 10 (1881), p. 83.
[2] A. R. H. Smith, "Dwelling Houses of Charleston" (1917), pp. 307–310.

English academic houses, being early exemplified in Coleshill. In the South the kitchen was henceforth placed outside the house in a detached building.

Elements of circulation received a development which, with the increased number of rooms, for the first time made privacy possible. Henceforth, as in Europe since about 1640, the ideal was, by means of hallways, to make it unnecessary to traverse any room to reach another. Further privacy and seclusion of the activities of servants were secured by the provision of a secondary staircase. This appears in Rosewell and Stenton before 1730, the Hancock house, Boston, 1737 (figure

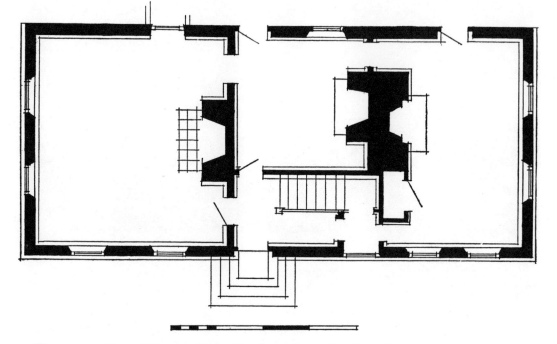

Figure 44. Plan of Graeme Park, Horsham, Pennsylvania. John Kirk, 1721 to 1722

40), the John Vassall house, Cambridge, 1759, Cliveden, after 1763, the Chase house, Annapolis, 1765, and elsewhere, but it remained exceptional even in fine houses.

In form the house of the eighteenth century, typically, was compact in mass, two rooms deep from the start in both stories, with ample hallways. Such a scheme, first used, as we have seen, in the Tufts and Sergeant houses about 1680, was not universally adopted with the opening of the new century, however, even in the most pretentious houses. With the tendency usual in the history of architecture, to greater conservatism in general form than in detail, some of these followed plans which belonged essentially to the previous period.

Thus the H plan, already familiar to us in Fairfield, and in the "Slate House," was retained in several notable houses, especially in Virginia, continuing until after

1750 (figure 41). Although this was the survival of an Elizabethan and Jacobean arrangement, it would be a mistake to suppose that it represents an arrear in relation to provincial England. The H plan remained in use there, also, such a notable example as Clifford Chambers falling well within the eighteenth century. Tuckahoe (figure 42), probably about 1710 and certainly before 1730, has slender wings

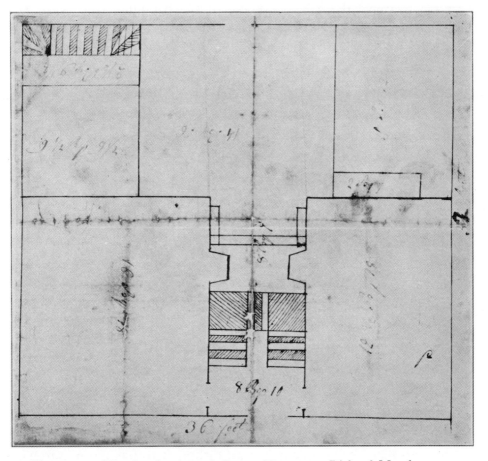

Figure 45. Plan for the Ayrault house, Newport. Richard Munday, 1739
From the original drawing in the possession of George C. Mason

a single room wide, with entry and stairs in the centre of each, and a hall, still occupying the traditional position of the old English hall in the central block. Its astonishingly detailed resemblance to one of the plates in Primatt's book (figure 30) can leave little doubt that it was derived precisely from this source. Stratford, also before 1730, has wider wings of four rooms each. The latest example is Elsing Green, rebuilt in 1758. In the North, also, this plan was not without a late representative in the country house built by William Browne in Beverly before 1744, still unfinished in 1750.

Although the date of 1714 on the weather-vanes of the Mulberry in South Carolina may not be wholly accurate, this unique building (figure 43), on land acquired in 1708, was certainly standing in 1725. In plan it is the most elaborate of the Jacobean survivals, having four nearly detached corner towers of one story, with roofs of fantastic shape. The suggestion that the Mulberry was "built after the picture of 'Seaton,' the English home of the Broughtons,"[1] is an erroneous one, in spite of the existence of projecting corner towers in Vanbrugh's famous design, executed 1720–1721.

Among rectangular houses, some, especially at first, remained but a single room in depth. These were chiefly among the minor houses, the dates of which are rarely established. Some important examples exist, however, especially in Charleston, where such houses were known as "single houses" by contrast with the thicker "double houses," and where they are placed characteristically with their ends to the street. The oldest datable one now standing is that of Colonel Robert Brewton, built prior to 1733; a much later one, that of Judge Robert Pringle. Both these have a central hall running through the house and containing the stairs. At Graeme Park, near Philadelphia, built by John Kirk for Sir William Keith in 1721–1722, the house is three rooms in length, but care was taken to make them all accessible from the stair hall, which is a shallow passage in front of the small central room (figure 44). Whitby Hall, also near Philadelphia, built in 1754, with two rooms down-stairs and a transverse hall, has the stairs projecting in a gabled tower.

A common form in which the house remained but a single room in depth was the L, with a wing or "ell" extended back at right angles to the house. An important dated example in which the wing forms part of the original construction is the Van Cortlandt house at Lower Yonkers, built 1748–1749. Here, as in the Philipse manor-house at Yonkers, there is a second stair hall in the wing, so that the rooms beyond have independent access, although to pass from one hall to the other one must traverse a room or step out of doors. An analogous arrangement exists at Woodford, built after 1756. As a later addition the ell frequently appears with all types of houses.

Among the houses two rooms in depth, the plan with a central chimney, obstructing circulation, survived for some time, even in pretentious houses. Thus it was followed in the house built by Richard Munday at Newport for Daniel Ayrault, a leading merchant, in spite of a shell doorhead and "Mundillion Cornish." Pencil lines on the plan (figure 45) and an increased estimate show that an alternative scheme with "Entry through; 2 stacks Chimneys" was considered but rejected on

[1] Ravenel, "Charleston," 1906, p. 65.

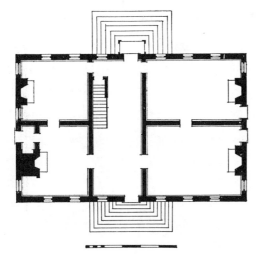

Westover, Charles City County, Virginia
Shortly after 1726

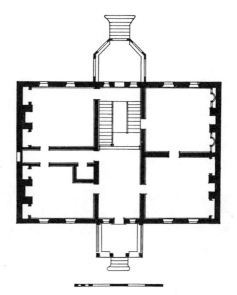

Gunston Hall, Fairfax County
Virginia.   1758

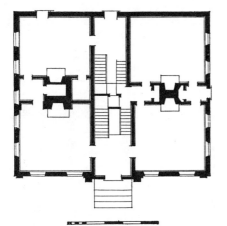

John Vassall (Longfellow) house
Cambridge, Mass.   1759

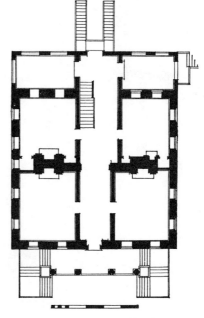

Miles Brewton house, Charleston
1765 to 1769

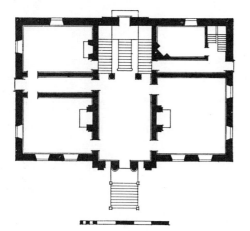

Chase house, Annapolis.   1769 to 1771

Figure 46.   Houses with a transverse hall

account of cost.[1]   Both this house and the similar one built for Ninyon Challoner,
1735, however, had back stairs which gave some privacy to the rear rooms above.

Among the houses where free access to all the rooms is provided, it would be

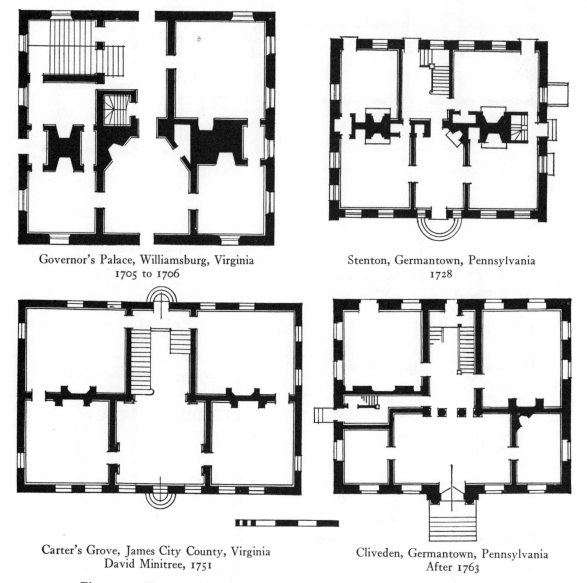

Governor's Palace, Williamsburg, Virginia
1705 to 1706

Stenton, Germantown, Pennsylvania
1728

Carter's Grove, James City County, Virginia
David Minitree, 1751

Cliveden, Germantown, Pennsylvania
After 1763

Figure 47. Houses with a developed front hall, and a stair hall at the rear

a mistake to suppose a general chronological sequence for the several types of
arrangement.   Rather we find, irrespective of general type, an historical progression, from functional arrangement with little regard for formal relationships, to
formal symmetry with attention to the composition of space.   This appears most

[1] Documents published by G. C. Mason, Jr., in *American Architect*, vol. 10 (1881), pp. 83–84.

clearly in the type of plan with a transverse hall containing the stairs, and that with a hall the fore part of which is given special development. Influenced by the general progression, the type with a hall expanded to one side tended to disappear toward the close of the period, and the type with a broad transverse hall kept free from stairs then had its use.

A house of four rooms to a floor, with a transverse stair hall, was the most common of Colonial types (figure 46). In the Royall house, Medford, this form

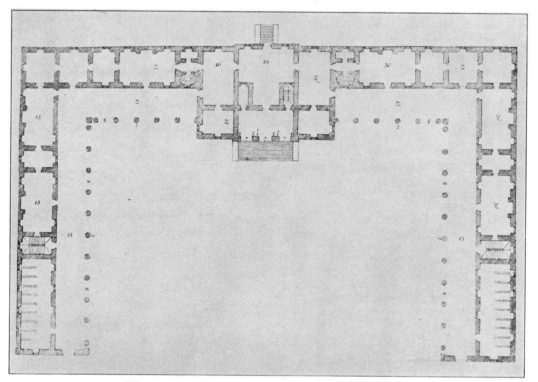

Figure 48. Plan from Palladio, Book II, plate 41

resulted from an actual doubling of the original depth (figure 19), and in others the form is not substantially different—the hall relatively narrow with little attention to its spatial effect. In some it is given a width more in proportion to the total depth. Noted datable examples, besides the Sergeant house from the previous century, are Westover, after 1726; the Hancock house, Boston, 1737; Gunston Hall in Virginia, 1758; the John Vassall (Longfellow) house at Cambridge, 1759; the Jeremiah Lee house at Marblehead, 1768; and the Chase house at Annapolis, 1769–1771. At Westover the hall derives its width, two of the seven equal bays of the front, at the expense of the rooms, less important, on one side. In certain other examples, where the fore part of the hall is symmetrical in relation to the doorway, the rear part is slightly narrowed or widened. As early as the Hancock house, however, and again at Gunston, the hall itself is perfectly symmetrical, although the stair rises along one wall and finishes on the other, so that the in-

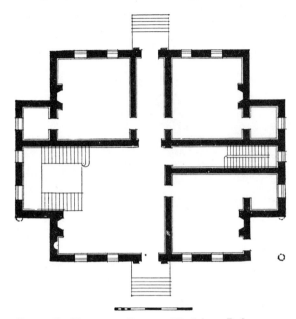

Rosewell, Gloucester County, Virginia. Before 1730

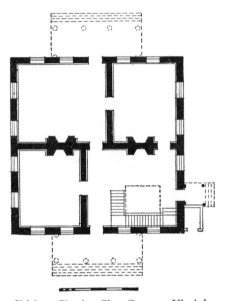

Shirley, Charles City County, Virginia

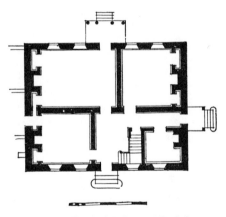

Kenmore, Fredericksburg, Virginia

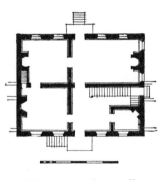

Brice house, Annapolis

Figure 49. Houses with a stair hall expanded to one side

terior spaces are unbalanced. At the Chase house, where the lower run is central and divides on the landing, the stairs are brought into relation to the balanced hall.

A number of Colonial houses have a hall with the front part treated as a room, the stairs in a separate and smaller space to the rear (figure 47). Early examples of this, such as the Governor's Palace at Williamsburg, and Stenton, are of much

76

irregularity. After the middle of the century the scheme is reduced to the symmetry seen at Carter's Grove and Cliveden. In this form it has some affiliation with such plans of Palladio as those of his Book II, plates 32, 41 (figure 48), and 61 (figure 73), in which the central apartments constitute an inverted T, although

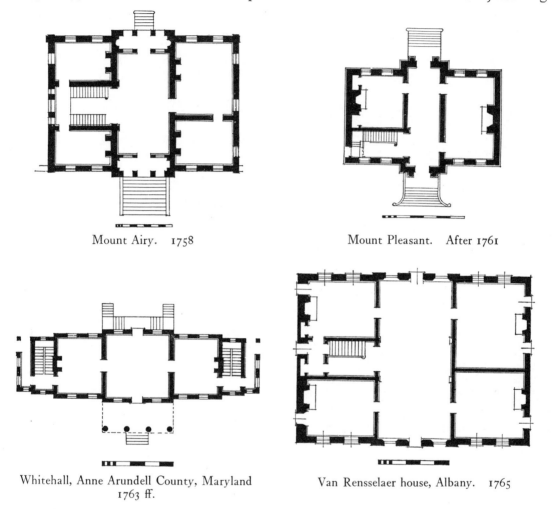

Mount Airy.   1758

Mount Pleasant.   After 1761

Whitehall, Anne Arundell County, Maryland
1763 ff.

Van Rensselaer house, Albany.   1765

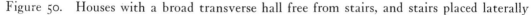

Figure 50.   Houses with a broad transverse hall free from stairs, and stairs placed laterally

none of these has the stairs in the stem of the T, as have the Colonial examples. At Carter's Grove an arch framed by pilasters connects the two parts; at Cliveden they are separated by a screen of columns.

Although of the half-dozen notable Colonial houses with a hall expanded to one side (figure 49) there is an authentic date only for Rosewell, there can be little doubt that the others all belong prior to about 1760.[1] The scheme was one in-

[1] The dates commonly assigned these houses are as follows: Shirley, 1700; the Brice house, Annapolis, about 1740; Kenmore, about 1750; the Moffat (Ladd) house, Portsmouth, 1763.

capable of that symmetrical co-ordination with the whole which was sought in the finest houses after that date, and thenceforth other schemes were preferred to it. The Hammond (Harwood) house, at Annapolis, in which the stairs are cut off by a wall, may perhaps be considered a continuation.

One of the favorite types after about 1760 was the plan with a broad transverse hall free of stairs, which were placed in separate compartments at the side (figure 50). The first dated example is Mount Airy, which reveals the fundamental resemblance of the scheme to one of Palladio's, embodied in his Book II, plates 33 (figure 51), 43, 44, 48, and 52. No doubt there were intermediate ancestors in English books, such as Gibbs's "Book of Architecture," plates 55, 59, and 62, but the ultimate progenitor is unmistakable. At Mount Airy there is even the sunk loggia familiar in Palladio. Other fine houses, with no staircase in the central hall, all from the 'sixties, are Mount Pleasant, the Van Rensselaer house, and Whitehall, the hall of the last rising through the two stories. So common, however, is the assumption that the splendid central staircase was an invariable feature, that legends of the former existence of such features have grown up to explain their lack!

Exceptional plans characterize a few houses, notably those of the governor at Annapolis and of Jefferson at Monticello,

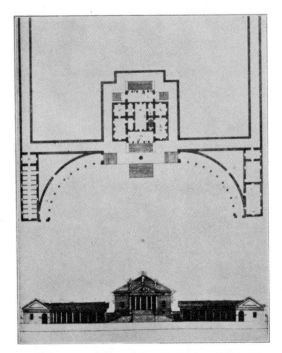

Figure 51.   Plan from Palladio, Book II
plate 33

erected in its original form in 1771 and following years. The Governor's house had a long drawing-room at the rear, across the full width of the main block, with a projecting bay in the centre. Wings, set back on the façade, form end pavilions on the rear. Monticello, as it stood down to 1796 (figure 52), likewise had its "parlour" in the centre of the garden-front, but the whole room projected in octagonal form—as illustrated in several designs in Robert Morris's "Select Architecture" (1759), which Jefferson owned—after the manner of a French *salon*.

The academic striving for formal organization brought the outbuildings into symmetrical relation with the main house. This was specially true of the large independent plantations of the South, where the outbuildings assumed greater importance (figure 53). It is sometimes difficult to determine absolute priority in the adoption of a given scheme, since outbuildings and house are not necessarily contemporary. The oldest building with a pair of offices symmetrically placed was the Governor's Palace at Williamsburg, itself built 1705–1706. They were connected with the main building by a wall, constituting a shallow forecourt in front of it. At Westover, Ampthill, and Carter's Grove (figure 54), a pair of offices stood isolated, in line with the main house. At Stratford and at Nomini Hall four iso-

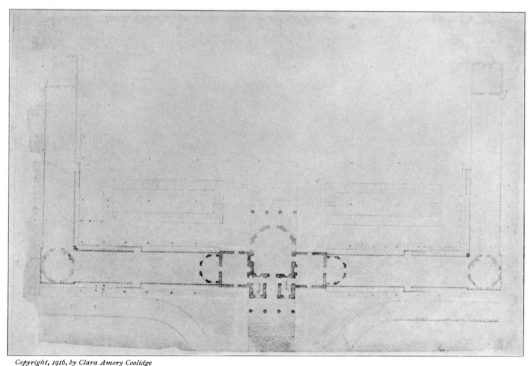

Copyright, 1916, by Clara Amory Coolidge

Figure 52. Monticello. Plan for the house and outbuildings. Thomas Jefferson, 1772
From the original drawing in the Coolidge collection

lated buildings marked the corner of a great square around the house, while at Mount Pleasant two outbuildings occupy a similar advanced position on one front. In the great houses of Annapolis and its neighborhood—the Brice, Paca, and Harwood houses, and Whitehall—the outbuildings were connected with the main house by lateral passages. With Mount Airy, 1758, appeared the Palladian scheme of advanced outbuildings connected with the house by curved passages, and this was adopted also in Tryon's Palace, 1767–1770, and in the enlargements of Mount Vernon begun on the eve of the Revolution. Jefferson likewise studied this scheme,[1] but preferred the other Palladian arrangement of long L-shaped passages flanked

[1] Kimball, "Thomas Jefferson, Architect," figs. 27, 28, 99.

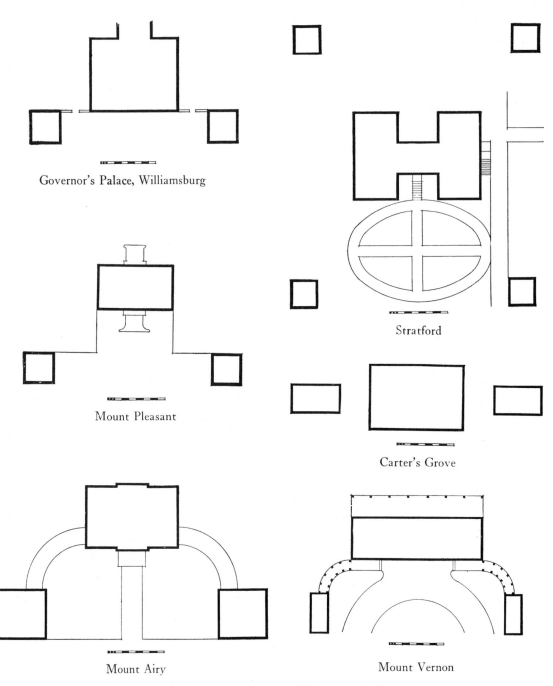

Governor's Palace, Williamsburg

Stratford

Mount Pleasant

Carter's Grove

Mount Airy

Mount Vernon

Figure 53. Relation of outbuildings to the house

by rooms and fronted by colonnades. Unlike those of the other houses, which rose from the same grade as the house itself, his service wings were reduced to the basement level to form terraces, above which rose merely decorative outbuildings.

Other elements than the rectangle were rarely involved in Colonial plans. Corners were sometimes cut off diagonally for fireplaces or cupboards, as at Stenton. No single instance of a circular or elliptical room, or of a curved projection on the exterior, is attested before the Revolution. Even the octagonal projecting bay, which appeared in English books about 1750, is found only in a few late examples:

From a photograph by H. P. Cook

Figure 54. Carter's Grove. 1751

Monticello, 1771; Lansdowne, 1773; and the Harwood house at Annapolis, also on the eve of the war, being the surely dated ones. The rear wing of the Roger Morris (Jumel) house in New York, an octagon of unequal sides, is shown by early descriptions to form part of the original edifice of 1765. The polygonal porch of the Schuyler house, Albany, is a later addition;[1] whether the same is true of the one at Gunston Hall is uncertain.

The stories in Colonial houses of the eighteenth century usually remained two in number, but houses of three stories became increasingly common, especially in the towns. In England academic country houses of three stories, ascribed to Webb

[1] G. Schuyler, "The Schuyler Mansion" (1911), p. 7.

—Thorpe Hall and Ashdown House—were erected about the time of the Restoration. As early as 1679 the Sergeant house in Boston seems to have had its full three stories, and by 1700, or soon after, the Hutchinson, Clark (Frankland), and Faneuil houses there had three. Jeremy Belknap wrote of the houses of Boston: "Those which were built after the fire of 1711, were of brick, three stories high, with a garret, a flat roof (*i. e.*, a deck) and balustrade."[1] At Charleston the Robert Brewton house, built before 1733, had three stories, which were not uncommon there henceforth. In the less closely built towns their coming was slower: at Salem there are datable examples (Orne and Pickman-Derby houses) in 1761 and 1764; at Marblehead (Jeremiah Lee house) in 1768; at Annapolis (Chase house) in 1769. In the country the earliest step in the same direction was the raising of the east

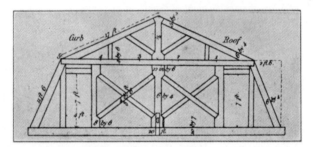

Figure 55. Diagram of a curb roof
From William Pain: *The Practical House Carpenter*

front of the old Usher house in Medford by Isaac Royall, between 1733 and 1737, so that it had three stories on that side, to one on the west (figure 19). Later the west front was raised to an equal height. From the 'fifties or early 'sixties comes the Cozzens (Bull) house near Newport; from between 1760 and 1769, the house of Governor Francis Bernard in Jamaica Plain,[2] Massachusetts; and from 1767–1770 Governor Tryon's Palace at Newbern, North Carolina—all of three full stories from the start. A basement partly above ground, still absent in Graeme Park, and the McPhedris (Warner) house, Portsmouth, in the 'twenties, became usual, as in such English houses as Coleshill and Thorpe Hall.

The heights of the stories showed a marked increase over those of the century previous. Whereas it was not uncommon before 1700 to have the bottoms of the summers in the lower story actually less than six feet from the floor, at Graeme Park in 1722 the parlor ceiling was eleven feet four inches in the clear. A foot more or less than this was the normal range in the lower stories of the finest houses be-

---

[1] *Collections of the Massachusetts Historical Society*, vol. 1 (1795), p. 190.
[2] F. S. Drake: "History of Roxbury" (1875), p. 428.

tween this and the Revolution—variations corresponding to wealth and pretensions rather than to any steady evolution. At Carter's Grove, 1751, the lower rooms had a height of thirteen and a half feet, and at Monticello, 1771–1775, the very exceptional height of eighteen feet. The second story was generally lower, ranging from nine to twelve feet, although where there were important rooms upstairs the roof space was occasionally turned to advantage for a coved ceiling. In

From a photograph by Frank Cousins

Figure 56. McPhedris house, Portsmouth. Before 1728

the Miles Brewton house, 1765–1769, such a cove attained the height of seventeen feet. Where there was a third story, this, as in England, was generally shorter than those below. Only in the case of the Clark (Frankland) house, if we may trust old views, was this as high as the rest, or higher.

The roof forms underwent significant transformations, a general tendency to flatter slopes, less total height, and level cornice lines dominating the development of particular types.

Of the gable roofs, which had previously been characteristic, the curb or gambrel form, flattened only at the summit, represented the survival of the old steep slope. Francis Price wrote of a figure in his "British Carpenter," 1733: "8B is called a kerb roof, and is much in use, on account of its giving so much room within side." English books of the middle of the century abound in diagrams for the trusses of such mansard roofs (figure 55),[1] with nothing to reveal that they were not intended to be carried out to a gable. In the McPhedris house at Ports-

From a photograph by Frank Cousins

Figure 57. Graeme Park, Horsham, Pennsylvania. John Kirk, 1721 to 1722

mouth, certainly before 1728, and probably finished by 1722, the brick wall of the gable rises above the roof according to earlier fashion, both along the slope and between the tall pairs of chimneys (figure 56). Elsewhere and later, a raking mould- ing extends along the gable. Usually this goes by the chimneys, also, although in the north gable of the Van Cortlandt house, Lower Yonkers, it is interrupted by the chimney, as late as 1748. Here, as in the McPhedris house, the eaves cornice

[1] *E. g.*, W. Salmon's "Palladio Londinensis," 1738 (first edition, 1734), pl. 34; Batty Langley's "City and Country Builder's . . . Treasury," 1745 (first edition, 1740), and "Builder's Jewel," 1752, pls. 89, 92; W. Pain's "Practical Builder," fourth edition, Boston, 1792, pls. 4, 5; etc.

is mitred against the façade without turning the corner. It was in Graeme Park (figure 57) and in the Hancock house (figure 58) that a more academic treatment was first used, a short horizontal return on the gable-end, which became universal in the best later houses of the type.

A truncation of the gable itself, analogous to that of the roof in these houses, securing the practical advantages of the vertical wall while reducing the effect of

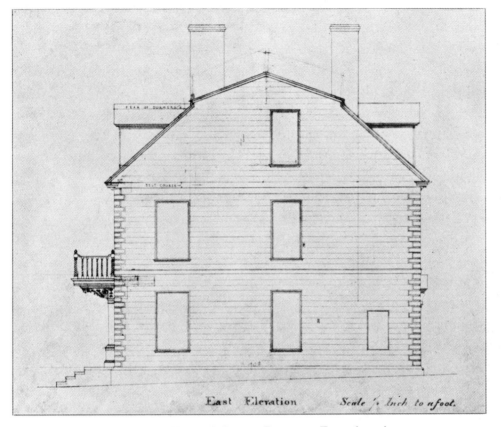

East Elevation   Scale ½ Inch to a foot.

Figure 58. Hancock house, Boston. East elevation
From a measured drawing by John Sturgis
Courtesy of R. Clipston Sturgis

height, occurs in several instances. This form of roof, sometimes called the jerkin-head, is spoken of in estimates for the Pinckney house in Charleston (figure 66) as a "hipp'd wall roof," and again as a "snug dutch roof."[1] In the earliest examples soon after 1700—the Charles Read house ("London Coffee-house") and the Joshua Carpenter house in Philadelphia, with their steep roofs, as well as the Mulberry (figure 43), where it is used in connection with the gambrel—the motive of its

[1] Smith, "Dwelling Houses of Charleston," pp. 361, 367.

origin clearly appears. Although unacademic, it continued in occasional use when the slope was less, as in the outbuildings of Stratford, in the Pinckney house, 1746, in Kenmore, near Fredericksburg, and even after the Revolution in Woodlawn, built by a son of the owner of Kenmore.

More commonly the gable, when retained, merely received a lower slope, conforming to that of a pediment. This was already true of the Sergeant and Penn houses before 1700. Among the more pretentious houses of the eighteenth century with a pitch roof few of the slopes exceed thirty degrees. The evolution of the gable end is the same as with the gambrel. At Tuckahoe (figure 42), soon after 1700, the cornice is cut off squarely; in the Governor Dummer's house at Byfield, Massachusetts, probably between 1712 and 1716,[1] it is mitred back against the façade. A short return around the corner occurs in the Grant house at East Windsor, Connecticut, 1758, and in the Johnson house, Germantown, 1768, both in general somewhat backward for their time. The ultimate form was the full pediment, with a horizontal cornice completely across the end, foreshadowed in the Sergeant house and even in the Penn house, where a heavy penthouse unites the eaves. The accepted relation of horizontal and raking cornices in a true pediment, with the cyma only along the rake, is one of the test-questions of academic architecture. It appears first in the central pavilions of Rosewell (figure 65) before 1730, and subsequently in houses of specially architectonic character. Its earliest certain appearance as the termination of a main roof is at Cliveden after 1763. Meanwhile in Pennsylvania, where the gable roof enjoyed a special vogue, a form appears intermediate between this and that of the Penn, Read, and Joshua Carpenter houses, with horizontal cornice also crowned by a cyma and covered by a small penthouse roof. This occurs in dated examples from 1744 to 1762; at Whitby, 1754, side by side with a grammatical pediment on the staircase tower.

Fully half of the more important Colonial houses of the eighteenth century had the hip-roof with a level cornice line all about, as in Coleshill, Thorpe Hall, and other English houses ascribed to Inigo Jones and Webb, and dated about 1650. This form was first adopted in America, as we have seen, just before 1700. The earliest examples rose to a ridge, and the ridge was retained until the Revolution in those houses in which the masses were relatively narrow, whether in an H plan or a long rectangle. Even where the house was more nearly square there were certain instances of keeping the ridge, as Westover (figure 59) after 1726 and Carter's Grove in 1751, with their vast expanse of roof surface. In general, however, such a roof was cut off at the top. Sometimes this was done in the true mansard

[1] Currier, "Ould Newbury," pp. 317–319.

Figure 59. Westover, James City County, Virginia. Shortly after 1726

form with steep lower slopes, and four visible upper slopes of less inclination, as at Ampthill, Chesterfield County, Virginia, about 1732; Shirley Place, Roxbury, Massachusetts, 1746; the Van Cortlandt house, Lower Yonkers, 1748; the John Vassall (Longfellow) house, 1759; and a number of fine houses of undetermined date, none of them substantially later than these. Even before this time, in exceptional instances, the roof was cut off by a deck, as nearly flat as might be, as in

From a photograph by Frank Cousins

Figure 60. Stenton, Germantown. 1728

the prominent English houses named above. This is the case at Stenton, 1728 (figure 60). After 1750 the deck was almost universal in the better houses of relatively square mass, whatever their location: Woodford, Mount Pleasant, and Lansdowne at Philadelphia, the Chase house at Annapolis, the Schuyler and Roger Morris houses in New York, the Timothy Orne house in Salem, Drayton Hall and the Miles Brewton house in South Carolina.

A significant feature of the roof was the balustrade that was frequently used with it. We have seen that Belknap mentions balustrades as used in Boston after 1711, bordering a flat deck. Such a flat deck balustrade first appeared in England at Coleshill, under the Commonwealth. The earliest Colonial example remaining is

88

that of the McPhedris house in Portsmouth, surely before 1728 and probably finished in 1722, which has a balustrade from chimney to chimney, along the curbs dividing the upper and lower slopes of its gambrel roof (figure 56). One likewise occurs with the gambrel in the Hancock and Pickman houses (1737 and 1750), where it also returns across the ends (figures 34 and 63). With the mansard roof (figures 67, 68) it appears in Shirley Place, Roxbury (after 1746), and the John Vassall

Figure 61. Royall house, Medford. East front. Between 1733 and 1737

house (1759); with the hip-roof having a deck—its truly functional use—in Woodford (after 1756), Mount Pleasant (figure 39, after 1761), and Lansdowne (1773–1777) at Philadelphia, in the Orne House at Salem (1761), and in the Roger Morris house in New York (1765). Simultaneously, to be sure, the same types of roof continued to be used also without a balustrade, as at Thorpe Hall: the mansard having none in the Van Cortlandt house (1748); the hip-roof with a deck having none in Stenton (1728), in Drayton Hall (before 1756), in the Miles Brewton house, Charleston (1765–1769), and in the Chase house, Annapolis (1769–1771).

Meanwhile the balustrade had appeared in another position, which was destined to be preferred in future, along the eaves. A terrace roof, covered with lead, with a balustrade above the cornice, had long been adopted in Europe for buildings of the greatest academic pretensions, as, in England, Whitehall and the Queen's House. It was adopted at Rosewell in Virginia by 1730. In minor English buildings for which a sloping roof was retained, a parapet or balustrade was nevertheless often introduced to approximate the fashionable effect. The oldest house in the colonies which has such an eaves-balustrade is the Schuyler house, Albany, 1761, and there is no special reason to suppose it did not form part of the original construction, although it is not specifically mentioned in those bills for the house which are preserved. The Pickman (Derby) house on Washington Street, Salem, built in 1764, had one from the start, for it is shown in a painting made just sub-

Figure 62.   Carved modillion from the Hancock house, Boston.   1737 to 1740
In the possession of the Massachusetts Historical Society

sequently. A parapet at the eaves appears also in an old view of Tryon's Palace, built 1767–1770, but any such feature did not become common in America until after the Revolution.

The dormer-window was widely used in the eighteenth century, and underwent characteristic modification. In many houses, to be sure, there were no dormers. This was generally where there were no rooms in the garret, owing usually to narrow masses or low hip-roofs, or where rooms there could be lighted from end gables. Only in very few cases, such as Shirley Hall, where dormers were kept off the front, yet used elsewhere, can any objection to them be inferred on grounds of appearance. The most common form of dormer, occurring throughout the period, was one with a square-headed window surmounted by a triangular gable or pediment. Other forms appear only during more restricted times. Thus an alternation of triangular and segmental pediments, as in Coleshill and Thorpe Hall in England, occurs in the McPhedris, Hancock, Clarke (Frankland), and Pickman houses, all in New England before 1750. Dormers having hip-roofs characterize certain Southern houses, such as Westover, and the Eveleigh house at Charleston, in the second quarter of the century. A semicircular-headed window rising into the tympanum of a triangular pediment was a form specially favored in fine houses of the last thirty years before the Revolution,[1] finding employment in 1746 at Shirley Place, Roxbury, and after 1760 at Mount Pleasant, Cliveden, the Roger Morris

Figure 63. Benjamin Pickman house, Essex Street, Salem. 1750
From an old lithograph: " J. C. F. del., Pendleton's Litho."

house, and the Miles Brewton house. At Mount Pleasant and Cliveden, in the 'sixties, the dormers are flanked by vertical consoles. Neither a dormer with a semicircular roof nor one with a Palladian window occurs in any attested instance before the Revolution.

A cupola was placed on the roof of some large Colonial mansions, as in many English houses, beginning with Coleshill and Ashdown. Among minor English ex-

[1] Hope Lodge, near Philadelphia, ascribed to 1723, has dormers of this type, otherwise unknown at such a date, and thus possibly later additions.

amples, the "Cupola house" at Bury St. Edmunds, dated 1693,[1] has an octagonal one with four arched windows and a roof semicircular in section. Governor Hutchinson wrote of a fire in the roof of his house in 1748, "the Lanthorne being in a blaze."[2] Existing cupolas in the colonies which seem to be contemporary with the houses are those of Shirley Place, after 1746; the Pickman house, Washington Street, Salem, 1764; and the Jeremiah Lee house, Marblehead, 1768. Whether that of Mount Vernon comes from just before or just after the Revolution has not been determined.

It is the detailed treatment of surfaces and openings which has hitherto received most attention in studies of Colonial architecture, yet the task still remains of giving an exact account of its evolution. For the exteriors we may say, in general, that the development is toward a higher and higher degree of formal organization.

At first this was an organization merely of the functional elements: wall surface, doorways, windows, cornice, angles, floor lines—any academic detail being confined to the treatment of these individually. In the spacing and size of openings, irregularity was more and more infrequent. At Graeme Park, in 1721, the arrangement of the front, like that of the interior, is not symmetrical; but at Westover (figure 59), soon after 1726, the façades are perfectly balanced, in spite of an unsymmetrical plan. The only later exceptions of importance are in the Royall house and Mount Vernon, both the product of remodellings. In the earlier houses a development can be noted in the number of elements elaborated. At Graeme Park (figure 57) all is of the utmost plainness. No feature projects from the wall surface; doors and windows alike have merely an architrave for frame, even the cornice is boxed in the simplest manner. At Stenton (figure 60), 1728, the cornice is enriched with block modillions and the internal divisions of the house are marked by projecting bands. At Westover, for perhaps the first time, the doorway is framed with pilasters. In the east façade of the Royall house (figure 61), 1733–1737, the windows likewise have a rich casing, including a cornice, and the angles are adorned with quoins. The Hancock house (figure 34), 1737–1740, has door and windows sumptuously framed and the modillions of the cornice are carved (figure 62). So much elaboration of the openings, however, remained exceptional.

It was more common for the wall surface itself to be enriched by groovings or "rustication." This was true not merely in masonry but imitatively in wood. Projecting quoins at the angles are found earliest in Colonel Robert Brewton's

---

[1] B. Oliver, "Old Houses of East Anglia" (1912).
[2] P. O. Hutchinson, "Diary and Letters of Thomas Hutchinson," vol. 1 (1884), p. 54.

house in Charleston, before 1733, in the east front of the Royall house, 1733–1737, in the Hancock house, 1737, and in the Roger Morris house—the last two of actual masonry, the other of brick faced with wood. Dated examples of rustication over the whole surface are, in masonry, the central pavilion of Mount Airy, 1758; in wood, the west front of the Royall house, probably before 1750, the Pick-

From a photograph by Frank Cousins

Figure 64.   Jeremiah Lee house, Marblehead, Massachusetts.   1768

man (figure 63) and Orne houses, Essex Street, Salem, 1750 and 1761, the Jeremiah Lee house, Marblehead (figure 64), 1768, and the entrance front of Mount Vernon, dating in its present form from about 1778.[1]

The most pretentious houses, as time went on, sought distinction rather by treatment with elements primarily formal in their very nature—"pavilions," pilasters, and porticos.

The first academic house in the colonies to have a projecting central "pavilion," was Rosewell (figure 65), before 1730, antedating any other by a score of years. At

[1] See letter of Lund Washington quoted by P. Wilstach, "Mount Vernon" (1916), p. 141.

93

Rosewell the pavilions, front and rear, are masses deep enough to affect the spaces of the interior, but a glance at the plan reveals that they were adopted for plastic exterior effect. This is obviously the case with the shallow central pavilions which appeared frequently after 1750: for instance, in the Pickman, John Vassall (figure 68), and Apthorp houses in Massachusetts; in Mount Pleasant and Cliveden at Philadelphia; in the Chase house at Annapolis; in Mount Airy and Tryon's Palace in the South.

From a photograph by H. P. Cook

Figure 65.   Rosewell, Gloucester County, Virginia.   Before 1730

Greater academic splendor was obtained by the adornment of walls and pavilions by an "order."   But two instances occur of an order embracing two stories above a story treated as a high architectural basement: the Matthew Cozzens, or Dudley house near Newport, built in the 'fifties or early 'sixties,[1] and Tryon's Palace,[2] 1767–1770. The favorite scheme was the "colossal order" rising from ground or pedestal to the main cornice. This first appeared in the Pinckney house in Colleton Square, Charleston (figure 66), 1746, and in Shirley Place, Roxbury (figure 67), built following that year.   In Shirley Place, in the west façade of the Royall house, before 1750, in the John Vassall and Apthorp houses in Cambridge, 1758

[1] Peterson's "History of Rhode Island" (1853), p. 149, and notes of Ogden Codman.
[2] J. Lossing, "Field Book of the Revolution," vol. 2 (1852), p. 570, note.

Figure 66.   Charles Pinckney house, Colleton Square, Charleston.   1745 to 1746
From Smith: *Dwelling Houses of Charleston*

Figure 67.   Shirley Place, Roxbury, Massachusetts.   After 1746
Courtesy of William Sumner Appleton

and soon after, the order consists of pilasters, each with an individual fragment of architrave and frieze, and perhaps also of pedestal. This was the way the orders were generally figured in the popular handbooks, by a single column with entablature and pedestal mitred back at either side. Their use in this form was not confined to the colonies: it may be seen even in such magnificent English houses as Stoneleigh Abbey (figure 69), to the central block of which the Royall façade is

From a photograph by Frank Cousins

Figure 68.   John Vassall (Longfellow) house, Cambridge.   1759

closely akin. It had the practical advantage of allowing more height for the windows of the upper story. This advantage was foregone in the central pavilion of the Pinckney house, however, as well as in the Apthorpe house in New York, ascribed to 1767,[1] where a full entablature completely encircles the house.

In the lateral arrangement of columnar elements the earliest examples were among the most ambitious. The Pinckney house has four pilasters forming a central frontispiece with a pediment, the front of Shirley Place has pilasters at every bay, with those of the end bays coupled, constituting end pavilions. In contrast

1 "Memorial History of New York," vol. 2 (1892), p. 432, note.

with these, the Royall house has merely a single pilaster at either end, the Vassall and Apthorp houses, one at each end and one at either side of the projecting central pavilion. At Shirley Place, moreover, the end pilasters turn the corners of the building, whereas in the Royall, Vassall, and Apthorp houses they are merely applied against the front as classical trophies. In the Hooper house, Danvers, Massachusetts (figure 70), and in the country-house of William Browne in Beverly,[1] a pair of engaged columns replace pilasters in flanking the central bay, and in the

Figure 69. Stoneleigh Abbey, Warwickshire

Apthorpe house in New York (figure 71), most architectonic of the group, pilasters mark each bay of the ends while engaged columns frame the recessed loggia of the front.

The extreme of academism everywhere involved use of the portico, with columns standing free. A small, tabernacle-like portico of two columns a single story in height had sheltered the door of the Sergeant house as early as 1679, and similar ones, more correct in detail, were again the chief ornaments of such splendid houses as the Orne house, Salem, 1761, and the Jeremiah Lee house, Marblehead, 1768.

---

[1] Dr. Andrew Hamilton, who visited it in 1744, says "the porch is supported by pillars of the Ionic order." "Itinerarium" (1907), p. 147. The foundations, of which a plan is published in *Historical Collections of the Essex Institute*, vol. 31 (1895), p. 212, seem to show that these pillars must have been engaged columns.

At Gunston there is a portico of four small columns, with an arch forming a Palladian motive, although this porch may be later than the house itself. The general unfamiliarity of wide low porches, even at the eve of the Revolution, is shown by some amusing references in the correspondence of the painter Copley with Henry

From a photograph by Frank Cousins

Figure 70. Hooper house, Danvers, Massachusetts

Pelham,[1] who was looking after the erection of Copley's house in Boston. Copley writes from New York, July 14, 1771:

Should I not add Wings I shall add a peazer when I return, which is much practiced here, and is very beautiful and convenient.

Pelham replied:

I dont comprehend what you mean by a peazer. Explain that in your next,

whereupon Copley responded:

You say you dont know what I mean by a Peaza. I will tell you than. it is exactly

[1] *Collections of the Massachusetts Historical Society*, vol. 71 (1914), pp. 131–137. Copley's plan and elevation are reproduced, facing p. 136.

such a thing as the cover over the pump in your Yard, suppose no enclosure for Poultry their, and 3 or 4 Posts added to support the front of the Roof, a good floor at bottom, and from post to post a Chinese enclosure about three feet high. these posts are Scantlings of 6 by 4 inches Diameter, the Broad side to the front, with only a little moulding round the top in a neat plain manner. some have Collumns but very few, and the top is gen-

Figure 71. Apthorpe house, New York City

erally Plasterd, but I think if the top was sealed with neat plained Boards I should like it as well. these Peazas are so cool in Sumer and in Winter break off the storms so much that I think I should not be able to like an house without. . . . I have drawn them in the Plan.

Copley's elevation shows one-story "peazas" at the sides like those now forming part of the John Vassall (Longfellow) house.

A two-storied portico of superposed orders, four columns in width, won for Drayton Hall in 1758 the appellation of a "Palace."[1] Here the upper columns stand on pedestals. In the Miles Brewton house in Charleston, near by, in 1765-1769, the same general scheme was repeated with far greater elegance: the width

[1] *South Carolina Gazette*, December 22, 1758, quoted by H. A. M. Smith in *S. C. Historical Magazine*, vol. 20 (1919), p. 93.

is no longer sprawling, the pedestals are omitted. In Jefferson's design for Monticello (figure 72), 1771, finally, the scheme—a favorite one with Palladio (figure 73)—was reproduced with strict Palladian accuracy both in proportions and in detail. The upper order seems never actually to have come to execution.[1] Not dissimilar was the portico of Lansdowne, built 1773–1777, and destroyed about 1866.[2]

The "colossal portico," of columns rising through the full height of the build-

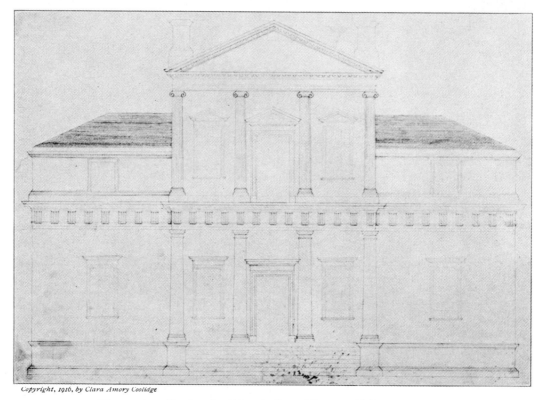

Copyright, 1916, by Clara Amory Coolidge

Figure 72.   Design for Monticello.   Thomas Jefferson.   1771
From the original drawing in the Coolidge collection

ing, is popularly thought of as specially characteristic of the Colonial house, but it will be found that only a single example can be proved to be prior to the Revolution. In many instances such a portico attached to a pre-Revolutionary house is a later addition. Thus the one at Whitehall has no relation to the mouldings of the main cornice of the house, which it intersects awkwardly; the one at the Woodlands, Philadelphia, would seem to date from the remodelling of 1788. Mrs. Mary Newton Stannard, who corrects the popular notion, cites Mount Vernon, Sabine

[1] Kimball, "Thomas Jefferson, Architect" (1916), p. 29.
[2] View and discussion in T. Westcott, "The Historic Mansions of Philadelphia" (1877), p. 334.

Hall, and Nomini Hall as among the few examples.[1] The portico at Mount Vernon, however, if our reasoning in the discussion of this house is correct, dates from between 1786 and 1787; the one at Sabine Hall seems also to be a later addition. The description of Nomini Hall by Philip Fithian, on which she depends, does not warrant the conclusion, the "Portico" which he mentions being evidently an enclosed porch with windows.[2] The sole authentic colossal portico from before the Revolution seems to be that of the Roger Morris or Jumel house in New York City (figure 74), which is almost certainly a part of the original fabric built in 1765.

The treatment of single elements will be discussed individually only in the case of those which show an unmistakable evolution. Most elaborate and important of these is the doorway, of which the opening, its filling, and its enframement all deserve analysis.

Doorways having a square-headed opening occur throughout the Colonial period, generally with a lintel, at least in appearance. The square-headed opening showing a structural flat arch is restricted to the first half of the century, appearing in the Mulberry, Stratford, the Hancock house, and Carter's Grove. The segmental arch is confined to much the same period: in Graeme Park, 1721, Stenton, 1728 (figure 75), and Whitby, 1754. On the other

Figure 73. Design from Palladio, Book II plate 61

hand, a semicircular arch does not appear until after 1756: in the side doorway at Woodford, in the Izard house, Charleston, in Gunston, Mount Pleasant, and Whitehall, in the Chase house at Annapolis, and others on the eve of the Revolution. There is but a single undoubtedly authentic example, itself late, of an elliptical arched door head before the Revolution, that of the Miles Brewton house in Charleston, built 1765–1769.[3] The familiar elliptical heads are otherwise entirely from Republican days.

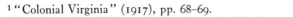

[1] "Colonial Virginia" (1917), pp. 68–69.   [2] "Journal of Philip Fithian" (1900), p. 129.
[3] The date of the Tristram Dalton house in Newburyport is wholly uncertain. A. Hale, "Old Newburyport Houses" (1912), p. 28.

The most significant difference within the bounds of the opening lay in the method of giving light to the hall at this point. In early houses a rectangular transom here was not uncommon: witness Graeme Park, Stenton, Rosewell, Westover, the Ayrault house at Newport, and the Daniel Pastorius house at Germantown, all between 1721 and 1748. A number of doorways about 1760 have lights in the upper panels of the doors themselves: those of the Williams house, Deerfield, as remodelled in 1756, the Ebenezer Grant house, East Windsor, the John Vassall

Figure 74.   Roger Morris (Jumel) house, New York City.   1765

and Apthorp houses in Cambridge. Meanwhile, in the arched door heads coming into use after 1757, semicircular transoms or fanlights now first appeared, superseding both the older forms. The elliptical arch of the Miles Brewton house also has its fanlight. No instance of side-lights, included within the main door opening, exists before the Revolution, although narrow windows at either side are combined with the door in an inclusive architectural motive in the Schuyler and Chase houses, from the late 'sixties, and others. Wooden bars were the rule in transoms prior to the War of Independence.

The enframement of doorways was at first merely an architrave, as in Tuckahoe, the Mulberry, Graeme Park, and Stenton (figure 75), all by 1728, and examples of this can be found in masonry houses down to the time of Whitby, 1754. Certain pretentious houses of this period had rusticated blocks instead of an architrave, notably Shirley Place, after 1746, with its heavy key-blocks. From

From a photograph by Frank Cousins

Figure 75. The doorway at Stenton. 1728

about 1725, however, it had become almost universal to have a more elaborate crown, with frieze and cornice in some form, generally supported by either consoles or an order. The two schemes appear almost simultaneously, consoles at Rosewell, pilasters at Westover, if these belong to the original work. Both occur in the North in the east doorway of the Royall house (figure 61), the console serving as key-block.[1]   Here, as later in the Hancock house and others, the order was relieved against a rusticated background.   Widely overhanging brackets are rare in American houses, the two dated examples being in the doorway of the Hancock house, where they support a balcony, and that of the Ayrault house, where they carry a hemispherical hood.   Both are from the late 'thirties.   English examples are numerous; one hood not dissimilar bears the date 1703.[2]   Engaged columns, bolder in relief, were first adopted in the Hancock doorway (figure 34), and after 1750 they rivalled the pilasters in frequency of use (figure 76).   With the addition of free-standing columns the door enframement became the portico.   Where the doorway involved an order there was generally a pediment, and this was ordinarily triangular.   The segmental pediment appears in doorways of the middle of the century, however, in the entrance front of Westover after 1726 (1749?) and the west front of the Royall house before 1750.[3]   The scroll pediment also—a reminiscence of Wren's baroque freedom—appeared over the garden door of Westover and the balcony door of the Hancock house.   Under the influence of the great Boston mansion, for which the trim had been cut in Middletown, it lingered in the Connecticut Valley as a dialect form beyond the middle of the century.   The Colton house at Longmeadow (1754), the Williams door at Deerfield (1756), and the Grant house at East Windsor (1757) illustrate this, as well as the fine undated example in the Metropolitan Museum (figure 77).

Window treatment followed lines of development essentially similar, but with its own special points of significance.   Thus the segmental arch was used through the same period as in doors, in the McPhedris house, Graeme Park, Stenton, Rosewell, Westover, and Carter's Grove, ranging from 1720 to 1751.   The proportions of the openings, however, varied with time in a way which is not true of the door openings.   Those of the houses down to 1732 are notably tall in proportion, as much as 2¾ : 1 at Graeme Park.   Such tall windows recur later only in the isolated instance of Gunston Hall, 1758.

The size of glass used in window-panes showed a general increase as the century progressed, but this increase was not regular and uniform for all houses of a given time.   Thus whereas in 1737 Thomas Hancock, countermanding a previous order, doubtless for smaller panes, ordered glass 11½ by 18 inches and 8½ by 12

---

[1] Side consoles exist in the door of the Dummer house, probably built between 1712 and 1716, which closely follows the doorway on p. 175 of Richards' "Palladio."

[2] J. Belcher and Macartney: "Later Renaissance Architecture in England," vol. 2 (1901), pl. 11.

[3] The fine similar doorway of the McPhedris house, Portsmouth, seems, from the way the belt course has been cut away for it, to be somewhat later than the house itself.

Figure 76. The doorway at Cliveden. After 1763

inches for his palatial house,[1] the panes of the Ayrault house in Newport, the same year, were to be 7 by 9,[2] and in a town ten miles from Boston in 1770 panes 10 by 14 excited the admiration and curiosity of the neighborhood.[3] The following table will show the prevailing tendency:

1721	Graeme Park	8 x 12½
1737	Ayrault house, Newport	7 x 9
1737	Hancock house, Boston	8½ x 12
		11½ x 18
1746	Pinckney house, Charleston	9 x 11
Before 1750	Royall house, west front	8 x 10
1748	Van Cortlandt house, Lower Yonkers	9 x 11
After 1756	Woodford	10 x 12
1758	Gunston Hall	12 x 18
1759	John Vassall house	12 x 16
After 1761	Mount Pleasant	9 x 12
After 1763	Cliveden	9 x 12
	Whitehall	13½ x 20
1765	Roger Morris house	12 x 16
1769–1771	Chase house, Annapolis	11 x 18
1770	Quincy house, Braintree	10 x 14
1771–1775	Monticello	12 x 12

The number of panes tended, of course, to vary inversely with their size, eighteen or twenty-four panes being generally characteristic of earlier or less pretentious houses, twelve panes the common number in the finer and later dwellings. For the chief windows, twelve lights were first used in the 'thirties, and they had become common by the 'fifties in the better houses, although at Philadelphia one finds Whitby, Woodford, Mount Pleasant, and Cliveden with twenty-four, the last after 1763. Throughout the Colonial period the sash bars remained heavy, being ordinarily 1¼ to 1½ inches in width.

Windows generally had a full architrave for casing, but in masonry houses this was ordinarily of wood and put in shelter between the masonry jambs. In certain instances after 1750, however, it was placed with greater regard for classical correctness, projecting in front of the plane of the wall. Thus at Whitby, 1754, the tower window has its wooden casing on the face of the wall; at Mount Airy, 1758, there are projecting architraves of cut stone; at Gunston and Whitehall the

[1] Arthur Gilman, "Thomas Hancock," *Atlantic Monthly*, vol. 11 (1863), p. 701.
[2] G. C. Mason, Jr., in *American Architect*, vol. 10 (1881), p. 83.
[3] "Memoirs of Eliza S. M. Quincy" (1861), p. 91.

windows of the hall are distinguished from the others by projecting architraves, which were used throughout at Monticello on the eve of the Revolution. In some of these instances and also occasionally in wooden houses the window was enriched

Figure 77. Doorway from Westfield, Massachusetts
In the Metropolitan Museum

by a cornice, or a frieze and cornice. The earliest case is in the east front of the Royall house, as early as 1737 (figure 61). Later examples remained always somewhat exceptional, as was the pedimented window, which first appeared in the west front of the Royall house, probably before 1750. Drayton Hall has pilasters also.

No house with its ordinary windows having semicircular arches was built in the colonies before the Revolution, but a single long arched window was often placed over the stair landing. There is such a one in the McPhedris house in the North and in Rosewell in the South, both before 1730, and others may be found down to the close of the period, although they tended to give way to the Palladian motive.

The "Venetian" or "Palladian" window, having a central arch rising above rectangular side openings, made its appearance in the colonies shortly before 1750 as a central feature of the façades, especially as a stair window. One is mentioned in the specifications of the Pinckney house in Colleton Square, Charleston, dated 1746.[1] Other Colonial examples are at Shirley Place, Woodford, Mount Airy, and Mount Pleasant (figure 39), in the Brewton house at Charleston and the Chase

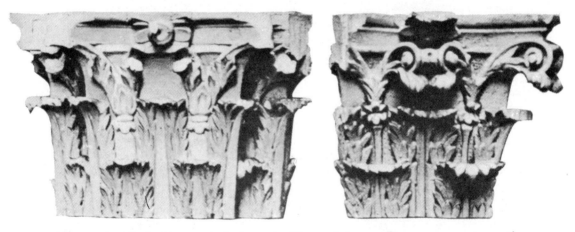

Figure 78. Corinthian capitals from the Hancock house, Boston. 1737 to 1746
Preserved by the Essex Institute and reproduced by its courtesy

house at Annapolis. In the Brewton house the central arch is doubled, and in the Chase house, latest of all, a large blank arch embraces the whole after a fashion then being adopted in England.

Outside window-shutters or blinds are common features among Colonial houses, although an equal number of houses may be found without them. No general rule may be framed regarding their presence, which is not even dependent on the absence of inside shutters. The Van Cortlandt and John Vassall houses, among others, have both. Whether all the shutters are contemporary with the houses is uncertain, but in the case of the Schuyler house, Albany, at least, we have bills of 1761 for fifteen pairs of "outside shutters."[2] Panelled outside shutters were practically confined to the Middle Colonies. The blinds with louvres used elsewhere in Colo-

[1] Smith. "Dwelling Houses of Charleston," p. 368.   [2] G. Schuyler. "The Schuyler Mansion," p. 6.

nial times, and indeed long after, generally had large slats and no cross-bar. Movable slats were not introduced until later.

The chimneys were slow to depart from the earlier tradition of elaboration in plan. Thus at Tuckahoe, Graeme Park, and Rosewell, all before 1730, the chimneys are T-shaped; this form occurs in one of the chimneys of the Hancock house,

From a photograph by H. F. Beidleman

Figure 79. The drawing-room, Graeme Park

1737, and even in one of those of the Van Cortlandt house, Lower Yonkers, 1748. Slender pilaster-like strips mark the ends of one broad face of the chimneys at Tuckahoe and in the McPhedris house, Portsmouth. Early chimneys of merely rectangular form exist, however, at the Mulberry and at Stenton, and they were normal after 1730, although an isolated instance of a pilaster strip occurs in such a fine house as Cliveden as late as 1763. The variety of forms of the chimney-cap between about 1730 and the Revolution are not significant of date. One having the profile of a small classic cornice, for instance, is found in a number of pretentious houses from Rosewell to Monticello, while others have but a simple plinth.

For exterior balustrades, turned balusters of ordinary academic profile were customary. The posts in early examples like those of the McPhedris and Hancock houses were likewise turned, and projected above the rail in a ball or knob. This style was retained in the John Vassall house, 1759. In the balcony of the Hancock house both balusters and posts have spiral turning like that of the stair rails inside. At Shirley Hall, after 1746, in the Pickman house, Essex Street, Salem, and at Mount Pleasant and Lansdowne, the posts were square dies like those of a balustrade of stone. After 1756 railings of "Chinese lattice"—slender bars forming patterns in the panels—made their appearance at Woodford, the Schuyler, Timothy Orne, and Roger Morris houses. Jefferson made drawings of Chinese lattice about 1771.[1] It continued in use after the Revolution.

The "orders" preferred in Colonial exteriors were the Tuscan or Doric and the Ionic—simpler of execution than the Corinthian. In the houses having the "colossal order," Doric is used in Shirley Hall, the Royall and Morris houses, Ionic in the other examples. In all the superposed porticos, also, it was the Doric and the Ionic which were employed. In the enframement of doorways, on a smaller scale, the Corinthian does appear; very well understood at Westover and in the Hancock and McPhedris houses, all before 1750 (figure 78); travestied quaintly in vernacular Connecticut River houses considerably after that date (figure 77). Among the Ionic capitals the angular type, with four pairs of scrolls placed diagonally—first codified in modern times by Scamozzi—was almost universal. Strangely enough, an example of the "antique" form with volutes parallel to the face occurs, crudely executed, in one of the Connecticut River doorways, that of the Charles Churchill house at Wethersfield. In the design for the portico at Monticello, 1771, its adoption was a conscious affirmation of Palladian standards.

Execution in wood in the colonies is generally supposed to have given the orders more slender proportions and the detail a special delicacy. This idea, an outgrowth of nineteenth-century functional theory, developed at a time when attention was focussed chiefly on the Colonial buildings of New England, and when the later history of English architecture was little known. Outside New England, however, as we have seen, the great majority of the finest Colonial houses are of masonry, and in a number of these even the doorways and other details are of brick and stone. On the other hand, many Georgian houses in England have doorways and cornices of wood. In neither country are the forms and proportions of wooden details in general modified in the direction of slenderness prior to the advent of the Adam style. The Doric pilasters of the west front of the Royall house,

[1] Kimball, "Thomas Jefferson, Architect," p. 130.

fifteen diameters in height, and the columns of the Roger Morris portico, some thirteen diameters tall, are quite exceptional. It is just as easy to find examples of less
than the normal academic proportions, which in general were closely followed. The
attenuation of classic forms by the Adams, based on Pompeian suggestions, which
had its beginnings only about 1760, appeared in the popular handbooks after 1780,

Figure 80. Drawing-room of the Miles Brewton house, Charleston. 1765 to 1769

and in America thus after the Revolution. The wide-spread change of proportions,
which then first took place, was English in its origin and independent of material.

In the Colonial interiors of the eighteenth century, as in the houses as a whole,
a formal academic treatment took the place of the direct revelation of structural
elements. As we have seen, however, this formal composition did not extend at first
or in any high degree to the organization of the interior spaces themselves, but was
largely confined to the wall surfaces and to the elaboration of individual elements
such as the doorways, the window casings, the ceilings, and especially the chimneypieces and staircases.

The instrumentalities of change and continued evolution were largely the same as for the plan and exterior—that is to say, chiefly the architectural publications and builders' handbooks. After 1700 and still more after 1725, these became rich in details of cornices, doorways, chimneypieces, and stairs, as well as consoles, cartouches, and other ornaments, and it is often easily possible, as we shall see, to identify the very book from which the forms used in a given house were derived. In the course of the century, and even in competing works of the same date, there

Figure 81. The stairs at Westover

are marked differences in the character of the forms exemplified and recommended. While the English Palladianism of Lord Burlington tended to banish from the exterior the baroque forms used by Wren, such as scroll pediments and broken forms generally, for the interior these persisted in company with the novel and florid *rocaille* ornamentation of Louis XV.

The assertion used often to be made that the interior finish, as well as the bricks, of the old mansions was imported.[1] We are not aware, however, of authen-

[1] Earliest in the account of Westover in William Dunlap's "History of the Arts of Design in the United States" (1834), vol. 1, pp. 286 ff.

112

tic instances of this except in the case of paper-hangings, hardware, and marble fireplace facings and mantels. It is true that Thomas Hancock wrote from his new house to England, March 22, 1739–40: "I pray the favor of you Enquire what a pr. of Capitolls will cost me to be carved in London of the Corinthian Order, 16½ Inches One Way and 9 yᵉ Other—to be well done,"[1] but we do not know that he ordered them. On the contrary, we learn from the bills of William

From a photograph by R. W. Holsinger

Figure 82. The dining-room, Monticello. Thomas Jefferson. 1771 to 1775

More against Hancock that when the lower room and the chamber were wainscoted in 1745, More made the two "pare of pilasters" of the Corinthian order.[2] Even paper-hangings began to be manufactured in the colonies by 1763.[3] Domestic marble remained unused here until some time after the Revolution, and the marble used in chimneypieces was of foreign varieties. In the case of Tryon's

[1] Arthur Gilman, "The Hancock House," *Atlantic Monthly*, vol. 11 (1863), p. 702.
[2] Hancock MSS., Boston Public Library. The pilasters are shown in a photograph in the Hancock Collection at the Old State House, Boston.
[3] Bishop, "American Manufactures," vol. 1 (1861), p. 209.

Palace, we learn expressly from a letter of 1769 that besides window-sash and lead for roofing, "four of the principal chimney pieces are arrived also from London, with the hinges, locks, and other articles for the finishing this much admired structure."[1] The one described is of marble.

In any attempt to trace the development of interior features there is special difficulty due to the frequency of later insertions and remodellings. Where addi-

From a photograph by H. P. Cook

Figure 83. Northeast room at Tuckahoe. Before 1730. Mantel, post-Revolutionary

tions were made after a long interval, as in the case of the post-Revolutionary mantelpieces at Tuckahoe, the Mulberry, and the two Van Cortlandt houses, the difference of style is unmistakable. There is also the possibility, however, of changes made soon after the first building. Thus, as we have just seen, although the Hancock house was occupied in 1740, the panelling of its great rooms was not done until 1745. In the case of Monticello, even more deceptive additions were made.

[1] *Colonial Records of North Carolina*, vol. 8 (1890), pp. 7–8.

For the dining-room window the inner architrave had been put up before 1775, but the frieze and cornice were added about 1803.[1]

Panelling was adopted in place of wainscot sheathing about 1700. Such panelling of rooms in wood throughout (figure 79) was proportionately commoner in the first half of the century than after that, although a number of late panelled rooms may be found: in the Van Rensselaer manor-house, the Jeremiah Lee house, the Corbit house at Odessa, Delaware, and several houses in Charleston. Some of

From a photograph by H. P. Cook

Figure 84.   The hall at Stratford.   Between 1725 and 1730

these, to be sure, are the most elaborate of the colonies: the "mahogany room" of the Lee house, with its rich carved pendent festoons, or the drawing-room of the Miles Brewton house (figure 80)—finest of all—with its proportions, doorways, chimneypiece, and portraits reminiscent of the splendid Double Cube at Wilton in England. Restriction of the panelling to two sides or one side of the room, or to the chimney-breast only, was chiefly a question of means or of the importance of the room. Limitation of panelling merely to a dado began in the stair halls, where awkward shapes were otherwise encountered. Although Tuckahoe and Westover

[1] "Thomas Jefferson, Architect," p. 167.

(figure 81) have stair halls completely panelled, these do not recur in dated examples at a later time. In the 'fifties, with Woodford and Gunston, appear for the first time houses without panelling and having only a plain dado.

The decreasing use of panelling, in some of the finest houses, was closely related to the development of paper-hangings. Perhaps the earliest use of them is mentioned in the well-known letter of Thomas Hancock, January 23, 1737-8, order-

Figure 85.   Drawing-room from Marmion, Virginia
In the Metropolitan Museum

ing some for his house, where he speaks of hangings brought over three or four years previous, with great variety of "Birds, Peacocks, Macoys, Squirrels, Monkeys, Fruit & Flowers."[1] The use of paper-hangings increased steadily down to the Revolution and after it.[2] Two of the most magnificent sets are those made specially for the Jeremiah Lee house, built 1768, and the Van Rensselaer manor-house, for which the bill, dated 1768, is preserved.[3] Both these include views of

[1] Quoted in full by Arthur Gilman, "The Hancock House," *Atlantic Monthly*, vol. 11 (1863), pp. 692-707.
[2] *Cf.* J. B. Felt, "Annals of Salem," second edition (1845), vol. 1, p. 406; and Bishop, "American Manufactures," vol. 1, pp. 208-210.
[3] M. T. Reynolds, "The Colonial Buildings of Rensselaerwyck," *Architectural Record*, vol. 4 (1895), p. 428.

Roman ruins in *rocaille* frames. Not all the rooms from which panelling was banished seem to have been intended to receive wall-paper, however. At Whitehall, the Chase house, and Monticello (figure 82), the chaste austerity of plastered walls seems to have been consciously preferred.

Where panelling was used, the customary type remained until 1765 that with a narrow sunk moulding and a bevelled raised panel, its centre flush with the surrounding rails. This was in accordance with the statement of Moxon in his discussion, "Of Wainscoting Rooms": "You may (if you will) adorn the outer edges of the *Stiles* and *Rails* with a small *Moulding*: and you may (if you will) Bevil away the outer edges of the *Pannels*, and leave a Table in the middle of the Pannel."[1] In rare instances throughout this time there were raised or "bolection" mouldings, themselves bringing the entire panel in front of the rails. These occur in the McPhedris house, the John Vassall house, and the Jeremiah Lee house. After 1765, in the Miles Brewton and Stuart houses at Charleston and in the Corbit house, Odessa, Delaware, appears the flat sunk panel, sometimes bordered with mouldings partly raised, partly sunk. The tendency was toward fewer and larger panels, the finest houses, such as Westover, Carter's Grove, the Van Rensselaer

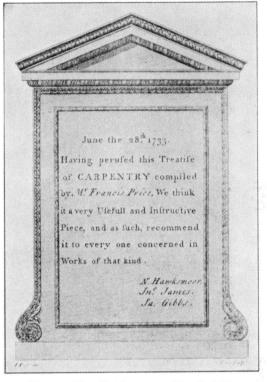

Figure 86. Tablet from *The British Carpenter*

and Miles Brewton houses having broad panels reaching from the dado to the cornice.

The dado cap itself was ordinarily carried along continuously, butted against the door and window casings; but in several early houses, such as Tuckahoe, the McPhedris house, and Stratford, it is interrupted short of these, being mitred against the wainscot. This still persists in the Van Cortlandt house in Lower Yonkers, and in parts of Carter's Grove, and it even recurs in the Lee house, Marblehead, in 1768, but at this late date it was highly exceptional.

Almost from the first introduction of panelling it was not uncommon for the wall treatment to include pilasters. They appear on either side of the fireplaces at

[1] "Mechanick Exercises: The Art of Joinery," second edition, with additions (1694), p. 106, and pl. 7.

Tuckahoe (figure 83), Westover (figure 102), the Hancock house, and many later houses, rising sometimes from the floor, sometimes from the dado. In the hall at Stratford (figure 84) they are used more ambitiously, completely surrounding the room at intervals measurably regular in effect, though not perfectly equal. A similar treatment, with Ionic pilasters, is found in the drawing-room from Marmion (figure 85), now in the Metropolitan Museum, and was apparently used likewise

From a photograph by H. P. Cook

Figure 87. Northwest parlor at Carter's Grove. 1751

in the Clark or Frankland house in Boston built by William Clark, who died in 1742.[1] These rooms remained unique, being rivalled in consistent "order" treatment perhaps only by the entrance hall at Carter's Grove, where uniform pilasters flank the doorways and the central arch. It was relatively rare elsewhere for pilasters to stand under a continuous entablature surrounding the room, as in these houses. Usually, even at a late period, they were employed, if at all, isolated and of different scales, as the individual elaboration of hall arches, doorways, and chimneypieces might suggest. In the Dalton house, Newburyport, and the Philipse

[1] S. A. Drake, "Old Landmarks of Boston" (1873), p. 165.

manor-hall at Yonkers, both of uncertain date, engaged columns, bolder in relief, replaced the pilasters. Free-standing columns on the interior occur during Colonial times only in two late houses of exceptionally formal disposition: Cliveden, after 1763, and the Chase house, Annapolis, 1769–1771. Those in the library of the John Vassall house seem to be additions by Andrew Craigie after the Revolution.

Arched doorways were occasionally used throughout the Colonial period. Specially characteristic of the time from 1725 to 1760, however, were the cupboard

From a photograph by Frank Consins

Figure 88. The great chamber, Graeme Park. 1721 to 1722

doors with arched heads frequently used to flank a fireplace. These occur in dated examples at Stenton, the Eveleigh house, Charleston, the Van Cortlandt house, Lower Yonkers, at Whitby and Mount Pleasant. Instances can be found, to be sure, after the Revolution also. A variant was the employment of open semicircular niches, of which perhaps the earliest domestic example is at Gunston Hall, 1758. Others, of more classical aspect, form part of the stair hall in the Chase house, a dozen years later.

In the usual square-headed doorways, the architrave was commonly treated with mitred "ears" at the top. From 1758, when they appear at Gunston, a frieze and cornice were frequently added to important doors, most usually with a broken triangular pediment. The frieze might be plain, curved, or even decorated with carving, but in doorways before the Revolution was not treated with end blocks or central panel. A pediment with cyma unbroken was found only in houses of exceptionally academic character: Graeme Park, Mount Pleasant, and Monticello. A door enframement with pilasters was unusual: there are instances at Gunston, Whitehall, and the Miles Brewton house, all dating after 1758. The William Brand-

From a photograph by Frank Cousins

Figure 89. Room to right of the hall, Jeremiah Lee house, Marblehead. 1768

ford (Horry) house in Charleston, built somewhere between 1751 and 1767, has folding doors framed by pilasters and an entablature. Doorways with consoles supporting the entablature were also rare in domestic interiors. Two dated examples are at Mount Pleasant and the Miles Brewton house, both after 1760.

Window casings rarely involved other members beyond an architrave. The architrave itself had ears less often than did the door casings. In two important instances, however, it is enriched by carved scrolls at the bottom: in Whitehall, and the Chase house at Annapolis, both from the 'sixties and but a few miles apart.

This was a familiar device in English work, perhaps the most conspicuous illustration in the handbooks being the plate bearing a recommendation of Francis Price's "British Carpenter," published in 1733 (figure 86). At the Van Cortlandt house, 1748, the windows have small cornices; at Carter's Grove (figure 87), 1751, they have a frieze and a cornice formed by breaking out the main cornice of the room. Gunston Hall, 1758, has the most elaborate window treatment internally: a pair of pilasters with full entablature. Interior panelled shutters folding into the jambs of the windows are well-known features of much Colonial work. The oldest examples are at Graeme Park. The specifications of the Ayrault house, Newport, 1739, call for "window shuts in all the rooms below,"[1] and those of the Pinckney house, Charleston, 1746, for "three panneled shutters" in the first floor windows.[2]

For framing the fireplace opening, as for windows and doors, the eighteenth century used a mitred moulding following more or less closely the classic architrave. The earliest example of this treatment, the Penn house, well before 1700, has a heavy curved bolection moulding, with a frieze and cornice providing a mantel-shelf (figure 28). Fireplace openings without a cornice or mantel-shelf long remained common. Counting those where mantelpieces were added after the Revolution, they include ones at Tuckahoe, the Mulberry, the McPhedris house, Stenton, the Van Cortlandt house in Lower Yonkers, Mount Pleasant, and in some rooms of Graeme Park (figure 88), Carter's Grove, and the John Vassall and Jeremiah Lee houses, the last as late as 1768 (figure 89). On the other hand, the Penn fireplace was not unique, even at an early day, in having a cornice, which exists on one fireplace at Graeme Park (figure 79) and on one at Carter's Grove, as well as in most later houses. The openings of the McPhedris and some of the Lee fireplaces, at least, had the bolection moulding, the others a typical architrave section of fascias and a small moulded back band. It was very characteristic of pre-Revolutionary work for the architrave to have ears, although occasional examples may be found without. Consoles above the architrave occur at Mount Pleasant and in the Lee house, both from the 'sixties, as well as at Kenmore and Mount Vernon, also before the Revolution. Consoles buttressing the sides of the architrave likewise exist at the Lee house and Mount Vernon, as well as at the Brice house in Annapolis. An order of small pilasters or columns supporting the mantel was known in the colonies prior to the Revolution only in imported chimneypieces of marble, to be discussed later.

It was customary to have a panelled chimney-breast above the fireplace. In

---

[1] Published by G. C. Mason, *American Architect*, vol. 10 (1881), p. 83.
[2] Smith, "Dwelling Houses of Charleston," p. 368.

the majority of examples until after 1750, especially where there was no mantel-shelf, the panels here often had merely the section of ordinary wainscot, identical with any used elsewhere in the room, or perhaps had the greater relief of a bolec-

From a photograph by Frank Cousins

Figure 90.   Mantel in room to left of hall, Lee house.   1768

tion moulding. This latter may be seen in some rooms of the Jeremiah Lee house as late as 1768. The majority of chimneypieces after 1750, however, had a special overmantel: a single large panel framed by an architrave, more or less elaborated. Two early overmantels are to be found at Graeme Park, built in 1721, but these are highly exceptional for their time. Ears on the architraves are almost universal, as elsewhere in Colonial times, and a pediment, always broken, was very common from the beginning. After 1760 the scroll pediment, or a similar treatment of

Figure 91. Chimneypiece from Swan's *British Architect* (1745), plate 51
Prototype of the Lee house mantel

the architrave, frequently occurs, contemporary with the employment of this feature in doors: at Mount Pleasant, the Schuyler, Van Rensselaer, Miles Brewton, Jeremiah Lee, and John Stuart houses. At Whitby, 1754, and Mount Pleasant

123

near by, after 1761, there is an "overmantel," notwithstanding the absence of a mantel-shelf, the architraves above and below being united by small projecting consoles. From about the same time flat consoles buttressing the overmantel were also adopted, as for the architrave of the fireplace opening itself: at Woodford, Gunston, the Miles Brewton, Lee, and Stuart houses. In a few chimneypieces, at the Brandford (Horry) house, Charleston, and the Brewton and Van Rensselaer houses, the overmantel is flanked by small pilasters. The exact date of the Horry house is uncertain, but it is surely after 1751 and before 1767; the others are after 1765.

Figure 92. Console from chimneypiece of parlor mantel in the Brice house, Annapolis

A special influence on Colonial chimneypieces was exercised by Abraham Swan's "British Architect, or Builder's Treasury of Staircases. Containing . . . a great Variety of New and curious Chimneypieces," of which the first edition was published in 1745, later ones in 1750 and 1758, and American editions at Philadelphia in 1775 and in Boston. Many of the chimneypieces with consoles which we have mentioned are derived with little modification from the plates of this book.[1] Thus that of the "mahogany room" in the Lee house, Marblehead (figure 90), follows plate 51 (figure 91) line for line; that of the dining-room at Mount Vernon, plate 50. The elaborate mantels in the Brice house at Annapolis, although not taken as a whole from single plates, are combinations of elements copied from Swan with special literalness. Thus in the living-room mantel the *rocaille* consoles at either side of the fireplace opening come directly from those shown in plate 51, and many motives of the other consoles, the frieze, and the overmantel are taken from plates 52 and 53. The consoles of the fireplace in the parlor (figure 92) are identical with those of plate 50 (figure 93), and the carved moulding of its architrave exactly follows the detail given on plate 51. The Brice house has been traditionally ascribed to 1740,[2] but it is obvious from these relationships that the interior finish, at least, dates from some time after 1745, at earliest.

The most elaborate of all the chimneypieces carved in the colonies (figure 94), that of the Council Chamber of the Governor Wentworth house at Little Harbor, near Portsmouth, with its termini supporting the mantel, is derived from plate 64 in William Kent's "Designs of Inigo Jones," a folio work of which several copies

---

[1] Its use at Annapolis has been already noted by T. H. Randall, "Colonial Annapolis," *Architectural Record,* vol. 1 (1892), p. 318.   [2] E. g., *ib.,* p. 335.

are known to have been in the colonies. There is a somewhat similar design in Swan's book, plate 54, but this has no overmantel and is otherwise not so nearly identical with the American example.

Facings of marble for the fireplace opening were often provided, the oldest houses having them being Stenton and Westover. Ordinarily these were plain slabs constituting the fascia of the architrave. At Whitby, built 1754, the soffit

Figure 93. Chimneypiece from Swan's *British Architect*, plate 50. With elements used in Mount Vernon and the Brice house

of the lintel slab is profiled more richly, and there is the suggestion of a moulded keystone. It was a facing like this, as we see by the photograph preserved at the Old State House in Boston, which is referred to in the bill of the joiner, William More, against Thomas Hancock:[1] "1746 June 28, To Cuting away the flore & fixing for ye Laying of your harthes & asisting the mason in puting up the fruntis^{peic} of marbel 3–0–0." Westover is unique in having a broad expanse of marble on

[1] Hancock MSS., Boston Public Library.

the chimney-breast, terminating in a pediment, and restored to-day with a panel and festoons above the fireplace (figure 102).

By the middle of the century whole mantelpieces of marble began to be im-

Figure 94. Chimneypiece in the Council Chamber, Wentworth house, Little Harbor

ported. At Carter's Grove, built 1751, one room had a full marble mantelpiece with frieze and cornice (figure 87), another merely marble architrave-facings. Bills for the Schuyler house include one of 1767 for "4 marble chimney pieces with hearths."[1] Governor Tryon enclosed in one of his letters of 1769 a description of the finest of the chimneypieces for his house:

[1] G. Schuyler, "The Schuyler Mansion," p. 6.

For the Council Chamber in the Governor's House at Newbern in North Carolina.
A large statuary Ionic chimney piece, the shafts of the columns sienna and the frett
on the Frieze inlaid with the same.   A rich edge and Foliage on the Tablet; medals of the

Figure 95.   Chimneypiece from Kent's *Design of Inigo Jones*, plate 64.   Prototype
of the Council Chamber mantel in the Wentworth House, Little Harbor

King & Queen on the Frieze over the Columns, the mouldings enriched, a large statuary
marble slab and black marble covings.
Messrs. Devol & Granger *fecit*.[1]

[1] *Colonial Records of North Carolina*, vol. 8 (1890), p. 8.

It is to be noted that this chimneypiece was flanked by a small order with columns. Analogous flanking members occur in the other marble mantels of this late period. One in the Van Rensselaer house has carved terminal figures; the one in the Miles Brewton drawing-room has pilaster-like strips crowned by consoles; the one in the parlor of the Chase house has half-pilasters. The Tryon chimneypiece also had another feature found at this time only in imported mantels: a frieze with a central panel and end motives, decorated with reliefs. Here there were medallions at the ends, foliage in the centre. In the Chase, Van Rensselaer, and

Figure 96. The stairs at Graeme Park
1721 to 1722

Brewton mantels, the central block has figure sculpture, the first popularly supposed to represent a scene from Shakespeare.

The stairs, so conspicuously placed in most Colonial houses, were developed as an artistic end in themselves, irrespective of whether there were important or public rooms above the ground story.

The adoption of an open string, with the ends of the treads showing, marked the change to the eighteenth century, although a few houses, such as Graeme Park (figure 96) and the Van Cortlandt house in Lower Yonkers, retain the closed string characteristic of the previous period. The ends of each step of the new stairs were treated either with a block, plain or panelled, or with a console-like scroll, or with both. All these varieties were also common in England. Plain block ends are generally early, as in the McPhedris house and Stenton; whereas panelled blocks may occur at any later time: 1761 in the Timothy Orne house, Salem. Scroll ends begin equally early, at Tuckahoe, Rosewell, and Westover. In the Hancock house, where the stairs (figure 100) established a new model of richness in so many respects, there were blocks and scrolls as well, and this was imitated in the Jeremiah Lee and other houses. The earliest examples of the scroll ends, at Tuckahoe (figure 97) and Rosewell, are carved somewhat in the manner of Gibbons, with foliage and flowers rather naturalistically treated, and this recurs at Carter's Grove in the middle of the century. At Westover there is a really academic, modillion-like scroll (figure 81), but this was unusual. The Hancock house initiated the use of a scroll block sawn to fantastic profile, in which a beaklike element predominates, and this was henceforth the commonest form, occurring at Whitby, Woodford, Mount Pleasant, Cliveden (figure 98), and in the John Vassall and Roger Morris houses. In the Miles Brewton house and the Jeremiah Lee house (figure 99), both in the later 'sixties, *rocaille* scrolls appear. Ordinarily the soffit of

Figure 97.   The stairs at Tuckahoe.   Before 1730

the stairs was unaffected by the form of the stair ends, but occasionally their profile was carried the full width of the stair. The Hancock house is the first instance. The other dated examples are late: the Orne house, 1761, for the block ends; the Chase house, 1769–1771, for the scroll ends.

The balusters of the eighteenth century were longer and more slender than those of the seventeenth, and were more closely spaced, generally three to a step. The turned part of all three began at the same height, so that there were three types with turning of unequal length. Sometimes the turning was of the ordinary sort, at right angles to the axis of the baluster, but in many instances the new device of spiral or swash turning was employed. Full directions for this are given by Moxon in his "Mechanick Exercises. . . . Applied to the Art of Turning" (1694).[1] It was used in the balusters of some of the first houses of the new century, such as Westover and Rosewell. In the Hancock house the three types of balusters were turned with different spiral patterns (figures 100 and 101), and this fashion was carried on in dozens of New England staircases down to the Revolution, as well as in the Schuyler house at Albany. Perfectly plain balusters were rare in Colonial days, although they may be found: square ones at Woodford and in the Chase house, round ones in the Roger Morris house.

Figure 98. The stairs at Cliveden
After 1763

Square newels, seen in Wren's Ashmolean Museum at Oxford, were frequently employed before 1750, as in the McPhedris house, Graeme Park (figure 96), Stenton, and the Van Cortlandt house in Lower Yonkers; they are rare after this date. Of the circular newels the earliest examples, at Tuckahoe and Rosewell, have carved foliage; many after 1735 have swash turning. A single spiral is used in the main newels of Carter's Grove and in the Schuyler house, and in newels at the turns in New England houses. The Hancock house initiated the *tour de force* of a double spiral in its main newel, the inner one twisting in the opposite direction from the outer, and this was imitated in many later New England houses. Elsewhere the later newels were generally left plain, as they were concealed by surrounding balusters supporting the end of a hand-rail which terminated in a horizontal scroll. This is first found at Westover; it became common after 1750. Even when this device was not used, the newel after 1730 was commonly set out beyond the line of the hand-rail, which curved to it. That of the Roger Morris house, set in front of the lower step, is a rare exception. In the last years before the Revolution there was a tendency to round the turns of the balustrade also. At the Miles Brewton house it makes a semicircle between the landing newels, although the front of the landing is straight; in the Chase house, for the

[1] "§ XXV. Of Turning Swash-Work," pp. 229–230, and pl. 18.

first time, it curves around without any intermediate newels. In the plan made for his house by the painter Copley in 1771,[1] it is the landing which is semicircular. Stairs themselves laid out on an arc of a circle do not occur before the Revolution.

The hand-rail at Graeme Park and Stenton, as in seventeenth-century Colonial houses and as in the Ashmolean, runs directly against the newel posts, but in fine

From a photograph by Frank Cousins

Figure 99. The stairs of the Jeremiah Lee house. 1768

staircases of later date it is customary to have curved easings, which first appear at Tuckahoe, Rosewell, and the McPhedris house. Similar curves were often introduced in the horizontal rail on the landings.

Stair rails with Chinese lattice instead of balusters, which may be seen at Boughton House in England, exist in America also, for instance at Bachelor's Hall in Maryland and at Brandon. The dates of both stairs are indeterminate, that of the latter probably after the Revolution.

From an early day it was universal in fine Colonial stairs to have a sloping

[1] *Collections of the Massachusetts Historical Society*, vol. 71 (1914), p. 136.

wainscoted dado against the wall opposite the stair rail. Graeme Park and Rosewell are perhaps the latest conspicuous exceptions.

The floors in houses of the eighteenth century began to receive a share in the
formal design. The most notable instance was the marquetry of the Clark or
Frankland house in Boston, built by William Clark, who died in 1742. The house
was demolished in 1833. "The floor of the eastern parlor was laid in diamond-

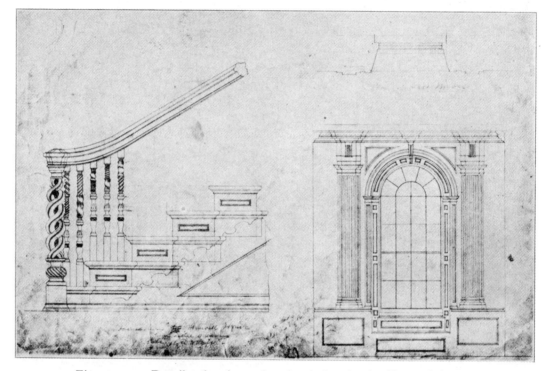

Figure 100. Details of stairs and stair-window in the Hancock house
From a measured drawing by John Sturgis
Courtesy of R. Clipston Sturgis

shaped figures, and had in the centre a unique and curious tesselated design . . .
encircling the coat of arms of the Clarke family."[1]

Stucco workers were rare in the colonies, and most plastered surfaces were left
plain, but in a few fine houses they were enriched with lavish ornament. The style
initiated by the French *rocaille* had been illustrated in several English works, such
as the "Designs" of Locke (1741) and Thomas Johnson (1758, 1761), and plates
showing *rocaille* ceilings were included in the general academic handbooks such as
Ware's "Complete Body of Architecture" (1756). Ceilings of this character ex-

[1] E. Nason, "Frankland," pp. 73–74. An independent description in S. A. Drake, "Old Landmarks of Boston," p. 165. The centrepiece was preserved and is reproduced in *Proceedings of the Bostonian Society*, 1887,
facing p. 27.

isted in the colonies at Westover, in the Miles Brewton and Huger houses in Charleston, and in the Philipse manor-house at Yonkers. At Westover the fantastic inner motives, while forming a composed pattern, are not continuous, but seem as if separately embedded in the ground (figure 102). Even if we assume them later than the fire of 1749, the ceilings there are unique for the time. In the other

ceilings mentioned, of which that of the Brewton house is surely contemporary with its building, 1765–1769, there is greater continuity and delicacy. Only in the Huger house are straight lines in the borders wholly abandoned. The Brewton ceiling had birds in relief, the Philipse ceiling, not only birds and animals but small pastoral figures, and even two large busts.

A change of style is visible in the ceilings of the Chase house at Annapolis, of Kenmore near Fredericksburg, and of Mount Vernon, *rocaille* shell work giving place to geometric patterns. In the Chase house, built 1769–1771, the stair hall (figure 103) still has, in the central circular panel, an attenuated *rocaille* motive, but in the adjoining panels there is an austere circle of classical husks, and in the drawing-room the central panel is composed of garlanded husks with a border of heavy flutings and pateræ, while all around the

Figure 101. Stairs from the Hancock house as now set up

Courtesy of William Sumner Appleton

ceiling has shallow octagonal coffers. Of the ceilings at Kenmore, the seat of Colonel Fielding Lewis, the myth is repeated that they were executed by a Hessian prisoner during the Revolution. That they were in reality earlier is shown by a letter of Lund Washington to Washington in 1775, which at the same time fixes the date of the earliest stucco work at Mount Vernon: "the stucco man" had completed "the new room," the chimneypiece, and the dining-room ceiling, which was "a handsomer one than any of Col Lewis's although not half the work on it."[1] All the ceilings at Kenmore, which form a series unsurpassed in America for richness, are in circular patterns made up of rather heavy acanthus rosettes and

[1] P. Wilstach, "Mount Vernon" (1916), p. 140.

garlands of husks, with occasional filling of acanthus scroll work. The pattern in the parlor (figure 104), both by its general form and by the crossed palm branches of one of the corner panels, betrays a derivation from plate 170 (figure 105) of Batty Langley's "City and Country Builder's and Workman's Treasury of Designs, or the Art of Drawing and Working the Ornamental Parts of Architecture," published in 1750, although the plate itself is dated 1739. These ceilings represent the fore

From a photograph by H. P. Cook

Figure 102.   The parlor at Westover

runners of the Adams in the reaction against the rococo. The dining-room ceiling at Mount Vernon, mentioned above, is of much the same character, although less crowded. In the ceilings of the west parlor and the banquet hall—the latter not raised until the summer of 1776 at earliest[1]—first appeared true Adam ornament, with a sunburst of husks, and with delicate festoons.

Plaster cornices were used in connection with the ceilings at Kenmore and in the dining-room at Mount Vernon; at Kenmore the overmantels of the saloon and the parlor were also modelled entirely in stucco. Both have a naturalistic treat-

[1] *Ib.*, p. 141.

134

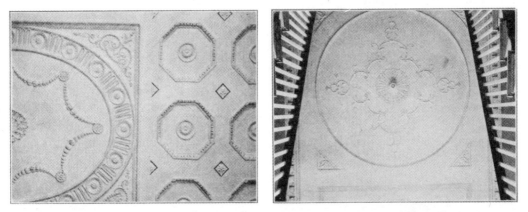

Figure 103. Details of hall ceiling in the Chase house, Annapolis

From a photograph by H. P. Cook

Figure 104. The parlor at Kenmore

ment, one with a garland and a basket of flowers, the other with a wreath encircling a landscape with scenes from Æsop's fables (figure 106). In Charleston there are instances of *rocaille* scrolls on the walls: over the stair window of the Miles Brewton house and in the drawing-room of Colonel William Rhett's house. One panel of the Rhett room has a more classical festoon.

Painting of interiors began to come into fashion about the second quarter of the eighteenth century.[1] Contrary to our usual notion, the color in Colonial days was not usually or initially white. For the Governor's Palace at Williamsburg it was ordered in council, May 2, 1727, "that the great Dining Room and Parlor thereto adjoining, be new painted, the one of pearl color, the other of cream color; that the window frames, outer doors and eves be also new painted." Of the houses in New York in 1748 Peter Kalm writes: "The alcoves, and all the woodwork were painted with a bluish grey colour."[2] The interior of Graeme Park still shows the traces of its original coat of gray-blue paint. Paint in contrasting colors, with marbling or graining, was not unknown. William Bentley, of Salem, wrote in his diary in 1816: "Visited the Woodbridge house, said to be 140 years old, to view Holliman's

Figure 105. Design for a ceiling from Langley's *City and Country Builder's and Workman's Treasury of Designs* (1750), plate 170

painting. He died about 1744. The great southeast room is pannelled on the north side around the fireplace. The ground is variegated white & black shaded. The panels brown framed in white. Above in the chamber the ground white & red variegated shades, frame & pannel as below. One beam till lately covered by a closet exhibits all the beauty of this man's colouring."[3]

In the Clark house, Boston, purchased by Sir Charles Frankland in 1747, there were "panels on each of which was painted armorial bearings, landscapes or ruins. . . . One of the panels of this room bore an exact resemblance of the building."[4]

[1] J. B. Felt, "Annals of Salem," second edition (1845), vol. 1, pp. 407–408.
[2] "Resa," Eng. tr., vol. 1 (1770), p. 250. [3] Vol. 4 (1914), p. 392.
[4] F. S. Drake, "Old Landmarks of Boston," p. 165; Nason, "Frankland," p. 73; J. Winsor, "Memorial History of Boston," vol. 2 (1881), p. 527.

Several of these are still preserved. In the drawing-room from Marmion in Virginia, now in the Metropolitan Museum, the panels bear paintings, some in decorative designs with vases, garlands, and horns of plenty, others with scenes on the

Figure 106. Chimneypiece in the saloon, Kenmore

terrace of a château. The legend that these were executed by a Hessian prisoner scarcely requires credence after what we have learned of Kenmore.

Summarizing the phases of style shown by interiors, we may observe that the fundamental treatment of the orders, so frequently used in wall decoration, doorways, and chimneypieces, remained that of the academic theorists. Proportions and profiles did not vary greatly, in the finer houses, from those established by Palladio, Vignola, and Scamozzi. Within the academic canon no one order has any special preference or priority: Corinthian, Ionic, and Doric are alike found in the earliest and in the latest houses of the period. As on the exteriors, only the Scamozzi type with angular volutes was used, except in the single case of Marmion. A baroque touch, familiar in Wren's work and the English vernacular, was characteristic: the prevalent breaking of architraves into ears, the use of broken and scroll pediments, the multiplication of consoles are instances. The influence of the rococo, as indicated by *rocaille* ornaments, began, if we leave aside the ceilings at Westover as possibly later than the house itself, not before 1745 at earliest and lasted until shortly after the Revolution, although in the most advanced houses it was disappearing just before the war. Related, and likewise at its height in the 'sixties, was the influence of Chippendale's "Chinese" manner, which we have seen appearing in the roof balustrades after 1756. An advertisement in the *South Carolina Gazette*, April 1, 1757, describes the James Reid house, offered for sale, as "new-built . . . after the Chinese taste."[1] The decoration of the Miles Brewton house, completed 1769, is full of Chippendale motives, in which rococo, "Gothic," and "Chinese" are mingled. It was such unacademic forms to which Jefferson referred in 1782, when speaking of Colonial houses, as "the burden of barbarous ornaments with which they are sometimes charged."[2] Only at Monticello, after 1770, were they expurgated in the interest of Palladian purism.

As in the case of the seventeenth century, one is eager to obtain a touchstone by which the date of houses for which no documents exist might be determined. Too often, of course, this is adopted as a royal way to knowledge, which it is hoped will replace the arduous search in old records. But, where these have really been shown to be non-existent or inconclusive, there remain many cases in which one must fall back on the criterion of style. Even then a single feature alone can rarely furnish the determination. Many, indeed, persisted with insignificant changes throughout the eighteenth century. But if the bearing of each significant feature is examined, and the period over which each occurs in authentically dated examples is noted, the time for which all these periods overlap must indicate within reasonable limits the date of the building.

An instance in which all documentary and structural evidence has been exhaustively studied without furnishing any sufficient ground for positive dating,[3]

[1] Quoted by Smith, "Dwelling Houses of Charleston," p. 358.
[2] "Notes on Virginia," see Kimball, "Thomas Jefferson, Architect," p. 35.
[3] Hall, "Philipse Manor Hall," pp. 210–247.

is the rich interior finish of the Philipse manor-house at Yonkers. In this case the number of elements furnishing evidence as to style is so large as to render inference conclusive. The striking general resemblance of the east parlor to the well-known room of the New River Water Company in London is less instructive than similarities in individual details with other American rooms at an equal remove from the metropolis of the empire. Thus all the dated examples of circular columns in interiors are from the 'sixties; of overmantels with consoles, after 1756; of scroll ped-

Figure 107. West parlor, Jerathmeel Peirce (Nichols) house, Salem. Samuel
McIntire, after 1779

iments in overmantels, between 1765 and 1769. The single actually dated example of a *rocaille* ceiling, in the Miles Brewton house, is from 1765–1769, and *rocaille* motives, such as occur in a few other places in the decoration, may be paralleled elsewhere about 1768. There can be little doubt, then, that, whatever the date of the walls of the house, the embellishment of the chief rooms was done not far from 1765.

The Royall house, another building respecting which the documents and structure have already been carefully studied, offers a case where a single element is exceptionally instructive. Comparison, instituted by Donald Millar, between the

Corinthian capitals of the room and a capital, nearly identical, from the Hancock house, preserved in Independence Hall, shows conclusively that these were carved by the same hand. Since this is the largest of the Hancock capitals, it is evidently

From a photograph by Frank Cousins

Figure 108. John Reynolds (Morris) house, Philadelphia. 1786 to 1787

one from the "Loer Rume" panelled by William More in 1745–1746. We may conclude that this work at the Royall house was done by More not far from that date.

Where the detail is less rich or less significant, it may scarcely be possible to date the work so closely by its style.

THE EIGHTEENTH CENTURY

The characteristics of the Colonial style long survived the Revolution. It took time for the novel ideas of the following era to be widely diffused and adopted. Many even of the finest houses built immediately after the Revolution are scarcely touched by any breath of innovation. Thus the Joseph Brown house in Providence, built shortly before 1789, is closely akin in style to the Van Rensselaer manor-house of 1765. The older rooms of the Jerathmeel Peirce (Nichols) house in Salem, the first work of Samuel McIntire, soon after 1779 (figure 107), would not betray that they had not been executed even a generation earlier. The large town house built by John Reynolds in Philadelphia in 1786–1787 shows likewise nothing fundamentally novel, although there are certain minor details not found before the Revolution (figure 108). Works like this justify the term "post-Colonial," which may properly be applied to all the less ambitious buildings down to 1800. With the reprinting of earlier English architectural books in America during and after the war,[1] many details of an earlier day were perpetuated even beyond this time. Long before it, however, they had become subordinate to new forms.

The prevailing belief has been that the most characteristic American architecture was the Colonial work of the eighteenth century, and that conditions peculiar to America at that time gave it a character more nearly our own than that of any later phase of style. Our study of the evidence forces the conclusion, on the contrary, that the special effect of these conditions in Colonial architecture has been much exaggerated. As in the first primitive shelters, there was little in the later buildings of the colonies which did not find its origin or its counterpart in provincial England or other parts of Europe of the same day.

There were, to be sure, Americanisms, there were local dialects differing from the king's English as did those of English districts themselves. The practised eye may recognize even the houses in which conformity is most complete—Mount Airy and Mount Pleasant, for instance—as Colonial, as American. The houses of the by-roads, the simple farmsteads lagging behind the march of progress, are unmistakable.

It is true none the less that the ideal of the Colonial style remained always conformity to current English usage. It is not the Colonial which constitutes America's really characteristic achievement in architecture. A truly American contribution to architectural style appeared only after the Revolution, and then it assumed a historical importance which has been little recognized.

[1] Swan's "British Architect" and some of his "Designs in Architecture" were republished in Philadelphia in 1775. A Boston edition of Langley's "Builder's Jewel" was still in print in 1804. John Norman's "Town and Country Builder's Assistant," published in Boston in 1786, has its text and plates copied largely from the same work.

HOUSES OF THE EARLY REPUBLIC

HOUSES OF THE EARLY REPUBLIC

THE Revolution brought a fundamental change in American domestic architecture, as in American art as a whole. How little this has been appreciated is shown by the extension of the term "Colonial" to cover all the work to 1820, or even later. The rank and file of builders, to be sure, continued to work at first, as we have seen, in much the same style as before, but the leaders were inspired by very different ideals, and these were rapidly diffused through the craft. Chief of them was the ideal of classical form. This involved much more than the adoption of the delicate Pompeian detail of the Adams; its ultimate goals were the unity and abstract quality of classical ensembles: the temple and the rotunda. Simultaneously with this formal ideal came the ideal of modern convenience, which had originated in the France of Louis XV. In the interplay of these two lies the key to the evolution of the American house during the first sixty years of the republic. So far as they were in conflict the issue in America was less a reconciliation between them than a triumph, in all its absolutism, of the formal, classic ideal.

The underlying reasons for change lay in political and cultural movements of the time, which could not fail to have far-reaching consequences in art: the transformation from colonies in provincial dependence on England to sovereign states soon welded into a nation, whose alliance lay with France. So far as America borrowed from contemporary art, she turned now less to England than to the Continent. There was not so much a transfer of allegiance, however, as a declaration of independence. The new states and the nation were republics, that regarded as their models not the monarchies of western Europe but the ancient democracies of Rome and Greece. In art also it was natural to turn to the classic forms of antiquity, which took captive the new republic more firmly than any of the older nations of Europe.

The belief has been wide-spread that the passing of the Colonial and post-Colonial styles marked the end of healthy development of traditional art as an outgrowth of contemporary culture, and that the classic revival which succeeded it was an exotic with no firm roots in American civilization. It is overlooked that the Revolutionary patriots—the Cincinnati—persistently, if sophomorically, identified themselves with the heroes of the Roman republic, and that the leaders of thought in the 'thirties had a consciousness of solidarity with ancient Greece which touched every department of life.

The classical revival was indeed a movement which had its beginnings abroad, and which there also had the same ultimate ideal, the temple. By priority in embodiment of this ideal, however, and by greater literalness and universality in its realization, America reveals an independent initiative. The origin and antecedents of American classic buildings of a public nature we have discussed in detail elsewhere.[1] It will suffice here to recall that the Virginia Capitol, designed in 1785, preceded the Madeleine in Paris, first of the great European temple reproductions, by twenty-two years; and that the Bank of the United States, built 1819 to 1826, antedated the corresponding foreign versions of the Parthenon, the National Monument at Edinburgh, and the Walhalla at Regensburg, by ten years or more. The adoption of the temple form abroad for buildings devoted to practical use came still later: in the Birmingham Town Hall (1831). In classicism America was thus not merely a follower; rather, a leader in pressing it to its extreme consequences.

In bringing the new style into being and determining its character, individuals played far more prominent rôles than during the Colonial period. The prophet of the new gospel was Jefferson, its earliest apostles were other distinguished laymen and amateurs. They not only established the ideals, but gave the first object lessons. Among those who contributed to more monumental treatment by designing their own houses was Washington himself. A native amateur of far wider activity and of great influence was Charles Bulfinch, who introduced the new style in New England after his youthful European travels. Other amateurs in architecture to design important domestic buildings were of foreign birth: the French engineer L'Enfant and the versatile Doctor William Thornton.

As the century drew to a close men of professional training in architecture first appeared in America. The earliest came from abroad: James Hoban from Ireland, and Stephen Hallet from France in 1789; Benjamin Henry Latrobe from England in 1796. Americans joined them as time went on. Bulfinch became a professional in the nature and extent of his practice if not in training; Robert Mills, after 1800,

---

[1] "Thomas Jefferson and the First Monument of the Classic Revival in America" (1915), esp. p. 48; "Thomas Jefferson, Architect," esp. p. 42; "The Bank of Pennsylvania," *Architectural Record*, vol. 44 (1918), esp. pp. 133–137.

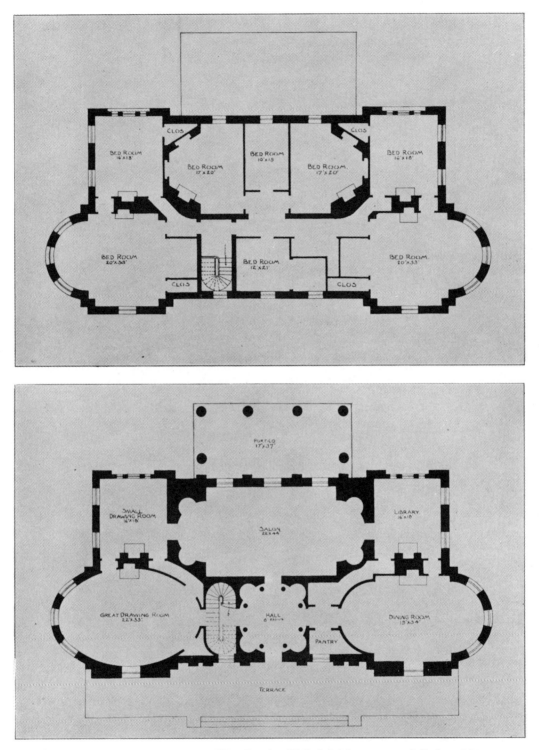

Figure 109.   Plans of the Woodlands, Philadelphia, as remodelled, 1788
From measured drawings by Ogden Codman.

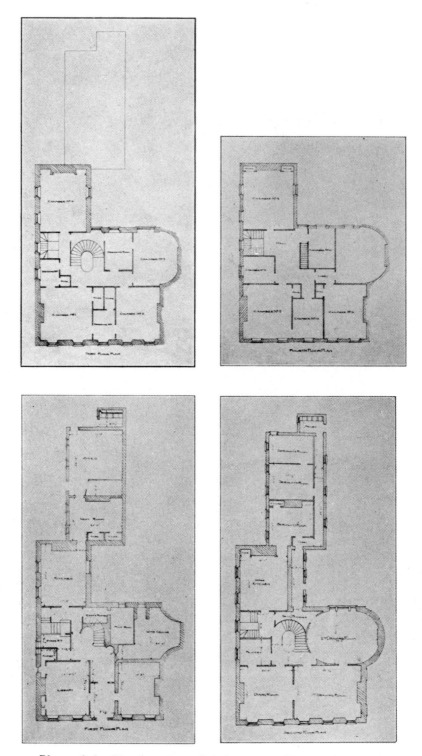

Figure 110.   Plans of the Harrison Gray Otis house, 45 Beacon Street, Boston.   1807
From measured drawings by Ogden Codman

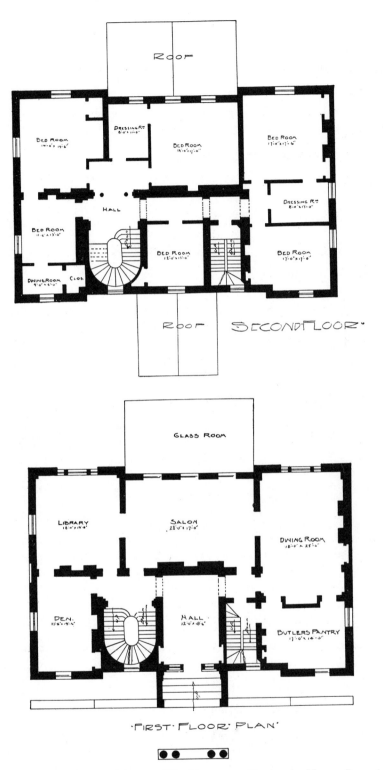

Figure 111. Plans of the Van Ness house, Washington. Benjamin Henry Latrobe, 1813 to 1819
From measured drawings by Ogden Codman

studied architecture under Hoban, Jefferson, and Latrobe to fit himself regularly for professional practice.

Gifted craftsmen showed in some instances remarkable power in assimilating the new ideas. Samuel McIntire in Salem after 1792, John McComb in New York after 1798, were little behind the pioneers and were themselves leaders of importance. Their practice tended to assume a professional character.

Books were of less relative influence than in the Colonial period, but remained much in use. The amateurs and craftsmen were still dependent on them for forms

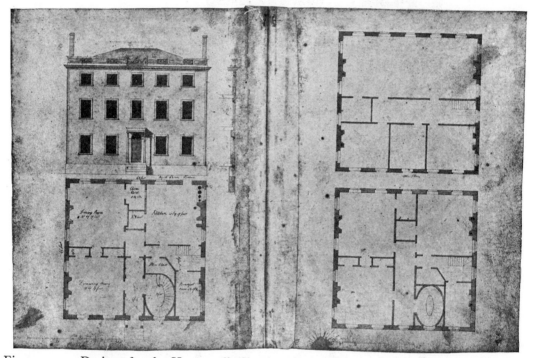

Figure 112.   Designs for the Hunnewell (Shepley) house, Portland.   Alexander Parris, 1805
From the original drawing at the Boston Athenæum

of detail, and now drew upon them more often for the arrangement of the ensemble. A stricter reading of Palladio was Jefferson's new point of departure. Gibbs's more monumental designs and the "Vitruvius Britannicus" now first came into their own. New publications made available the details of the style of the Adams. This was popularized especially by the later works of William and James Pain, such as the "Practical House Carpenter," which seems to have been owned by McIntire and other builders. No less than four of Pain's works were republished in America before 1804.[1] A native version of Adam forms was embodied by a Mas-

[1] "Catalogue of All the Books Published in the United States" (1804), reprinted in A. Growoll, "Book Trade Bibliography in the United States" (1898). Besides "The Practical Builder," Boston (1792), and "The Practical House Carpenter," Boston (1796) and Philadelphia (1797), these include "The Builder's Easy Guide" and "The Builder's Pocket Treasure."

sachusetts builder, Asher Benjamin, in his first two works: "The Country Builder's Assistant" (Greenfield, 1796)[1] and the "American Builder's Companion" (Boston, 1806).[2]   In the more literal revival of Roman and Greek forms the publica-

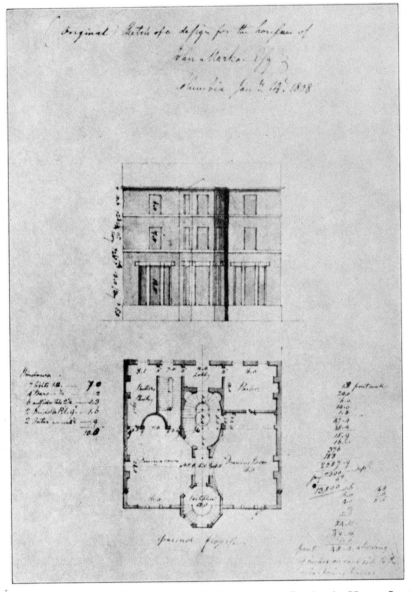

Figure 113.   Sketch for the Markoe house, Philadelphia.   Benjamin Henry Latrobe, 1808
From the original drawing in the possession of Ferdinand C. Latrobe

tions of ancient monuments were indispensable. To supplement the drawings of Roman buildings by Palladio and Desgodetz[3] had come since the middle of the

[1] Reissued 1797, 1798, 1805.   [2] Reissued, with lower proportions for the orders, 1820.
[3] Jefferson acquired a copy in 1791. *Cf.* Kimball, "Thomas Jefferson, Architect," p. 93.

eighteenth century those of Greek and eastern temples. The Library Company of Philadelphia had already acquired by 1770 copies of the first volume of Stuart's "Antiquities of Athens" (1762), of Major's "Ruins of Paestum" (1768), and of Wood's "Palmyra" and "Balbec." Jefferson secured many of the same works between 1785 and 1795.[1]

In one way or another the new forces were felt everywhere within a few years after the Revolution, but there was independent initiative in the several sections, and considerable resulting diversity. The different strands—inspiration from the classic, whether directly or through the English version of Pompeian decoration, influence from France toward freer composition of plan and space—were variously interwoven. The South, under Jefferson's leadership, was first to feel the direct classicism of the revivalists, but in the end the temple form and Greek detail everywhere prevailed.

For the evolution of the style we have a source of knowledge scarcely available in the Colonial period. To supplement the buildings still remaining, and mitigate the historical loss by destruction, there are preserved not only engravings and photographs, but large numbers of the original drawings and designs. Many of these bear a date and a signature, so that a new precision is possible in attributions, as well as clearer light on the nature of the artistic intent.

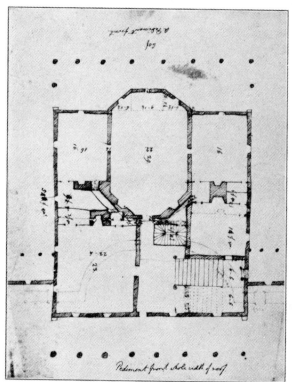

Copyright 1916, by Clara Amory Coolidge

Figure 114. Study for remodelling the Governor's Palace, Williamsburg. Thomas Jefferson, about 1779

From the original drawing in the Coolidge Collection

The materials, brick and wood, remained largely the same as in Colonial times, disguising the fundamental contrast which often exists between the forms of the two periods. Brick houses became more common in the New England towns, their great increase in Salem coming about 1805.[2] The number of houses of cut

[1] Kimball, "Thomas Jefferson, Architect," pp. 34, note, 92–101.

[2] "List of Brick Buildings Standing in Salem at the Beginning of 1806," Salem *Gazette*, February 4, 1806.

stone grew slightly, but they were still to be counted almost on one hand: the President's house in Washington, the Parkman and David Sears houses in Boston, Colonnade Row in New York. The house begun in 1793 by Robert Morris in Philadelphia was unique in being, in large part, of marble. In the treatment even of materials previously used, however, there were some characteristic innovations as time went on. Chief of these was the increasing use of stucco, sometimes ruled to imitate ashlar. An early example is Solitude in Philadelphia, 1784. The great

vogue of stucco, however, really began after 1800, with the buildings of Latrobe and his pupil Mills, under the influence of Soane. By the 'thirties red brick was scarcely shown any more. In New England, where stucco was not adopted, the brick was painted gray. Some important houses where such painting seems to have been done at an early date are Franklin Crescent in Boston, the Gore house in Waltham, and the Andrew (Safford) house in Salem. In the North, where wood continued to be used for pretentious houses, it was also common for the façade to be covered with smooth boarding with close joints, instead of clapboards or shingles. This innovation appears in the wooden front added by McIntire after 1789 to the Pickman (Derby) house on Washington Street, Salem, and is a familiar feature in the work of Bulfinch and his followers.

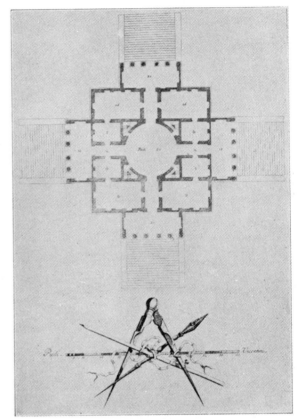

Figure 115. Plan of the Villa Rotonda for Almerico
From Palladio, Book II, plate 14

The new standard of convenience, first embodied by the French at the beginning of the century, brought many improvements in the provisions of houses after the Revolution. The old scheme of a transverse stair hall dividing four nearly equal rooms of uncertain destination, lingered on until 1800 or even later, but it tended to give place to more flexible arrangements, varying with the orientation, and having more varied elements, more compact circulation, and greater privacy.

Differentiation in the functions of rooms and adaptation of the individual room to its specific use proceeded much further than in Colonial houses. No other document is so enlightening here as the memorandum prepared by Jefferson in 1792 detailing the accommodations desirable for the President's house in Washington:

President's house

Antichamber area		10	squares of full elevation
Audience room		15	
Parlours	1 of	15	
	1 of	10	
Dining Room	1 of	10	
		——	60 squares of full elevation

Parlours	1 of	7½
	1 of	5
Dining Room	1 of	5
Study		5
Library		10
Clerks rooms 2		10
Bedrooms with anti-chamb. & Dressing room to each—4 of		32
Bedrooms single 6		24
		98½

Making altogether squares of
half elevation to be counted as   49½

109 squares or
105 f. sq.

Servants apartments, the kitchen and its appurtenances to be in an interval of 7 f. pitch between the floor of the house and cellars, consequently to be sunk a foot or two beneath the surface of the earth.

Cellar, woodrooms etc. to be below the servants apartments.

Estimated in squares of 10 feet or 100 square feet.[1]

Although the provision of state dining-room and private dining-room, public and family parlors, and clerks' rooms here is due to the official character of the house, the number and variety of the rooms otherwise do not surpass those of many fine private houses of the time, such as the Woodlands (figure 109), the Harrison Gray Otis house on Beacon Street, Boston (figure 110), or the Van Ness house in Washington (figure 111).

[1] District of Columbia Papers, Department of State, vol. 6, part 2, no. 138.

Refinements in the accommodations of the sleeping-rooms were the provision of one or more with an alcove for the bed, or with a separate dressing-room. Both these features were practically unknown in America before the Revolution, although Jefferson in 1771 had written "Dressing Room" in the large room preceding the bedroom in his plan for Monticello. The *chambre à l'alcove*, an invention of the French under Louis XIV, was exceptional in England, although occasional examples may be found from the time of Wren onward. It occurred increasingly in English books toward the close of the eighteenth century.[1] At the same time it appeared in American designs, earliest perhaps in 1788 at the Woodlands, where three of the bedrooms have an alcove. Jefferson, fresh from France, introduced it in his house in New York, 1789,[2] and actively advocated it,[3] including it in numerous designs. At least in his own houses, Monticello and Poplar Forest, the alcoves were actually built. Other designers also favored the scheme,[4] and Latrobe employed it in the Van Ness house in Washington, built 1813–1819. Suites of bedrooms and dressing-rooms, sometimes with two bedrooms and a small vestibule, were provided in the Woodlands, the Van Ness house, and the Harrison Gray Otis house, Beacon Street, built by Bulfinch in 1807.

A shallow recess in the dining-room for the sideboard was another characteristic feature of houses after 1795. Jefferson used it in remodelling Monticello in 1796; Bulfinch, in the house for Ezekiel Hersey Derby in Salem by 1799; Alexander Parris, in houses in Portland from 1805 and in the David Sears house in Boston in 1816; Latrobe, in the Van Ness house and elsewhere.

The elements of circulation were also elaborated, at the same time that the entrance hall, reception rooms, living quarters, and service arrangements were segregated, in the plans of leading designers, with a care hitherto unthought of. Lateral passages or corridors were provided, especially in houses of increased length, such as the Woodlands, the White House in Washington (figure 119), Monticello as remodelled, and the Van Ness house, giving a *dégagement* from the corner rooms to the hall. The main stairway tended to be secluded from the entrance hall, where it had invited even the chance comer to the upper rooms. In some cases where it remained in direct connection with the hall, it was at least pushed to one side in a compartment of its own, as at the Woodlands. This was a favorite arrangement with Bulfinch, which he used in his own house and in the plan he

[1] J. Paine, "Plans of Noblemen and Gentlemen's Houses" (1783), pl. 42; G. Richardson, "Original Designs for Country Seats" (1795), pls. 37, 55, etc.

[2] Kimball, "Thomas Jefferson, Architect," p. 47 and fig. 121.

[3] See his letter to Madison, May 19, 1793, *ib.*, p. 56.

[4] It occurs in the designs of unknown authorship reproduced in F. Cousins and Riley: "The Woodcarver of Salem" (1916), facing p. 29; and in Latrobe's plan for completing the White House, 1807.

made in 1795 for Elias Hasket Derby; it was widely imitated in New England, for instance in the Hollister house at Greenfield, attributed to Asher Benjamin and to 1797, and in the houses at Portland by Alexander Parris from 1805 (figure 112). Still further in the direction of seclusion were stairs opening from the lateral passages, as in the White House, in Monticello, in the Swan house in Dorchester, Massachusetts (figure 122), in Thornton's most elaborate study for Tudor Place in Georgetown, and in the Van Ness house, ranging in date from 1793 to 1813. So ingrained is the Colonial tradition in the matter that this retired position of the stairways at Monticello is still ascribed to absent-mindedness of the "philosopher" Jefferson.

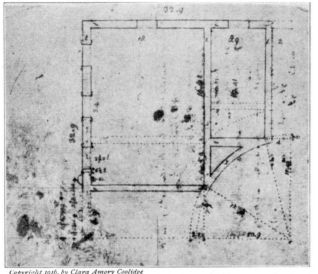

Figure 116. Study for a Governor's house in Richmond on the model of Palladio's. Thomas Jefferson about 1783

From the original drawing in the Coolidge Collection

For service a second stair gradually became universal. Where the kitchen was in the basement, as was often the case, the back stairs connected it with the dining-room, either directly, as in the Perez Morton house in Roxbury, or through a butler's pantry, as in the Swan house near by, the Markoe house in Philadelphia (figure 113), and the Van Ness house. A butler's pantry was also interposed between dining-room and kitchen where both were in the same story; in the Crafts house, Roxbury, and the John Gardner house, Salem, both from 1805. Service through the main hall was only tolerated in the best houses when other considerations clearly outweighed this disadvantage, as in the David Sears house in 1816 (figure 127).

Orientation and exposure of the rooms were considered with a new freedom from *parti pris*. Where the street frontage was on the north, it was not uncommon for the chief rooms to be toward the rear, constituting a "back front" or garden front, as in the Derby, Gore, and Brockenbrough houses, for instance. In all these the hall was not carried through to the garden side, but the desirable exposure there was used for a file of rooms *en suite*. So much preferred did such an arrangement become that in some cases where the best exposure was toward the street the hall was displaced from the centre to leave it free for the living-rooms. In the Swan

156

house the entrances are at the ends of the front, in the Harrison Gray Otis house on Mount Vernon Street, Boston, 1800, and in the David Sears house, 1816, the door is moved to the eastern side. Where the street ran north and south, or in any case when the lot was relatively narrow, the house might be turned end to the street, facing on a side yard. This was a scheme inaugurated by Bulfinch,[1] and followed, among others, by McIntire in the Dow and Felt houses at Salem in 1809–1810.

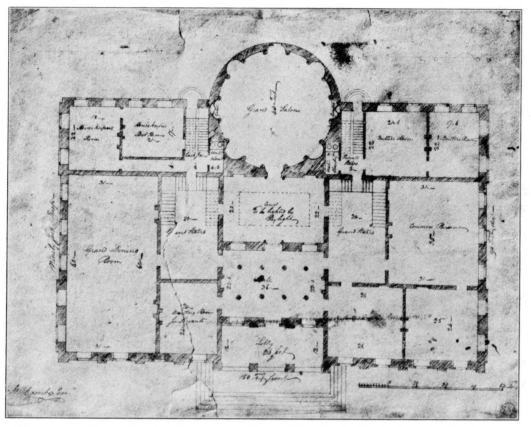

Figure 117. Study for the Government House, New York City. John McComb, 1789
From the original drawing in the possession of the New York Historical Society

The great majority of houses continued to have all the living-rooms on the same floor with the entrance hall. A certain number had the living-rooms divided between that floor and the one above, as had occasionally been the case before the Revolution. They included not only houses in Charleston, of which this scheme had been particularly characteristic, but others elsewhere, such as the Morton house in Roxbury, by Bulfinch. The tendency, French in ultimate origin, was to

[1] See the design, watermarked 1796, with his handwriting, published by Cousins and Riley, "The Wood-carver of Salem," facing p. 23, and wrongly attributed to McIntire.

place the more important rooms *en suite* in a *bel étage* up one story, the entrance being at the ground level. This was the arrangement in the houses of great leaders of fashion such as that of William Bingham, of Philadelphia (figure 170),[1] built before 1788, and of Harrison Gray Otis in Boston, built on Beacon Street in 1807, as well as in such other aristocratic houses as that of Jonathan Mason on Mount Vernon Street and those on Park Street. All of these Boston town houses were the work of Bulfinch.

These tendencies to specialization and flexibility of arrangement were limited in their application by the counter-tendency to ideal classic symmetry. When the

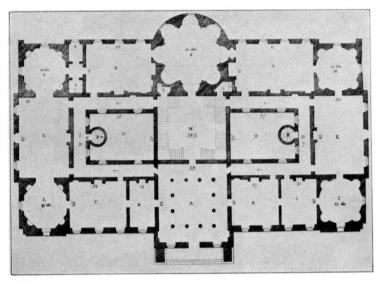

Figure 118. "Plan of a mansion for a person of distinction"

From Crunden's *Convenient and Ornamental Architecture* (1785). The prototype of McComb's design for the Government House

exterior mass was the first consideration, convenience might have to be subordinated and some of its new possibilities sacrificed. Even then, however, the situation was scarcely different from that of Colonial days. The four-square Colonial house was as schematic in arrangement as the revivalist temple. The interplay of the formal tendency with the practical we have now to trace.

In form, the really significant houses of the new republic belong to several novel and distinct general types. Two of these were based on classical ideals, the more important of them modelled on the temple: a simple rectangular mass with a columnar portico of its full width and height, crowned by a pediment. Its beginnings fall during the blackest days of the Revolution, in one of the earliest designs made

[1] *Cf.* the description in Griswold, "Republican Court" (1856), p. 262.

in the independent states. About 1779 Jefferson, on becoming governor of Virginia, made studies for the remodelling of the old Governor's Palace at Williamsburg. Of these, the one obviously representing an ideal (figure 114), recognized as beyond immediate reach, shows a portico on either face eight columns broad, with the legend "Pediment front whole width of roof." The idea of imitating the form of the temple in a domestic building was at this time quite absent abroad.

Figure 119. Accepted plan for the President's house, Washington. James Hoban, 1792
From the original drawing in the Coolidge Collection

Playful reproductions of temples had indeed been built in the English landscape gardens since the time of Vanbrugh, and Campbell had proposed in the "Vitruvius Britannicus," a church on the model of a temple, "Prostile, Hexastile, Eustyle,"[1] but anything so radical as a dwelling-house on these lines had not been suggested by the most ardent foreign classicist. For the moment the idea could not germinate. It was years, indeed, before Jefferson himself advanced it again in so uncompromising a form. It is important to note, however, that even before his

---

[1] Vol. 2, pl. 27, and p. 2.

foreign journey and his epochal design for the Virginia Capitol, he had formulated the ideal which was ultimately to rule in American domestic architecture.

Almost equally early, and from the same hand, came the suggestion of the other ideal type of the Palladians and classicists, the *rotonda*: a building symmetrical in all directions about a central vertical axis, and preferably crowned by a dome. Its ultimate basis was the Roman circular temple, which Jefferson regarded as the model of "Spherical," as the rectangular temple was of "Cubic architecture."[1] The modern embodiment in domestic architecture, the *villa rotonda*, suggested in the designs of Giuliano da San Gallo and Serlio, had been first completely devel-

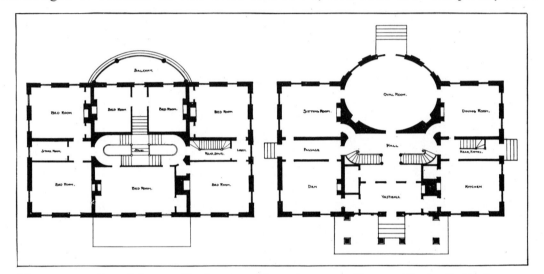

Figure 120.   Barrell house, Charlestown, Massachusetts.   Plans.   Charles Bulfinch, 1792
From drawings by Ogden Codman

oped and executed by Palladio in the famous villa for Paolo Almerico near Vicenza (figures 115 and 132). A square mass with four porticos, about a circular, domical hall lighted from above, the monumental features actually exceeding in area the rooms for use—it is a scheme less practical than purely ideal, an extreme expression of abstract enthusiasm for classical form.

From Palladio's plates the scheme was copied in northern Europe, with a literalness or a freedom of modification dependent on the degree of academic fervor. In the royal pavilion at Marly (1680–1686), the most purely ideal of the buildings of Louis XIV, the absolute identity of the four sides was retained, but the exterior dome and the projecting porticos were alike omitted, while pilasters of the full height of the walls were carried entirely around.   In England, at least four houses of the type were projected in the decade from 1720 to 1730, generally with some or

[1] "Account of the Capitol of Virginia," in "Works" edited by Lipscomb and Bergh, vol. 5, p. 134.

even all of the porticos omitted, and with other concessions to economy or use. Two, however, retained an exterior dome: Mereworth Castle, by Colin Campbell, following Palladio's plate of the villa for Almerico with the utmost literalness throughout; Lord Burlington's villa at Chiswick, otherwise less complete, having an octagonal saucer dome with steps.

Among Jefferson's studies after the transfer of the government of Virginia to Richmond, when he was chairman of the Directors of the Public Buildings (1780–

Figure 121. Jonathan Mason house, Boston
From an old lithograph. Courtesy of Ogden Codman

1783), apparently for a Governor's house there, is the quarter-plan of such a *villa rotonda* (figure 116).[1] Although somewhat reduced in scale and showing but a single frontispiece of four columns, it follows exactly the interior arrangement of Palladio's design. Like the temple scheme, this plan did not come to execution at the time, but it was not forgotten, as we shall see, and was destined ultimately to have an important future in America.

Earlier than these classical types in its embodiment in executed buildings was a scheme of which the inspiration was essentially French. This was the plan with

[1] *Cf.* Kimball, "Thomas Jefferson, Architect" pp. 33 and 140.

a projecting saloon, occupying a place of honor in the centre of a garden front, opposite the entrance. Created by Le Vau at Vaux-le-Vicomte under Louis XIV, the type, with an elliptical *salon*, was adopted almost universally in France in the style of Louis XV, and became the favorite device of the rococo in Germany, at Sans Souci (1745), Solitude, and Monrepos (1764). In England, the scheme, with an octagonal saloon, had been illustrated in some of Robert Morris's books, "Archi-

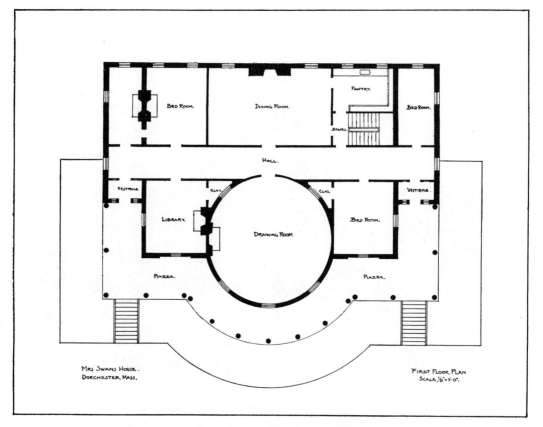

Figure 122. Swan house, Dorchester, Massachusetts
From a measured drawing by Ogden Codman

tecture Improved" (1755) and "Select Architecture" (1759). Made classical by using a circular room surrounded by columns and surmounted by a saucer dome, it was adopted by James Paine in his unexecuted design for the garden façade of Kedleston (1761), and by Robert Adam in the River House at Sion. In this classical form it appeared in France in the Hôtel de Thélusson, built 1780, and the Hôtel de Salm, 1782–1786.

The house with the projecting saloon had likewise owed its introduction in America to Jefferson, who, as we have seen, adopted an octagonal projection in building Monticello (figure 52) just before the Revolution. It was taken up independently by others, who were the first to employ the curved projection. This appears in both the lateral façades of the Woodlands, as remodelled in 1788: a house which, although somewhat limited in the central part by existing walls, is remarkable in its freedom and novelty of composition in plan, both as regards convenience and privacy, and as regards variety of spatial effects (figures 109 and 196). The

Figure 123. Swan house, Dorchester
Courtesy of Ogden Codman

entrance is to a circular vestibule surrounded by columns, with niches on the diagonals. To the left, beyond the stairs, and to the right, are the great drawing-room and the dining-room, one elliptical, the other with semicircular ends, both jutting out boldly on the exterior. Beyond the vestibule is the saloon, likewise with semicircular ends. It does not itself extend beyond the plane of the building, but has a great projecting portico in the centre of the river front.

A "grand salone" on the axis, of circular form, was first employed by John McComb in a drawing which seems to belong to the series of studies he made for the Government House in New York in 1789 (figure 117). It is the most elaborate of the group, fully commensurate with the purpose of the house as a residence of the President. Identity in many elements leaves no doubt that the design, with the saloon, was derived from plates 52–53 (figure 118) of John Crunden's "Convenient and Ornamental Architecture" (1785). The other studies,[1] progressively less pretentious as they approach the character of the building as executed, lack the circular saloon, although two of them retain a projecting bay, octagonal on the exterior, in the middle of the garden front. Like Crunden's plan, most of the studies of McComb have one or more interior rooms dependent on top light.

The earliest American examples of the scheme with an elliptical saloon on axis were James Hoban's winning competitive design for the President's house in Washington (figure 119) and Charles Bulfinch's for the house of Joseph Barrell in Charlestown (figure 120), both in 1792. Hoban, an Irishman by birth, had some training as a youth in the architectural school of the Dublin Society, and had been working for the past few years in South Carolina.[2] His design for the President's house was derived in the main, as we have shown elsewhere,[3] from Gibbs's "Book of Architecture," plates 52 and 53. From Gibbs's plan Hoban retained on the interior only the arrangement of the vestibule and adjoining stairs. In the centre of the garden front, where Gibbs has a long drawing-room, he interpolated an ellipse. As, however, he placed this, like the ellipse at the Woodlands, endwise to the façade, it was inadequate to serve as the main reception-room, necessarily located elsewhere, and in its original form it made but an insignificant projection on the exterior.

In the Barrell house, on the other hand, as in the leading European examples, the ellipse lies lengthwise of the garden front. Bulfinch had doubtless seen the Woodlands when he visited Philadelphia in 1789 and dined with the leading families,[4] but he had made the tour of France in 1786, giving special attention to architecture,[5] and it may be assumed that his inspiration came directly from abroad. The plan, as reconstructed on ample evidence, places the stairs in the centre of the house, lighted from the top, so that vestibule, stairs, and saloon form a suite of varied spatial effect along the central axis, with minor rectangular rooms on the flanks.

In the later development of the more ambitious and characteristic houses, the type which soonest gained a strong foothold was the one with a projecting saloon,

---

[1] McComb collection, New York Historical Society, nos. 54–57.

[2] No domestic designs of his there have yet been identified. It is questionable, also, whether any of the houses there with curved projections were prior to 1792. *Cf.* Smith, "Dwelling Houses of Charleston," ch. VI.

[3] "The Genesis of the White House," *Century Magazine*, vol. 95 (1918), pp. 524–528.

[4] E. S. Bulfinch, "Life and Letters of Charles Bulfinch" (1896), pp. 75–76.

[5] *Ib.*, pp. 42, 51.

most commonly of oval or circular form. Under Bulfinch's leadership it became especially frequent among fine houses in Boston and New England. He himself seems to have been the designer of at least five such houses: those of General Henry Knox in Thomaston, Maine, 1793, of Perez Morton and James Swan in Roxbury and Dorchester, ascribed to 1796 and thereabouts,[1] of Jonathan Mason in Boston, and of Harrison Gray Otis in Watertown, 1809. All of these had the projecting saloon in the centre of the garden front. The Knox house is almost a duplicate in plan of the Barrell house, but has the elliptical bay enclosed in the

Figure 124. Gore house, Waltham, Massachusetts. Garden front. Between 1799 and 1804
Courtesy of Miss N. D. Tupper

second story as well as in the first. In the Mason house (figure 121) it rises through all three. The Morton (Taylor) house has an octagonal projecting room, the ellipse, truncated in this case so that it does not project, being reserved for the up-stairs drawing-room. The Swan house (figures 122, 123, and 146) is unique among the executed houses in having a circular room as the projecting feature, its wall rising two stories on the exterior, above a low surrounding colonnade which crosses the front. In this house the saloon is in the centre of the entrance front, with the entrances themselves pushed to either side. The Gore house in Waltham (figure 124), as rebuilt between 1799 and 1804, which may also be by Bulfinch, not only has a projecting elliptical saloon, but has a room opposite it, on

[1] F. S. Drake, "The Town of Roxbury" (1878, reprint 1905), p. 135.

the entrance front, the inner side of which is elliptical. The entrance hall and stairs here are placed at one end of the front.

Samuel McIntire, of Salem, whose work hitherto had continued Colonial traditions, was quick to take a leaf from Bulfinch's book. Among his drawings are

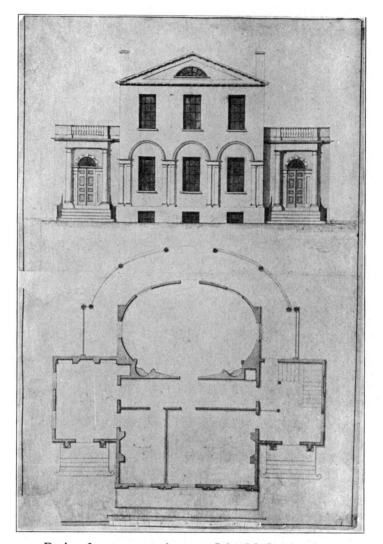

Figure 125. Design for a country house. John McComb, about 1798 to 1800
From the original drawing in the possession of the New York Historical Society

sketches from the oval room in the Barrell house, and a plan of the Thomas Russell house in Charlestown showing its elliptical stair. In a country house in Waltham for Theodore Lyman, who purchased the land in 1793, McIntire applied his newly acquired vocabulary of spatial forms by using a projecting oval room. Otherwise the plan is on conventional lines, being traversed by corridors. As suggestions for the famous mansion-house built by Elias Hasket Derby in 1795–1799, the owners collected designs from many sources. The plan made for it by Bulfinch has a suite of rectangular rooms across the garden front, approached by a passage with the stairs at one side. Not satisfied with this, McIntire, who made the final designs, introduced the innovations which Bulfinch had made elsewhere: the oval saloon of the Barrell house, preceded by the elliptical stair hall of the Russell house, making an axial suite of great variety and interest.

In other parts of the country the scheme was likewise a favorite. Jefferson,

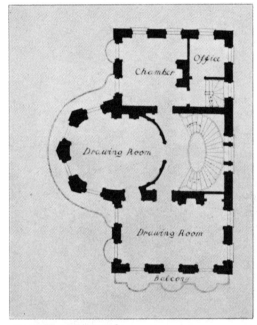

Figure 126. Plan of the Russell house
Charleston. Finished 1811

From a drawing by Albert Simmons in Smith's
Dwelling Houses of Charleston

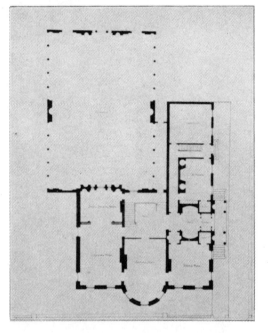

Figure 127. David Sears house, Boston
1816. Alexander Parris, Architect

From a measured drawing by Ogden Codman

whose house in Paris had had an oval *salon* to the garden,[1] twice employed it in studies and designs,[2] although in neither case does it seem to have come to execution. The Hôtel de Salm, with its circular *salon*, which he so greatly admired, gave him one idea for the President's house in Washington.[3] Elliptical saloons occur among the designs of John McComb, of New York, the most interesting (figure 125)[4] being datable by the paper employed as about 1798–1800. It has the entrance hall and stairs at one end of the front, the saloon projecting almost its

[1] Kimball, "Thomas Jefferson, Architect," fig. 118. [2] *Ib.*, figs. 120 (1793 ?), 181 (1803).
[3] *Ib.*, fig. 131. [4] McComb collection, New York Historical Society, no. 109.

full depth on the garden side, surrounded by a veranda with small columns much like that of the Swan house. In Charleston the Nathaniel Russell house, completed before 1811, has an oval drawing-room, projecting endwise with a polygonal exterior, in the centre of the garden façade (figure 126). For Tudor Place in

Figure 128.   Robert Morris house, Chestnut Street, Philadelphia.   Pierre Charles L'Enfant
1793 to 1801
From the engraving by William Birch, 1800

Georgetown Thornton made a series of studies with oval saloons on axis which are exceptional for rich combination of elements of varied shape.[1]

In other houses where the saloon had not a full elliptical or circular form, it had none the less a semicircular or segmental end forming a projecting bay. This was common in Soane's "Plans" (1788). One of Jefferson's ideal studies shows

[1] The most ambitious is published by G. Brown, *Architectural Record*, vol. 6 (1896), p. 64.   Others are among the Thornton papers in the Library of Congress, Manuscripts Division.

the form.[1] His disciple, Robert Mills, used it in the Wickham (Valentine) house in Richmond, 1812. In Boston it was employed by Alexander Parris in the house he designed for David Sears in 1816 (figure 127).

Sometimes an octagonal or semi-octagonal room was the central projecting feature. Jefferson continued frequently to employ it: in designs believed to be for Woodberry Forest, Orange County, Virginia, the estate of William Madison, 1793,[2]

From a photograph by Frank Cousins

Figure 129. The Octagon, Washington. William Thornton, 1798 to 1800

in those for rebuilding Shadwell, 1800–1803, for Poplar Forest as originally proposed, and that of Barboursville, 1817.[3] The scheme also occurs many times in the ideal studies which Jefferson made, probably during his return voyage to America in 1789.[4] Bulfinch also used it, as we have seen, in the Morton house, 1796.

The use of curved elements on the exterior was not confined to emphasis on a central saloon toward the garden. The splendid house begun by L'Enfant for Rob-

[1] Kimball, "Thomas Jefferson, Architect," fig. 225.
[2] *Cf. ib.*, p. 56. The drawing reproduced there as fig. 171 has been thought to be for this house. If so, it was modified in execution, not to speak of later remodellings.
[3] *Ib.*, figs. 173, 185–192, and 205–206 respectively.   [4] *Ib.*, figs. 217–224, 230.

ert Morris (figure 128), 1793–1801, had end "pavilions" with curved faces, analogous to those of the Hôtel Moras (Biron) in Paris. The last of the town houses built by Bulfinch in 1807 for Harrison Gray Otis, on Beacon Street, Boston, on a restricted site, has an oval drawing-room at one side overlooking the rear garden. The Joseph Manigault house in Charleston, reputed to have been designed by Gabriel Manigault, has the dining-room ending in a curved bay, and the stairs in a semicircular bay at the front. The Middleton-Pinckney house at Charleston has

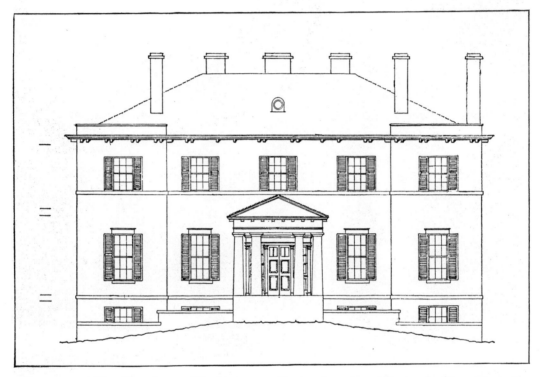

Figure 130. Van Ness house, Washington. Front elevation. Benjamin Henry Latrobe
1813 to 1819
From a measured drawing by Ogden Codman

similar features. Sometimes in a pair of symmetrical houses a bay was placed at either end of the front, as in the house at 55 Beacon Street, Boston, long occupied by the historian Prescott, or the one formerly standing at Summer and Arch Streets, the home of Edward Everett. A special group is formed by the town houses on corner lots which have a corner entrance in a circular pavilion. The most noted of these is the so-called Octagon House in Washington (figure 129), designed by Thornton for John Tayloe, and built in 1798–1800. As in the case of Tudor Place, Thornton made an elaborate series of preliminary studies. The plan selected for execution has a circular vestibule on the corner, with the stair hall

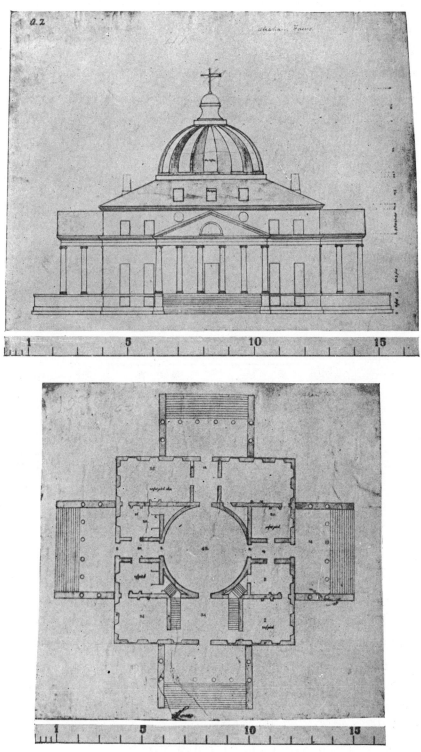

Figure 131. Competitive design for the President's house, Washington
Thomas Jefferson, 1792

From the original drawing in the possession of the Maryland Historical Society

behind it on the diagonal axis, between wings with rectangular rooms. The Richter house at Portsmouth, New Hampshire, was substantially similar in mass, except for a veranda with light columns around the circular bay.

The octagonal bow also appeared in other combinations. The study of these specially fascinated Jefferson, as his ideal sketches reveal.[1] At Farmington, 1803, and Ampthill in Cumberland County, Virginia, 1815, he terminated the façade with lateral bays.[2] In a number of studies about 1809, he used a pair of similar bays facing the front, with the entrance recessed between.[3] Some of these studies

Figure 132.   Elevation of the Villa Rotonda for Almerico
From Palladio, Book II, plate 15

show also a central octagon bay in the rear. The type became a popular one in Richmond, witness a description of houses there in the middle of the century: "Others appear to be triangles made of three two story hexagonal towers, with a portico filling up the open space at the base of the triangle, and the pointed roofs joining one another. This style seems to have effected a large number of the houses of the city of any great age, giving them and it a singular appearance."[4] At least two examples still exist in Richmond, the Hancock (Caskie) house at the corner of Main and Fifth Streets and the McRae house, which assumed its present form by 1809,[5] at the corner of Ninth and Marshall Streets.

[1] Cf. especially figs. 216 and 217 in Kimball, "Thomas Jefferson, Architect."
[2] Ib., figs. 183–184, and 203–204.   [3] Ib., figs. 198–202.
[4] J. P. Little, "Richmond" (1851).   [5] Data kindly furnished by Edward V. Valentine.

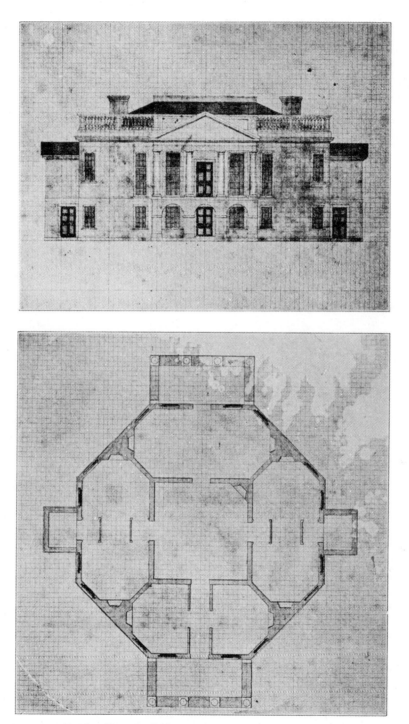

Figure 133.   Poplar Forest, Bedford County, Virginia.   Plan and elevation
Thomas Jefferson, 1806 to 1809
From a drawing by Cornelia Jefferson Randolph in the possession of the University of Virginia

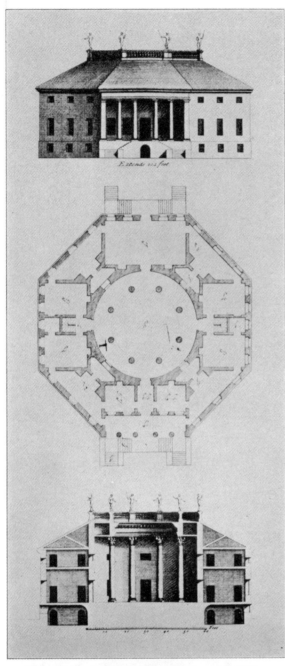

Figure 134. Octagonal design ascribed to Inigo Jones

From William Kent's *Designs of Inigo Jones* (1727)

Projecting pavilions of merely rectangular form likewise continued in some currency. Aside from frontispieces of columns or pilasters only on an unbroken wall, there are shallow central projections on a half dozen important houses. The early ones, such as the John Brown and Joseph Nightingale houses in Providence, have pediment-crowned pavilions which are very narrow relative to their height of three stories—as in the Chase house just before the Revolution. In the Morton and Crafts houses in Roxbury, after 1800, and in the Wickham house in Richmond, 1812, the buildings are lower, the bays wider. Pairs of end pavilions, found in Colonial America only in the Governor's house at Annapolis, terminated the entrance fronts of the Woodlands, the President's house at Philadelphia, and both fronts of the Van Ness house (figure 130).

The *rotonda* plan which Jefferson had proposed for the Governor's house at Richmond was the form which he finally preferred for the President's house in Washington, and embodied in an anonymous competitive design (figure 131).[1] It closely follows the Palladian prototype, as shown in Leoni's edition of his works (figure 132), with the tall exterior dome and all four porticos. Failing of selection by Washington and the commissioners, the idea was later embodied by Jefferson in an unexecuted design for which Robert Mills, then a youth under his instruction, made

[1] Kimball, "Thomas Jefferson, Architect," pp. 53, 154–156; "The Genesis of the White House," *Century Magazine*, vol. 95 (1918), pp. 524–528.

drawings in 1803.[1] The scheme was too purely formal in its balance to meet with favor until ideals of abstract unity had become established through the strengthening of classical influence generally. Not until after central balance and a central dome had become common in the design of churches and other buildings was the type of Palladio's *villa rotonda* adopted in dwelling-houses. After 1830, however, buildings on this model—square, with a central hall, circular or polygonal

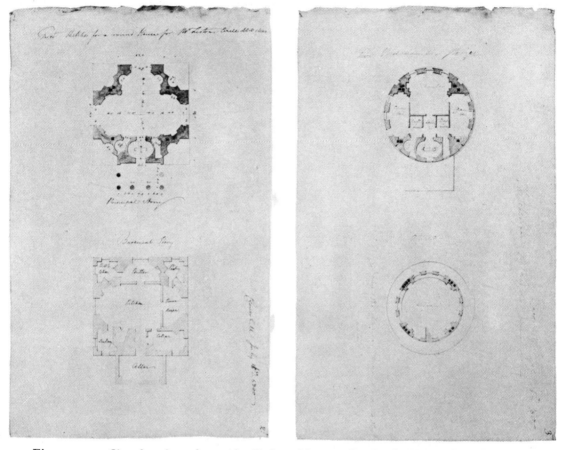

Figure 135. Sketches for a house for Robert Liston. Benjamin Henry Latrobe, 1800
From the original drawings in the possession of Ferdinand C. Latrobe

in shape, often lighted from above—became numerous. A magnificent example was Belmont, Nashville, Tennessee, designed by William Strickland about 1850, with an unbroken cornice supported by a Corinthian order. Many others could be cited, such as Waverly, near Columbus, Mississippi, or a house standing until recent years on the hill in Providence, Rhode Island.

Meanwhile the house composed about a central axis had been exemplified in a less ambitious form, better fitted for acceptation. Before 1804 Jefferson had

[1] Kimball, "Thomas Jefferson, Architect," fig. 181.

proposed for Pantops, one of his farms, a house in the form of a single regular octagon, and this he erected on another estate, Poplar Forest, beginning in 1806 (figure 133). Although it is in a sense the logical outcome of his experiments with octagons and with the *rotonda* type elsewhere, the direct suggestion seems to have come from a design ascribed to Inigo Jones (figure 134),[1] showing an octagonal building on a larger and more elaborate scale. Jefferson's simplification was extremely ingenious, giving a square top-lighted room in the centre and octagonal-

From a photograph by R. W. Holsinger

Figure 136.   Pavilion VII, University of Virginia, Charlottesville, Virginia
Thomas Jefferson, 1817

ended rooms around it, meeting at the central point on each side. As finally developed for Poplar Forest, there were porticos at front and rear. Although octagonal churches were built soon after by Bulfinch and Mills, the octagonal form was not widely taken up for houses until 1850, when Orson Squire Fowler popularized it by his book, "A Home for All, or a New, Cheap and Superior Mode of Building."[2] He had built himself a house on the Hudson on this model about 1844. The scheme

[1] Plate 17 in vol. 2 of W. Kent, "Designs of Inigo Jones" (1727), a book which Jefferson owned.
[2] See Fanny Hale Gardiner, "The Octagon House," *Country Life in America*, vol. 23 (March, 1913), pp. 79–80.

then had an enormous following. Octagonal houses were scattered everywhere, in New England, in the Northwest, many still with Greek detail. Even to-day few old Michigan towns are without one or more, built in the 'fifties and 'sixties. In cruder examples the bedrooms are arranged around a central chimney, very much like so many pieces of pie.

The logical, if not the sensible, extreme of the *rotonda* type is obviously a house in the form of a circle. Temples or casinos of circular form were features of the

From a photograph by R. W. Holsinger

Figure 137. Pavilion II, "Ionic of Fortuna Virilis," University of Virginia
Thomas Jefferson, 1818

English landscape gardens, and were imitated on the Continent, as in the "English Pavilion" at Pillnitz. Some of these pavilions were not mere summer-houses, but had living accommodations for the owner and two or three servants. John Plaw's "Rural Architecture," published in 1794, of which Bulfinch owned an edition,[1] included drawings of a circular house on Lake Windermere, "designed and built by the author." There were few of the leading American designers who did not at least toy with such an idea. Jefferson made a sketch as early as 1794, as a

[1] E. S. Bulfinch, "Charles Bulfinch," p. 83.

forerunner of the Poplar Forest scheme, of a casino in circular form: a round central room with a colonnade encircling it part-way, the remaining segments having two elliptical rooms inscribed in them.[1] McComb devised a scheme closely similar.[2] Latrobe designed for the British minister, Robert Liston, in 1800, a circular casino of four stories, showing the greatest ingenuity in interior arrangements (figure 135).[3] None of these seem to have reached execution, but later at least one

From a photograph by H. P. Cook

Figure 138. Arlington, Alexandria County, Virginia

such was erected, the Enoch Robinson house at Spring Hill, Somerville, Massachusetts. On the lower floor were an oval parlor and a circular library; up-stairs the bedrooms opened on a central rotunda.[4]

It was long after Jefferson's first suggestion at Williamsburg before the temple was again taken as a model for a dwelling, but when it finally was, it quickly became the universal type. Its victory was rendered possible by the adoption mean-

[1] Kimball, "Thomas Jefferson, Architect," fig. 133.
[2] McComb collection, New York Historical Society, no. 254.
[3] Drawings in possession of Ferdinand C. Latrobe, of Baltimore.
[4] Drawings are published by G. E. Woodward, "The House, A Manual of Rural Architecture" (1869), at p. 92. *Cf.* the description in "Notes and Queries" of the Boston *Transcript*, 1918, no. 3895. A recent account, with a photograph and drawings, is in *Old-Time New England*, vol. 11 (1921), pp. 173–175.

while of the form of the temple for public buildings, without real parallel abroad. Jefferson's Virginia Capitol at Richmond, 1785–1789, modelled on the Maison Carrée, and Latrobe's Bank of Pennsylvania, 1799–1801, with the Greek order of the Erechtheum, had made the temple form familiar and had habituated people, al-

Figure 139. Andalusia, Bucks County, Pennsylvania. Portico, 1834 to 1836
Courtesy of Edward Biddle

ready filled with classical enthusiasm, to its imitation in buildings devoted to practical use. The step of building a house like a temple was finally taken by Jefferson himself in several of the pavilions of the University of Virginia, which he designed "to serve as specimens of orders for the architectural lectures." To be sure, these pavilions were not houses merely, since each contained the classroom as well as the lodgings of a professor, but with the enlarged living quarters for men with families, the domestic use was physically the more important. The first pavilion (figure 136), which followed a suggestion from William Thornton, itself had, in Jefferson's conception of it as showing itself above the dormitories, the form of a Doric prostyle temple of six columns, and a "pediment the whole breadth of the front"; but it was raised above a story of arches, giving it a conventional academic character. The next two pavilions, which followed sugges-

From a photograph by H. P. Cook

Figure 140. Berry Hill, Halifax County, Virginia. 1835 to 1840

tions by Latrobe, having columns the height of both stories, had neither of them the temple pediment of full width. The temple form in its entirety, which does not appear in any of Latrobe's sketches, was first adopted by Jefferson in the fourth pavilion to be built, begun in 1819. By 1822 three such temples, the Pavilions I, II (figure 137), and IV were completed,[1] each with four columns across the front.

It was not long before the new example began to be followed in some of the most pretentious houses elsewhere, even though they did not share the same semi-public functions or the same didactic purpose. George Hadfield, whose training

[1] For the documents and drawings concerning the design and building of the university, see Kimball, "Thomas Jefferson, Architect," pp. 74–77, 186–192; W. A. Lambeth, "Thomas Jefferson as an Architect" (1913).

in Rome had given him a preference for a single colossal order, already evident in his proposals for the Capitol, carried out before his death in 1826, the portico of Arlington, with a front of six Greek columns of enormous massiveness, modelled on those of the great temple at Paestum (figure 138). Disproportionate as it seems

Figure 141. Wilson house, Ann Arbor, Michigan. After 1836

from near at hand, no other house than Arlington could carry so well across the river to the city, Washington, or so well hold its own at the other end of a composition from the Capitol.

The extreme step in the imitation of the temple, the adoption of a peristyle instead of merely a prostyle arrangement, was taken by Nicholas Biddle in rebuilding his country house, Andalusia, in 1834–1836. Biddle had been in his youth the first American to travel in Greece,[1] and was deeply interested in the fine arts. In his magazine, the *Port Folio*, in 1814 had appeared an essay, "On Architecture," by George Tucker, urging an uncompromising imitation of Grecian architecture.[2] For the Bank of the United States, of which Biddle became a director in 1819 and president in 1823, Latrobe had presented in 1818 a design based on the Par-

Figure 142. Dexter house, Dexter, Michigan. 1840 to 1843

thenon, which, as executed with little change, Biddle greatly admired. Even this, however, lacked the lateral colonnades, which Latrobe considered impractical in a modern building. No such consideration restrained Biddle in remodelling his house, to which he added a wing toward the Delaware on the pattern of the "Theseum," its cella flanked as well as fronted by columns (figure 139).

It remained only to model a house on the Parthenon itself, with its front of eight columns instead of six. This was done by James Coles Bruce at his planta-

[1] W. N. Bates, "Nicholas Biddle's Journey to Greece in 1806," *Proceedings of the Numismatic and Antiquarian Society of Philadelphia*, vol. 28 (1919), pp. 167–183.

[2] *Port Folio*, n. s., vol. 4 (1814), pp. 559–569. *Cf.* P. A. Bruce, "History of the University of Virginia," vol. 2.

tion, Berry Hill, in Halifax County, Virginia, in the years following 1835 (figure 140). Mr. Bruce spent some time in Philadelphia, just before inheriting the estate and undertaking the new house, and was influenced by Andalusia in his choice of a type.[1] The porticos were carried across both front and rear, although not along the flanks. A roof with pediments on the fronts was scrupulously provided, although the house is far broader than it is deep. On either side of the great lawn are the

Figure 143. Hill house, Athens, Georgia

office and schoolroom, each likewise in the form of a Greek Doric temple. Nowhere else, perhaps, is the ante-bellum plantation to be found in equal architectural magnificence.

These are only outstanding examples. A host of others, many scarcely inferior in importance, had meanwhile sprung up under the stimulus of enthusiasm for things Greek given by the War of Greek Independence, 1821–1827. At the time of the Greek war, as John Bassett Moore has pointed out, American sympathy was so great that a gentleman from western New York declared he could furnish, from his sparsely settled region, "five hundred men, six feet high, with sinewy arms

[1] His nephew, Philip Alexander Bruce, the distinguished historian of Virginia, informs me that he "often heard it stated in the family that the house was modelled on Andalusia."

and case-hardened constitutions, bold spirits and daring adventurers, who would travel upon a bushel of corn and a gallon of whiskey per man from the extreme part of the world to Constantinople."

No one region had any special monopoly on the use of the temple form for houses. It was employed in New England quite as much as in the South. The towns which prospered in the 'thirties and 'forties, such as the whaling ports of

Figure 144. Anderson house, Throgg's Neck, New York. J. R. Brady, about 1830
From a contemporary lithograph in the possession of the New York Historical Society

New Bedford and Nantucket, still have many examples. Others are listed among the works of Alexander Jackson Davis and Ithiel Town, between 1829 and 1833.[1] A critic unsympathetic with the style writes of its progress about Boston in 1836:

"Of late it has become much the fashion to build country houses in the form of a Grecian temple, with a projecting portico in the front, resting on very magnificent columns. This style prevails at Cambridge. These classic models, which surround the college, are imitated closely in Cambridge-Port. Two or three specimens of this style are to be seen on the road which forms the continuation of the old Concord turnpike through the Port. One of them, in particular, we have noticed, as it has been in progress. It is a small edifice, the whole length of which, including the portico, may possibly be 30 ft., and the breadth 15 ft. The

[1] Dunlap, "Arts of Design" (1918 ed.), vol. 3, pp. 212–213.

front of this little building is adorned with four massive columns, with elegantly carved Ionic capitals, the cost of which can scarcely have been less than that of the rest of the house. There seems to be a prevailing passion for columns throughout the country. One gentleman in an interior county, has surrounded his house with them, and his example has been followed in a house in East Boston."[1]

In the backwoods states beyond the Alleghanies and the Ohio the imitation of the temple was even more universal than on the seaboard. When the wave of Eastern emigration of the 'thirties swept out along the newly opened Erie Canal and

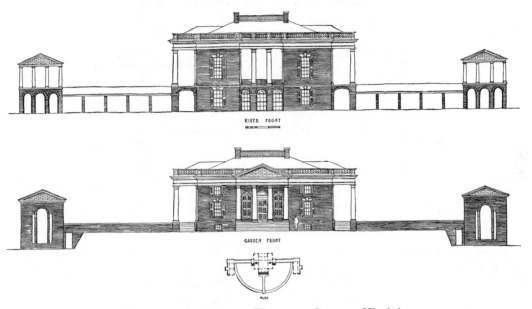

Figure 144A. Bremo, Fluvanna County, Virginia
From measurements and sketches by Pleasants Pennington

across the lakes, it brought with it this ruling ideal. In Michigan Greek enthusiasm was particularly strong. The names of towns—Ypsilanti and Byron, Ionia and Scio—perpetuate famous personalities and places in the Greek struggle for freedom. Judge Woodward, in his first sketch for the organization of the state university, preferred for it a Greek title, the Catholepistemiad! When the institution came actually into being, its several departments were housed in as many porticoed temples of the Muses. Little after the log cabins of the first settlers, side by side with them in many instances, rose ambitious dwellings in the form of the temple. In the most pretentious of these, Greek proportions and detail were strictly followed. The house of Judge Robert S. Wilson in Ann Arbor (figure 141) has four columns of the Ionic order—it is the "Temple of the Wingless Victory." Judge Samuel Dexter's patriar-

[1] H. W. S. Cleaveland in the *North American Review*, October, 1836.

chal mansion (figure 142), overlooking the town which bears his name, is the amplest and most imposing in the state, with six tall columns of a slender Greek Doric.

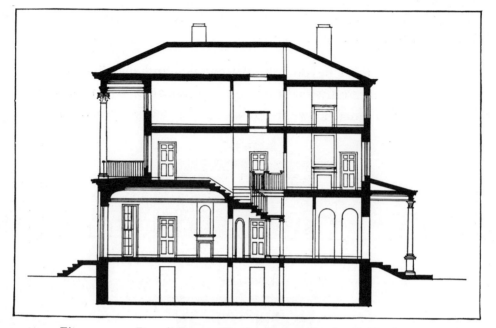

Figure 145. Barrell house, Charlestown. Charles Bulfinch, 1792
From a drawing by Ogden Codman

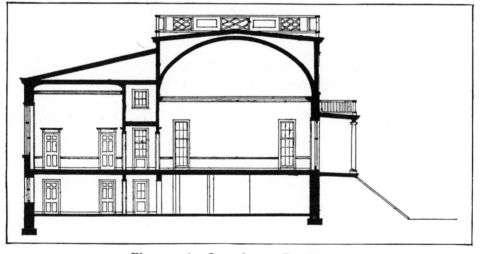

Figure 146. Swan house, Dorchester
From a measured drawing by Ogden Codman

In this diffusion of the temple scheme books played an important part. Besides the folio publications of the Greek temples and the handbooks which popularized the forms of the Greek orders, there were works which gave actual designs for modern houses on the temple plan. Chief of these was Minard Lafever's "The Modern Builder's Guide," published in New York in 1833. With forms so thoroughly established owners were able to proceed with no other architectural assistance than that of the carpenters and builders, and the scarcity of professional architects, their total absence in outlying regions, was thus not onerous. The few professional architects of the time—Mills in Carolina, Strickland and Walter in Philadelphia—generally eschewed abdicating their creative liberty to the temple scheme in dwelling-houses, so that it represents a genuinely popular preference of laymen and amateurs.

From a photograph by R. W. Holsinger

Figure 147. Monticello, as remodelled 1796 to 1809. Thomas Jefferson

Various modifications of the strict or normal arrangement of the temple had wide currency. One of the most common was the omission of the pediment, producing a scheme analogous to that of the Bourse in Paris. Although the houses where this was done were generally wider than they were deep, no doubt the dislike of visible roofs, as we shall note, and the desire to make it possible to conceal them behind parapets, had an influence. The river front of Mount Vernon may perhaps be regarded as the earliest example; Pavilion V of the University of Virginia as the first complete one. Such Southern houses, with porticos fronting or surrounding a cubical mass, are well known, especially in Georgia, Alabama, and Mississippi. The town of Athens, Georgia, above all others—significant by its very name—is filled with fine specimens. They include the most superb of all, the Hill house, with its peristyle of tall Corinthian columns (figure 143). Less familiar are the equally numerous houses of the sort in the North, especially in towns which had great growth in the second quarter of the century. The work of Elias Carter, builder and architect, of Worcester, Massachusetts, embraces many, from 1830 and the following years.[1]

The number of columns on the front was not always an even one, with an opening on the axis. Considerations of plan sometimes made it preferable to have an

Figure 148. Dyckman house, New York City
Courtesy of Alexander McMillan Welch

even number of openings with an odd number of columns. The arrangement could have been familiar to the more cultivated and studious architects of the time in engravings of the "Basilica" at Paestum. A model house with five columns is shown in Lafever's "Builder's Guide."[2] Such a house was the Van Vorst mansion in Jersey City, demolished after 1890.[3] Others with three columns are not uncommon in Michigan, the "cella" being only one room and a hall in width.

Another modification of the basic temple scheme was the addition of wings.

[1] H. M. Forbes, "Elias Carter, Architect, of Worcester, Mass.," *Old-Time New England*, vol. XI (1920), pp. 59–71. [2] Pl. 73. [3] W. J. Mills, "Historic Houses of New Jersey" (1902), p. 28.

At Arlington the wings were perhaps structurally a part of the pre-existing house. Elsewhere they were no less needed to increase the accommodations of the rather inelastic temple cella. Their extreme development is in the magnificent Parker (Bennett) house in New Bedford, ascribed to 1834,[1] where the central mass with six Ionic columns on either front is connected by wings with end masses, likewise of two stories and in the form of the prostyle temple. More usually the wings were short and of a single story, as in the Anderson house at Throgg's Neck near New York, about 1830, of which J. R. Brady was the architect (figure 144). Buildings substantially of this type were shown by Lafever, and were widely copied in western New York, in the old Northwest, in Kentucky, even in Wisconsin. Often there was only a single wing, as an appendage at right angles to the main mass.

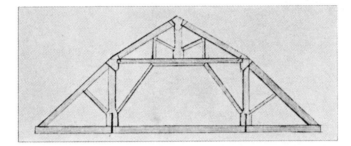

Figure 149. Diagram of a low curb roof
From William Pain's *Practical Builder*

The extreme simplification of the temple-house lay in omission of the main portico itself, usually from motives of economy. Even when this took place, however, the building retained unmistakable signs of its origin, being characteristically narrow and deep, its gable to the street, in contrast to the Colonial house which turned its broad side, with level eaves, to the front.

Outbuildings after the Revolution continued often to be combined with the house by wings (figure 162): the Lyman and Gore houses, Homewood, Woodlawn, and Tudor Place, ranging from 1793 to after 1810, repeat the general scheme of the older houses at Annapolis. Isolated buildings symmetrically arranged were also employed, as in the Derby mansion and at Berry Hill. The scheme of outbuildings below grade, constituting terraces fronted by colonnades, which Jefferson had developed at Monticello, was used in certain important houses elsewhere under his influence. Thus during his occupancy of the White House, in 1804, he designed the lateral terraces for the service quarters.[2] At Bremo, for which he

---

[1] D. Ricketson, "New Bedford in the Past," sketches written in 1878 (1903), p. 41.
[2] Kimball, "Thomas Jefferson, Architect," figs. 175–177, and pp. 66, 175.

made a design, his friend, John Hartwell Cocke, built similar terraces terminated by porticoed pavilions (figure 144A). The Hermitage at Savannah had perhaps the finest ensemble of plantation buildings, grouped about a shaded lawn dominated by the house. To left and right were the overseer's house and the slave hospital, then the quarters in uniform brick pavilions joined by walls, in disposition all very much like the University of Virginia.

The number of stories after the Revolution generally remained two in the case of country houses and three in the case of town houses, but there were tendencies

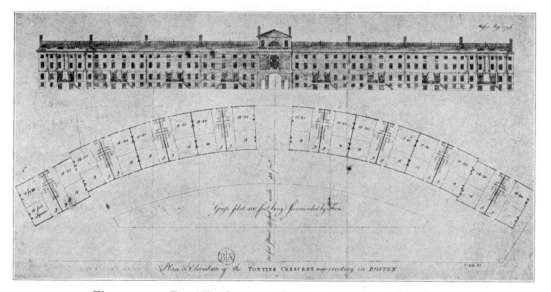

Figure 150. Franklin Crescent, Boston. Charles Bulfinch, 1793
From an engraving in the *Massachusetts Magazine,* 1794

both to greater height and to less. In Boston, New York, and Philadelphia four stories were not unusual after 1800. The Jonathan Harris house in Boston, building in 1797, even had five, "a height unknown in the town."[1] On the other hand, in the country certain houses were restricted to a single story, as Roman houses were supposed to have been. This was an idea which goes back ultimately to Palladio, and was brought by Jefferson from the Paris of 1785, when the Hôtel de Thélusson and the Hôtel de Salm were building. On his return he removed the upper story of Monticello.[2] Where he had a free hand, as in the design of Edgehill, 1798, and Ampthill, 1815, he placed all the rooms on one floor. At Poplar Forest, also, the house shows but one story to the entrance front. Instances could be

---

[1] W. Bentley, "Diary," vol. 2 (1907), p. 242. The drawings preserved by the Bostonian Society show that one of the five stories was a basement.
[2] Kimball, "Thomas Jefferson, Architect," p. 57.

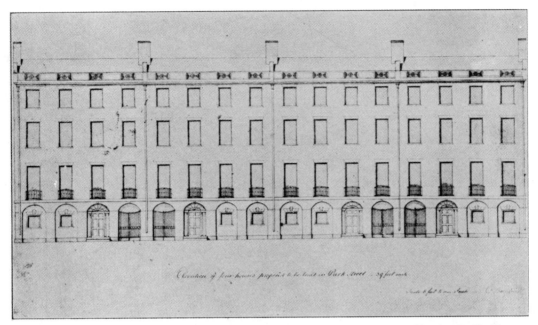

Figure 151. Houses nos. 1–4 Park Street, Boston. Elevation. Charles Bulfinch
1804 to 1805

From the original drawing in the possession of John Collins Warren

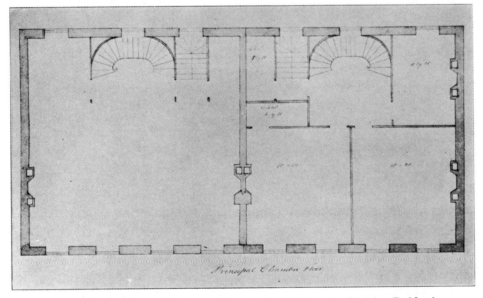

Figure 152. Plan of houses nos. 1–4 Park Street. Charles Bulfinch
1804 to 1805

From the original drawing in the possession of John Collins Warren

multiplied in which the scheme was taken up by others: in the Mason house on Analostan Island at Washington; in the houses of Sir Edwin Cust and others near Detroit.

In the matter of heights of stories the most significant change was the achieving of freedom to have a variety within a single one, conforming to the uses of different rooms. For the private rooms great height was no longer considered desirable—the conception of intimacy, developed in the period of Louis XV, had an effect. When Monticello was remodelled, the height of the old rooms was cut in half for the new ones by the device of the mezzanine, which Jefferson had already proposed in his *rotonda* study for the President's house. For the main saloons, on the other hand, greater height and stateliness were desired. The various *rotonda* designs secured this by the central hall, rising even into the roof of the house and lighted from the top. For the houses having the projecting saloon various devices were adopted. In the Barrell house Bulfinch made the saloon higher than other rooms on the floor by the height of its cove (figure 145), over which he carried stairs in an ingenious manner. In the Swan house (figure 146), where the dining-room rose through two stories, the circular saloon was still higher, masked on the exterior by false windows. The Jonathan Mason house in Boston had a similar arrangement, with panels opposite its dome (figure 121).

The roof forms were affected by the classical tendency in two different ways. The older Palladian classicism would tolerate no visible roof but a spherical one; the literal classicism of the revivalists brought in the temple with its broad expanse of roof.

In contemporary Europe visible roofs had long been taboo in buildings of academic pretensions. Although Palladio's published designs for villas and palaces all show pitch roofs without eaves-balustrades, his "Basilica," like the Library of St. Mark and the palaces of Michelangelo on the Capitol, had only a balustrade visible above the cornice; and this scheme of roof *à l'italienne* had been an index of the spread of academic influence. It marked the first designs of Inigo Jones; it appeared in France for the first time in the garden front of Versailles and the colonnade of the Louvre. By 1721 it had filtered down into the popular handbooks. In Godfrey Richards's version of "The First Book of Architecture of Andrea Palladio," Chapter L discourses "Of Flat Roofs," and a figure shows the construction, which, with the coverings then available, involved a slope of some twenty degrees, concealed by a parapet. We have seen that, in the colonies, Rosewell had a concealed roof and a parapet as early as 1730.

An aversion to visible roofs was among the strongest feelings of one large group

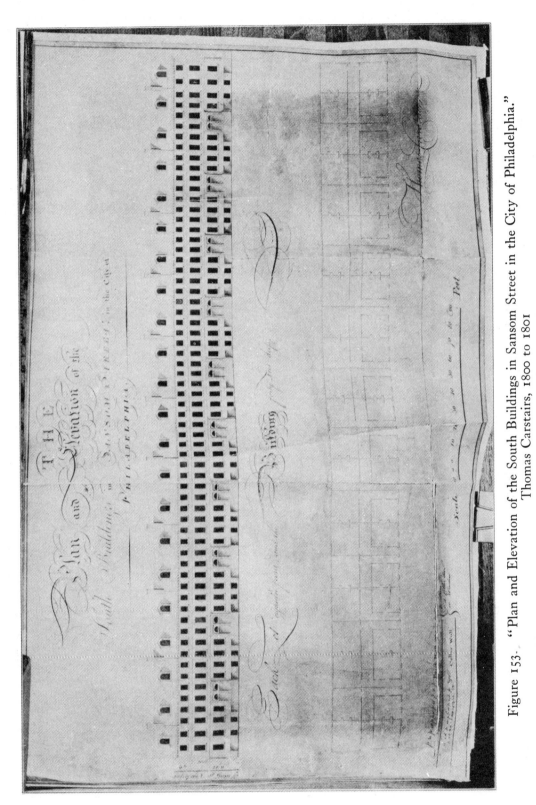

Figure 153. "Plan and Elevation of the South Buildings in Sansom Street in the City of Philadelphia."
Thomas Carstairs, 1800 to 1801
From a drawing in the Ridgway Library

of architects and laymen in the early republic. Cooper has expressed and satirized this feeling in "The Pioneers" (1822),[1] in describing the mansion of Marmaduke Temple, joint product of an amateur and a builder, erected just before 1793 in the wilderness of central New York. We have seen that the use of an eaves-balustrade began just before the Revolution. In the first ambitious houses after the war this feature was adopted almost universally, and the roof itself was now kept low enough to be out of sight. The Peirce (Nichols) house in Salem (figure 154) and Washington's portico at Mount Vernon are early examples.

To make a roof really flat, so that it might serve as a terrace walk, as contemplated for the outbuildings of Monticello and the White House, and for the colonnades of the University of Virginia, presented great technical difficulties which have only been overcome in recent years by the aid of bituminous coverings. Jefferson devoted much attention to the problem, and devised a scheme of narrow transverse valleys below a level grating.[2] At best they proved unsatisfactory, and those of the University were soon covered by sloping roofs.

Not until the adoption of the temple form in the professors' houses at the University of Virginia did the visible roof again begin to come into vogue. For a time there was a struggle for mastery, in which, as we have noted, the temple was often robbed of its pediment and provided instead with a parapet. With the complete triumph of the temple ideal, antagonism to revealing the roof was overcome.

An exterior dome was a feature which Jefferson greatly admired in the Hôtel de Salm,[3] as in the Villa Rotunda. His own *rotonda* studies included hemispherical central domes like the one shown on the building in Palladio's plates. In the remodelling of Monticello (figure 147) he sought to assimilate it to the scheme of the Hôtel de Salm by placing over the projecting saloon a saucer dome with steps, which he had already mooted during the Revolution for a garden house,[4] the form of the dome in that case being "taken from Inigo Jones's designs, pl. 72." Another similar dome was included in his design for Barboursville,[5] but it seems not to have been carried out. Jefferson was not alone in proposing or executing such domes in domestic architecture. McComb showed an exterior saucer dome in his studies for the Government House in New York, and Alexander Parris built one in 1816 over the saloon of the David Sears house. The cupola, essentially a little dome on a tall drum, likewise received in a few houses such as Hampton, Maryland, and the Hasket Derby house, a treatment more in harmony with its monu-

---

[1] Chapter III.   [2] Kimball, "Thomas Jefferson, Architect," figs. 176, 177, and p. 195.
[3] Letter to Comtesse de Tessé, March 20, 1787. Lipscomb, "Writings of Jefferson" (1907), vol. 6, p. 102.
[4] "Thomas Jefferson, Architect," fig. 62.   [5] *Ib.*, figs. 205–206.

mental origins, but after 1795 the more classical form of the saucer dome was preferred.

In less pretentious houses older roof forms persisted long after the Revolution, but not without undergoing significant modifications. Thus the gambrel, which then had a great vogue in the regions about New York City, was made lower and flatter. The Dyckman farmhouse on Manhattan, built after 1783, well illustrates

Figure 154. Jerathmeel Peirce (Nichols) house, Salem

this, an outstanding characteristic of what has come to be known as the "Dutch Colonial" style (figure 148). It is scarcely Colonial in the strict sense, and not Dutch in origin at all. Nothing analogous is known in Holland. On the other hand, diagrams of the low curb roof of this type were common in English handbooks after 1733.[1] It appears in American reprints after the war (figure 149)[2] when its popularity is to be explained by the general tendency toward reducing the height of roofs.

[1] E. g., F. Price, "British Carpenter" (1733), pl. I k; W. Salmon, "Palladio Londinensis" (1734), pl. 34; B. Langley, "City and Country Builder's . . . Treasury" (1745 ed.), supplementary plates; "Builder's Jewel" (1746), pl. 92, etc.
[2] E. g., W. Pain, "Practical Builder" (Boston, 1792), pl. 7.

A development of republican days new in America was the block of several houses of unified design. The first of these, Franklin Crescent in Boston (figure 150), was designed and financed by Bulfinch, beginning in 1793. It was likewise

From a photograph by Frank Cousins

Figure 155. The Woodlands, Philadelphia. Entrance front as remodelled, 1788

the most ambitious. Sixteen houses of three stories and a basement were arranged in a solid crescent, the pair at each end brought forward to constitute a pavilion, and a special motive placed in the centre, arching a cross street. Opposite, facing the crescent, were two pairs of larger semi-detached houses of similar treatment. When in 1801 the town of Boston, in which Bulfinch was chairman of the Select-men, sold the lots on Park Street, cut from the Common, to private owners, the deeds contained the provision "that all buildings to be erected on said bargained premises shall be regular and uniform with the other buildings that may be erected on the other lots." Under this condition Bulfinch designed, among others, the

Figure 156. Morton house, Roxbury. 1796
Courtesy of Ogden Codman

block at the foot of the street containing four houses (figure 151). Within a few years he had also designed houses farther up, including the Amory (Ticknor) house at the corner of Beacon Street (figure 165), which may certainly be assigned to him on grounds of style. Then, in 1810, he gave the designs for "Colonnade Row" along the south side of the Common, nineteen houses, with nine others in two far-ther blocks, beyond. All told, they gave the Common of that day a harmonious frame unequalled in America, and not unworthy of comparison with the civic improvements which Bulfinch had admired abroad.

Other cities and architects soon took up the idea. In Philadelphia, in 1800 and 1801, William Sansom built "the first row of houses on a uniform plan . . . on Walnut Street north side, between Seventh and Eighth, and in the Street between Walnut and Chestnut, from Seventh to Eighth, afterwards called Sansom Street." [1] The first of these two was designed by Latrobe. [2] The design for the second, by Thomas Carstairs, is still preserved, and shows a block of eleven pairs of houses, without other general composition than an exact repetition (figure 153).

Figure 157. Crafts house, Roxbury. Peter Banner, 1805
From a measured drawing by Ogden Codman

In New York McComb designed a block of six houses, the centre pair raised higher than the others, with a pediment. [3] Robert Mills in 1809 designed a block in Philadelphia on Ninth Street between Walnut and Locust. [4] Most important of the later blocks was Colonnade Row or Lagrange Terrace on Lafayette Place in New York. The exterior treatment of these will be discussed later.

The plans of these houses with party walls varied according to their width. Those of eighteen and twenty feet, including Carstairs' and McComb's, could

[1] Scharff and Westcott, "History of Philadelphia," vol. 1 (1884), p. 511.
[2] Cf. his letter of January 12, 1816, in the possession of Ferdinand C. Latrobe.
[3] McComb collection, New York Historical Society, no. 11.
[4] Drawing in the possession of Alexander Dimitry, shown me by courtesy of Mrs. Austin Gallagher.

have only two rooms on a floor, the stairs between, and on the street floor an entry parted off from one side of the front room. In Bulfinch's crescent (figure 150), where the houses were twenty-seven feet wide, this entry was carried through and contained front and also back stairs. The houses on Park Street, thirty-six feet wide, had the entrance through a full basement story to stairs at the rear, and

Figure 158. President's house, Philadelphia. 1792 to 1797
From the engraving by William Birch, 1799

thus could have two parlors occupying the full width of the front on the main floor—a favorite arrangement with Bulfinch (figure 152).

In the treatment of surfaces, supports, and openings the scheme which ultimately prevailed in republican times was the puristic classical one of plain walls, windows simply framed, and orders used according to their original structural function, with free-standing columns. The academic elements employed in Colonial times to enrich and organize the wall surface fell into disuse: rustication almost at once, engaged orders by about 1800. Another mode of organization, by shallow surface arches, taken up meanwhile, continued much later in vogue, but likewise ultimately gave way. Interest in detail was thus concentrated, increasingly from the Revolution, on the windows and doorways themselves, in which a greatly increased variety of form and grouping compensated for the decrease in enrichment of surface.

Rustication of any sort was highly exceptional after the Revolution. No important instance of a façade grooved or rusticated throughout occurs after the en-

Figure 159. Accepted elevation for the President's house. James Hoban, 1792
From the original drawing in the possession of the Maryland Historical Society

trance front of Mount Vernon, completed during the war. McIntire's early designs include one, but it does not seem to have been executed. Even angle quoins were very rare. They occur before 1800 in the Joseph Nightingale house at Providence, and a few other examples. After the beginning of the new century such a use of them as in the Radcliffe (King) house in Charleston is almost unique.

Projecting belts, to mark one or more of the floor lines, were common in brick houses until 1810, and were imitated in wood, as in the Samuel Cook (Oliver) house in Salem. They now uniformly turned the corners, instead of stopping short of them, as had been equally frequent in Colonial days. A subdivision of three stories by a single band above the ground story was often made after the Revolution, to suggest an architectural basement, even where no order was used above.

The earliest characteristic instances are in the curved houses of Franklin Crescent, and in the Octagon. Where two stories were grouped in such a way, panels were sometimes introduced opposite the intervening floor, above the windows. The Bingham house (figure 170), the Woodlands (figure 155), the Octagon (figure 129), and Homewood—all before 1800—have plain panels there, those of the brick houses white against the surrounding red. From about the beginning of the century such

Figure 160. Study for the Elias Hasket Derby house, Salem. Charles Bulfinch, 1795
From the original drawing in the possession of the Essex Institute

panels were occasionally carved: in the Hersey Derby, Parkman, and Jonathan Mason houses (figures 166 and 121) designed by Bulfinch, in Woodlawn, and in the David Sears house by Parris, the last from 1816. By this date, however, a surface free of bands and panels alike was almost universally preferred: the later houses of Salem are smooth from water-table to cornice.

Pilasters did not vanish at once from the façades. In the "colossal" form, running the full height of the building, as they had done in Shirley Place, the Royall house, and many other Colonial houses, they occur in McIntire's early work, at the corners of the Jerathmeel Peirce (Nichols) house (figure 154) and of

Figure 161. Harrison Gray Otis house, 85 Mount Vernon Street, Boston. Charles Bulfinch
1800 to 1801
Courtesy of Ogden Codman

the Pickman house on Washington Street as remodelled for Elias Hasket Derby about 1790. The Langdon house in Portsmouth, built before 1782, likewise has corner pilasters. The Woodlands (figure 155), 1788, and the Morton house (figure 156), 1796, have each a central motive of tall pilasters on the entrance front, and the Crafts house (figure 157) follows the Morton design with the substitution of close-coupled columns. The Mason, Prescott, and Everett houses in Boston had very slender pilasters flanking their curved projecting bays. Pilasters above an architectural basement, as in two exceptional instances before the Revolution, are

Figure 162. Lyman house, Waltham, Massachusetts. Samuel McIntire, after 1793
Courtesy of Ogden Codman

characteristic of the last decade of the century, especially of the style of Bulfinch and his followers. The President's house in Philadelphia (figure 158) and the river front of the White House in Washington, each begun in 1792, both have them. The engaged columns of the central pavilion on its north front (figure 159) likewise originally rose above a high basement. For Franklin Crescent (figure 150) Bulfinch adopted an engaged order, columns for the central pavilion, pilasters for the end pavilions and the houses opposite; and he repeated the motive with varied lateral groupings in his designs for the Knox house, the Hasket Derby (figure 160) and Hersey Derby houses, his own house, and the Harrison Gray Otis house on Mount Vernon Street (figure 161), the last in 1800. All these have the pilasters

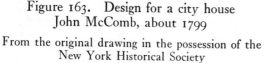

Figure 163. Design for a city house
John McComb, about 1799

From the original drawing in the possession of the
New York Historical Society

running through the two upper stories. McIntire lost no time in adopting the new arrangement, in the Lyman house (figure. 162) and in the remodelling of the Assembly House, both from 1793, but in both the order embraces but a single story. Later imitations of both schemes exist in the Pierce house in Portsmouth, in houses at Salem, Portland, and New Haven, but after 1800 the motive was no longer used by the leaders in Boston, any more than in the South.

The first use of blind arcades was

Figure 164. Design for a city house
Charles Bulfinch, after 1800

From the original drawing in the possession of
the Massachusetts Institute of Technology

as substructure for pilasters above a basement. A basement with open arcades below an order was the motive of Gabriel's famous palaces of the Place de la Concorde, which Bulfinch had seen, and which influenced his designs for public buildings. A similar treatment with blank arcades and an engaged order had been current in England since Lord Burlington's design for General Wade's house; the Adams had made it specially their own by such works as the house for Sir Watkin Wynn. All these had semicircular arches with single square-headed windows beneath. Soane employed segmental arches, with grouped and mullioned windows. These appear below the order in Bulfinch's first house, the one for Joseph Barrell (figure 184). His design for the Hasket Derby mansion (figure 160), in 1795, followed the Provost's House in Dublin—a copy of General Wade's—Malton's view of which, published the same year, formed part of Bulfinch's library. He likewise used basement arcades, sometimes circular, sometimes segmental, under the pilasters of his own house, the Hersey Derby house, the Otis house on Mount Vernon Street (figure 161), and the houses opposite Franklin Crescent. In his houses at the foot of Park Street (figure 151), in 1804, the basement story has the segmental arches,

Figure 165. Thomas Amory (Ticknor) house, Park Street, Boston, 1803 to 1804
Courtesy of Ogden Codman

although the upper stories are plain. McIntire did not adopt the arcaded basement, but arches as well as pilasters were taken over in the later imitations of Bulfinch's work.

John McComb, of New York, who used the arcaded basement in a design about 1799 (figure 163), seems to have led in adopting arcades framing the windows of the main story, in another of the same date. Both[1] show blind arches supported on pilasters or pilaster-like piers. Bulfinch used an arcaded main story with plain piers in a study on paper watermarked 1800[2] (figure 164), filling the lunettes also with glass. The Amory (Ticknor) house at Park and Beacon Streets (figure 165), surely to be attributed to him, and his Parkman houses in Bowdoin Square (figure 166) soon followed. All these have a tall basement below, although a preliminary design for the Parkman house has not. Asher Benjamin, in his "American Builder's Companion" (1806), which codified Bulfinch's innovations, shows two city

[1] McComb collection, New York Historical Society, nos. 104 and 109 respectively.
[2] Bulfinch collection, Department of Architecture, Massachusetts Institute of Technology.

houses with arcades in the main story[1]—with basement and without. With Banner's Crafts house (figure 157), 1805, the arcades were taken up in lower, country dwellings in New England also. Less elaborate examples are the Phelps house at Andover and a house at Orford, New Hampshire. In the South, Woodlawn and, later, Arlington (figure 138) have arcades along the wings; the Russell house in Charleston has them all about in the main story, one flight up. Latrobe's Burd

Figure 166. Parkman houses, Bowdoin Square, Boston. Charles Bulfinch, after 1806
Courtesy of Ogden Codman

house in Philadelphia (figure 167), built in 1801 and long destroyed, was exceptional in having blank arches in both of its lower stories, its only fellow being the Larkin house in Portsmouth (figure 168) from 1817—so similar and yet so subtly different.

Where the façade is unbroken—without pavilions, arcades, or an order—the general composition might depend either on uniform repetition of a window motive across the front, or on special types of windows on the central axis. A uniform range of five single windows was the ordinary Colonial scheme; it never ceased to

[1] Plates 33, 35.

206

have excellent examples, such as, in Salem, the Nathan Read house, 1793, the John Gardner house (figure 169), 1805, and the John Forrester house (Salem Club), 1818. After using more varied schemes in two earlier houses for the same client,

Figure 167. Burd house, Philadelphia. Benjamin Henry Latrobe
1800 to 1801
From an old photograph at the Ridgway Library

Bulfinch came back to it in the Harrison Gray Otis house on Beacon Street, Boston, in 1807. A modification after 1800 was the use of three uniform units, each in itself multiple, as in the Larkin house and others. Such a uniform treatment did not necessarily require that the front should have an odd number of bays, especially if the entrance was elsewhere. Street fronts two or four bays wide, with the door on the side of the building, were common in New England after 1805. One is figured in Benjamin's "American Builder's Companion." Bulfinch had already used fronts of four bays, even with the door in one of them; and this not only in double or multiple houses where balance could be secured by reversing adjacent fronts, but in the single house for Hersey Derby.

While special window motives were used in the centre of façades during Colo-

Figure 168. Larkin house, Portsmouth. Finished 1817

nial times, it was ordinarily in a pavilion, projecting or marked by pilasters. After the Revolution it became common to use them in an unbroken front, repeating the wider and more important opening of the door in the centre of the lower story. The first instance was the Bingham house in Philadelphia (figure 170), before 1788, modelled on Manchester House in London (figure 171) and having a Palladian window in the second story, a semicircular window in the third. An early manuscript design by Bulfinch (figure 172) shows a similar treatment which was embodied in the Harrison Gray Otis house on Cambridge Street in 1795, and in a house at the corner of Summer and Arch Streets, as well as in the Pickman (Shreve-

Little) house, Salem, in 1819. An analogous Southern example, later, is the Russell house in Charleston. Examples of such a treatment in two-story houses, or in the two lower stories of three, are common after 1800. In the Orlando Fairfax house at Alexandria, based on a plate in *The Builder's Magazine* (1774),[1] the central windows of the two upper stories are embraced in a single tall blind arch rising through both.

Many of the individual elements of the façades underwent significant trans-

From a photograph by Frank Cousins

Figure 169. John Gardner (Pingree) house, Salem. Samuel McIntire, 1805

formations. Windows, doorways, and cornices all had characteristic differences from the Colonial forms, and in some respects continued in rapid evolution.

Windows in the Colonial period had been almost universally single and square-headed, the only exceptions, aside from the early segmental ones, being the arched stair-windows and the Palladian motives, which were confined to an axial position. In contrast with this the houses of the early republic frequently had arched windows, windows of semicircular, circular, and even elliptical form, and triple groupings of many sorts, used in the side rooms as well as in the centre.

[1] Plate 117.

Ranges of arched windows, oblong with semicircular heads, appear in 1788 at the Woodlands, on the river front, and soon after in the President's house at Philadelphia (figure 158), in Monticello as remodelled, in Woodlawn, and in the Burd house, Philadelphia (figure 167), as well as later in the Larkin house, Portsmouth (figure 168), and in Arlington (figure 138).

Palladian windows of the sort common in academic and Colonial buildings con-

Figure 170. Bingham house, Philadelphia. Before 1788
From the engraving by William Birch, 1800

tinued in use after the Revolution, although rarely after 1800. The Bingham house, the John Brown house in Providence, the George Read II house in Newcastle have them, in quite the old form, with pilasters, entablatures over the side bays, and an archivolt over the central arch. Later examples, in the wings of Homewood and in the Nathaniel Silsbee house on Salem Common (figure 173), built in 1818, have no enframing order beyond the jambs, and merely a band of voussoirs bent over all three divisions.

More commonly in republican days the Palladian window was framed by a shallow bearing arch. This motive, a favorite one with the Adams, had been used once, we may recall, in the colonies just before the war—in the Chase house at Annapolis. It was now adopted when the Woodlands was remodelled (figure 174), and successively in the President's house at Philadelphia and in Bulfinch's Hasket Derby design. All these, before 1800, still had pilasters and entablature under a semicircular arch. Later examples are modified in two ways. The order is

Figure 171. Manchester House, London
From an old view

omitted in favor of plain mullions and bands, still keeping the large semicircular arch above. This is the scheme in Latrobe's Burd house (1801), in the Larkin house (1816), and the Fairfax house at Alexandria. Or the bearing arch is made elliptical, coming down on the head of the archivolt below, as in the John Andrew (Safford) and Pickering Dodge houses in Salem, 1819 and 1822 (figure 176), which keep the order, but with slender engaged columns.

Triple windows all square-headed, though with the side-lights narrow, as in the Palladian scheme, came into use after 1790, and increasingly after 1810.

Totally unknown before the Revolution, they appeared in 1788 in Soane's "Plans," and during following years in many derivative publications. Their first use in America, as we have seen, was in the bow of Bulfinch's Barrell house, under its segmental arches. In 1796 the Morton house, Roxbury, had one, with a transom; in 1805 the Crafts house (figure 157) had another. In Latrobe's domestic designs, such as the Markoe house in Philadelphia (figure 113), 1808–1811, and the Van Ness house (figure 130), begun 1813, they were the favorite form. From him they passed to his pupil, Mills, who used them in the Wickham and Brockenbrough houses in Richmond. Thornton took them up in Tudor Place and they were widely used elsewhere, nowhere more beautifully than in the house at 1109 Walnut Street in Philadelphia (figure 175), a masterpiece which deserves to be better known.

Figure 172. Design for a city house
Charles Bulfinch, after 1796

From the original drawing in the possession of
the Massachusetts Institute of Technology

Such triple windows were also used with a bearing arch—in Soane and derivative English books; in many of the buildings of Latrobe, Mills, and Thornton, just mentioned. Generally they were in the main story, with square-headed triple windows above them.

The sill in Colonial windows had been always at some distance from the floor; after 1788, especially in Bulfinch's work, it was frequently dropped to the floor level so that one might pass out to porches and balconies or to the ground. Usually this was made possible by ordinary guillotine windows with three sash, but occasionally casement sash or French windows were used, as in Solitude, 1784, in Bulfinch's Morton house, the Gore house, and Latrobe's Van Ness house.

The position and form of the window-frame in masonry walls underwent a subtle yet significant change. In Colonial times it had always been in the form of a classic architrave, occasionally projecting in front of the wall but normally flush, between the jambs. Only a few were set back, revealing the masonry jamb, and these were still relatively broad, with the form of an architrave. The flush architrave persisted to 1800 and later in houses of post-Colonial character, but in the progressive work it was replaced by a narrow and simple frame set back from the face of the wall. This type, long used in England with windows having a stone architrave, was retained there when there was none, as commonly in designs of the Adams. It appeared in America, along with the first Adam detail, in the Woodlands and in the Barrell house. Parris, who introduced it into Portland in 1805, shows in his details for the Hunnewell (Shepley) house an architrave frame for the second story, but a narrow frame for the first (figure 177). In Benjamin's

From a photograph by Clifford, 1855

Figure 173.   Nathaniel Silsbee house, Salem.   1818 to 1819
Courtesy of the Essex Institute

"American Builder's Companion," the following year, only the narrow frame was shown. Sash-bars were also made narrower, as in England—a feature of Adam slenderness.

Any exterior enframement of windows in masonry walls by an architrave, frieze, or cornice was commonly omitted. Of the few exceptions, the White House was an adaptation of earlier, academic designs; the entrance fronts of the Gore house (figure 178), the Amory house (figure 165), and the Otis house on Beacon Street have the type of enframement radically different from Colonial forms. All three are also exceptional in having consoles over a narrow supporting strip. The novelty in the case of the Boston houses, all after 1800, was that the strip came directly at the jamb, without an architrave—an arrangement not characteristic of Adam's

From a photograph by H. F. Beidleman

Figure 174. Window at the Woodlands, 1788

work, which Bulfinch must have got elsewhere. The only enrichment of the plain hole which normally held the window in brick walls was in the treatment of its arch or lintel. Over Colonial windows there had generally been a plain brick arch, even a keystone of stone was exceptional. Plain flat arches were rare in republican days, although the Octagon, built 1798–1800, has them throughout. A white keystone alone was not thought sufficient. Most houses have the whole arch in white, with a single or double keystone and perhaps other voussoirs marked off. Perhaps the earliest example is the Reynolds (Morris) house in Philadelphia, 1786. The Russell house, Charleston, 1811, has an additional elaboration in that the outermost voussoirs, like the key-block, also rise above the top of the arch. About 1819 came the substitution of lintels, with raised centre and ends ornamented by

From a photograph by Philip B. Wallace

Figure 175.   Window of the house at 1109 Walnut Street, Philadelphia

a key pattern. They are found in Salem in the Silsbee house, finished in that year, and in the Pickering Dodge house (figure 176), among others.

In wooden walls an elaborate window enframement remained in favor until wood fell into disuse for the better houses, about 1805. A few windows are framed in rusticated quoins, notably those of the wings of the Lyman house, after 1793, but rustication was on the way to abandonment.   Post-Colonial buildings such as the Jerathmeel Peirce house in Salem and the Langdon house in Portsmouth, Adam buildings like the Hasket and Hersey Derby houses in Salem, Oak Hill in Danvers, the Morton and Crafts houses in Roxbury, all have a frieze and cornice over the principal windows. The later of these, by Bulfinch and his followers, may be readily distinguished from Colonial work by their delicate proportions. The friezes are commonly terminated by small end blocks and may be enriched by fluting or carving.

The Colonial types of doorways rapidly vanished from pretentious houses. The single rectangular opening, either with or without a rectangular transom, is scarcely to be found after 1790, until the adoption of the temple scheme brought it back in the University of Virginia. Glass panels in the doors likewise disap-

Figure 176. Pickering Dodge (Shreve) house, Salem. 1822 to 1823

peared. The pediment, which had been so universal a feature in the enframement of later Colonial doorways, scarcely persisted longer except in local vernacular work. The baroque scroll pediment had been disused on exteriors before the Revolution.

The door with an arched transom persisted as a means of illuminating the hall, for which was introduced also a new device, the side-light. In the form and grouping of these features, largely under the influence of the Adams, lay the variety and evolution of the doorway after 1788. In that year the first side-lights were provided in the doorway of the Bingham house in Philadelphia (figure 170). Bulfinch used side-lights in some form customarily from 1792; McComb adopted them

216

in New York before 1800, and they were employed in Charleston from the same period. Both in the fanlights and in the side-lights leaded designs, as in Adam's work, were ordinarily substituted for the wooden Colonial sash-bars.

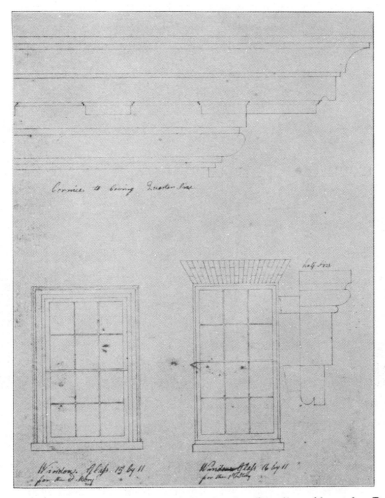

Figure 177. Hunnewell (Shepley) house, Portland. Details. Alexander Parris, 1805
From the original drawing at the Boston Athenæum

Semicircular fanlights—the form preferred by the Adams themselves—were the first to be used, in the Bingham house and the Woodlands, and, with or without side-lights, they remained the most common until about 1800 (figure 179). Meanwhile in New England elliptical fanlights had come into vogue. The innovation in America seems to have been due to Bulfinch, who went out of his way to use the elliptical form over the door in his design for the Hasket Derby house (figure 160). McIntire had used it in 1793 in his Nathan Read house, designed largely under Bulfinch's inspiration. Elliptical or segmental fanlights remained

217

universal in New England until 1820. With but a single exception—that of the Morton house—they all had the side-lights. Elsewhere and later, square-headed doorways with side-lights, and usually a transom, made their appearance: first perhaps in McComb's house for Alexander Hamilton, The Grange, in 1801. The Greek revival made this the accepted form (figure 180).

In earlier triple doorways there were either plain mullions and transoms or at

Figure 178. Gore house, Waltham. Entrance front. Between 1799 and 1804
Courtesy of Miss N. D. Tupper

most pilasters on the mullions, as in Bulfinch's design for the Hasket Derby mansion. In the Salem houses of 1818 and following years, however, slender engaged columns and entablatures of great richness were adopted (figures 176 and 191), and heavier columns often repeated the scheme during the Greek revival.

The enframement of the door, like its shape and filling, underwent modification. The favorite late Colonial form, with a pediment into which a curved transom broke up, was unusual after 1793, although in a few doorways, such as that of Montpellier, remodelled in that year, a pediment was made thus to span one of the new elliptical fanlights (figure 186). Even in other relationships a pediment on the door-casing soon became rare.   Instead, there was generally a full horizontal entablature.   A pair of light pilasters or engaged columns and an entablature framing a doorway with semicircular transom occurs on numberless city houses of

Figure 179.   Doorway of the Gore house
Courtesy of Miss N. D. Tupper

the period of Franklin Crescent and Sansom's buildings; and, under a portico, on not a few country houses such as Homewood and Upsala, both begun in 1798.   On the other hand, it was not uncommon, even without a portico, for a triple arched doorway to have an archivolt only, as in the Bingham house, the George Read II house in Newcastle, and the Gore house, or merely to be placed filling one of the bays of a shallow arcade, as in the Hersey Derby house or the houses at the foot of Park Street, Boston. In such a case even the archivolt was absent. Similarly the classicists simplified the treatment of the rectangular opening: Jefferson, under the porticos of his University, used an architrave only; Latrobe, in triple square-

Figure 180. Doorway of the Dexter house, Dexter, Michigan. 1840 to 1843

headed doorways, omitted it in favor of plain square jambs (figure 181). The Greek designs made frequent use of square antæ (figure 180).

A portico of some form over the door became almost universal after 1790. In the North until 1825 it remained ordinarily no more than an elaboration of the doorway itself, its small columns and pilasters constituting the door enframement. Such porticos continued a Colonial tradition: sometimes without change, as in the Jerathmeel Peirce and Samuel Cook houses in Salem, the John Brown house in Providence, the Octagon, and the Hunnewell (Shepley) house in Portland; usually with greater variety and richness of form. The first and one of the most elaborate of the new door porticos is that of Governor Langdon's house in Portsmouth, before 1782, which has the square central bay widened by quadrants, with, in all, four columns and four corresponding engaged columns (figure 182). In 1793 McIntire, inspired by the great semicircular portico of the Barrell house, adopted a door portico of this form in the Nathan Read house in Salem, and this was later imitated there in the houses of William Gray, 1801, John Gardner, 1805 (figure 169), Gideon Tucker, 1806–1809, and others, as well as elsewhere in New England. The Gardner and Tucker porches have supplementary pilasters at either side. Related with these were the porches with an overhanging semicircular canopy,

Elevation of the front of Commandants quarters to the East.
Latrobe

Figure 181. Commandant's quarters, Pittsburgh arsenal. Benjamin Henry Latrobe
From the original drawing in the Library of Congress

used by Bulfinch in the Morton house (figure 156), 1796, and elaborated in the Andrew house, Salem, in 1819. Sometimes a rectangular portico with four columns in front was still treated as itself the door enframement: with coupled columns and coupled pilasters behind. Such were the porticos of Oak Hill (1801) and the Otis house on Beacon Street, Boston (1807). The later Salem houses generally reverted to a portico of two columns only, depending for richness, as we have seen, on elaboration within the door-arch (figure 176).

Other porticos with columns a single story in height gave more monumental expression to doors which already had their own special enframement. McIntire proposed such a portico of four columns, with a pediment, in studies of 1780; Solitude had one on the garden front soon after; Woodlawn, The Grange, the Wickham and Van Ness houses furnish later examples (figure 130). All these were rectangular, with four columns.   Semicircular examples of the same general scale may also be found in the Joseph Manigault and Wilson Glover houses at Charleston. In Tudor Place, after 1810, and later in the Bulloch house at Savannah (figure 183),

From a photograph by Frank Cousins

Figure 182.   Porch of the Langdon house, Portsmouth.   Before 1782

the semicircle of the portico is continued by a great niche hollowed about the door after the manner of Soane.

A special case of the portico of one story was what had come to be known as a piazza: a covered veranda with a longitudinal range of light posts or columns. We have noted the prevalence of this form in New York before the Revolution and its introduction into Boston by Copley.   It remained characteristic of the vernacular style about New York, which has become known as the "Dutch Colonial." Here its position was along the front, perhaps along the rear also, under an extension of the main roof—as in the Dyckman house in Manhattan (figure 148), soon

Figure 183.   Portico of the Bulloch house, Savannah

after the war, the Board (Zabriskie) house in Hackensack, 1790, and countless others.   In New England the customary position was the one established by Copley, along the sides of the building, where we find it in the Morton and Crafts houses.   In the far South there could not be too many verandas, and we find them even encircling the house at every story.

The first examples of a portico above a high academic basement, interestingly enough, were the semicircular or segmental ones: Bulfinch's Barrell house (figure 184), 1792, McIntire's executed design for the Hasket Derby mansion, and the south portico of the White House, as proposed by Jefferson and Latrobe in 1807 and built in 1824.[1] All these have two stories embraced in the order. The first rectangular portico of the sort was on the garden front of Poplar Forest, 1804, the next in Pavilion VII of the University of Virginia (figure 136), erected in 1817 after a suggestion of Thornton. In both the portico is of but one story in height, with a width, at the University, of six columns. A few subsequent instances may be found, of one story and of two.

Porticos with superposed orders, like those of the finest Palladian houses on

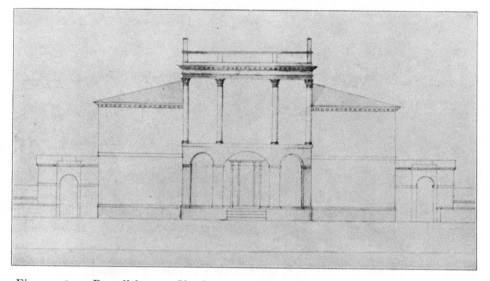

Figure 184. Barrell house, Charlestown. Elevation. Charles Bulfinch, 1792
From an original drawing in the Library of Congress

the eve of the Revolution, were uncharacteristic of the early republican period. Jefferson abandoned the idea of crowning his Doric at Monticello with an Ionic. Verandas in several stories, as we have seen, were common in the far South, but these had ordinarily small architectural pretensions. Not until the classic revival was waning did the placing of one order above another again become sanctioned.

An approach to the truly colossal portico is furnished by Jefferson's houses: Monticello, as remodelled (figure 147), Edgehill, designed by 1798, the entrance front of Poplar Forest, and Ampthill in Cumberland County—in which the portico ran the full height of a building of one story. At Monticello, and later at Barboursville, there were mezzanines, to be sure, and at Farmington, where the new rooms

[1] W. B. Bryan, "History of the National Capital," vol. 2 (1916), p. 64.

behind the portico constituted a single story equal to two of the older part, they were twenty-seven feet in height.

Already before these houses, others having two stories throughout were dignified by a portico of their full height—like that of the Morris house in New York, which had been unique before the Revolution. The great portico at the Woodlands (figure 185) seems to date from the remodelling of 1788. The Government House

From a photograph by H. F. Beidleman

Figure 185. The Woodlands, Philadelphia. River front, as remodelled 1788

in New York, begun the next year, followed McComb's studies in having one from the start. Madison, under the advice of Jefferson, added one to Montpellier (figure 186) in 1793,[1] and the owners of many other Colonial houses did likewise. For the White House, the great north portico projected by Latrobe in 1807 was built in 1829.[2] A width of four columns was universal, the portico being merely a central pavilion, narrower than the front of the house. The decisive further step was taken, as we have seen at Mount Vernon and in the Pavilions V and I of the University of Virginia, where the porticos were made the full width of the front. From this point the history of the portico became that of the mass of the house itself.

[1] Kimball, "Thomas Jefferson, Architect," p. 56.
[2] Bryan, "History of the National Capital," vol. 2, p. 238.

Differences in the form and proportions of the orders are among the most obvious of the changes from the Colonial to republican work. The example of the Adams was here all-powerful at first. Elements and arrangements familiar in their work became common in America, beginning before 1790. Thus the Ionic capital with parallel volutes and a decorated necking was first adopted on the entrance front of the Woodlands (figure 155), and soon in Franklin Crescent. Both of these also have an order without an architrave, and a decoration of friezes with flutes and circular paterae. The Corinthian capital with a single row of leaves was

From a photograph by R. W. Holsinger

Figure 186. Montpellier, Orange County, Virginia. Portico, 1793

taken up in Bulfinch's Morton house (figure 156) and widely used by McIntire, among others. In the front portico at Homewood the favorite palm capital appears.

Columns were attenuated systematically in the work under Adam influence, not sporadically in a few instances, as before the Revolution. The Corinthian pilasters in Adam's house for Sir Watkin Wynn in London are somewhat over eleven diameters in height, instead of the academic ten. The same proportion is to be found in the Corinthian order of the Barrell house and the Ionic of the Woodlands. It was not long before it became almost universal to add one or two diameters, at least, to the academic proportions, as Asher Benjamin did tacitly in "The Country Builder's Assistant," and expressly—"lengthening the shafts two diameters"— in the "American Builder's Companion" (1806). In the Gideon Tucker porch in

Salem (1809) McIntire made the Corinthian columns as slight as fourteen diameters, and in the Pickering Dodge doorway (1822) those on the mullions have the extreme slenderness of seventeen.

From this attenuation Jefferson held aloof. The orders in his Virginia houses

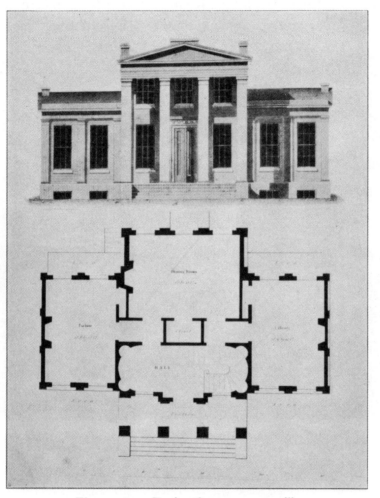

Figure 187. Design for a country villa
From Lafever's *Modern Builder's Guide*, 1833
The prototype of many houses with wings and square antae

and in the University were of strict Palladian outlines and proportions, often of the heavy Tuscan. Latrobe, first to use the Greek orders, gave the columns of the Van Ness porch (figure 130), after 1813, the full Parthenon ratio of diameter to height. In some of the most pretentious houses on the model of the Greek temple—Arlington and Andalusia, for instance—the Doric columns were quite of antique solidity of proportion, but in many others they were lightened somewhat. This practice was justified by Asher Benjamin in "The Practical House Carpenter . . . being . . . the Grecian Orders of Architecture . . . fashioned according to the Style and Practice of the Present Day" (1830). He writes in the preface that the Doric column "was generally made, by the Greeks, about five diameters in height; but the same order was generally made, by the Romans, from seven and a half to eight diameters in height. It is therefore evident that the latter proportions come nearer to

Figure 188. Smith house, Grass Lake, Michigan. 1840

our practice than the former one, especially when the orders are used in private houses." Benjamin's Greek Doric was some six and three-quarter diameters high.

Different periods had their preferences among the orders. Thus the protagonists of the Adam style generally chose the Corinthian or the Ionic, whereas the designers of the first Greek houses preferred the Doric. The Greek Ionic was soon taken up, but the full Greek Corinthian, of the "Lysicrates" type, although used by Latrobe in the House of Representatives in Washington in 1817, did not come into general use for houses until after the striking exemplification of it on the exterior of Girard College, 1833–1847.[1]

[1] The Russel house at Middletown, Connecticut, by Ithiel Town and Alexander Jackson Davis, was described in 1833 as "Corinthian amphiprostyle from the Monument of Lysicrates." Dunlap, "Arts of Design" (1918 ed.), vol. 3, p. 213, and note.

Square piers or antae were sometimes substituted for circular columns, as less difficult to make and less expensive. The first notable instance is the long portico at Mount Vernon, added between 1784 and 1787. Many of the best vernacular houses in New Jersey, such as the Vreeland house at Nordhoff, have a treatment substantially similar. Lafever in his "Builder's Guide" (1833) applied the scheme to the house in imitation of the temple (figure 187), and examples evidently in-

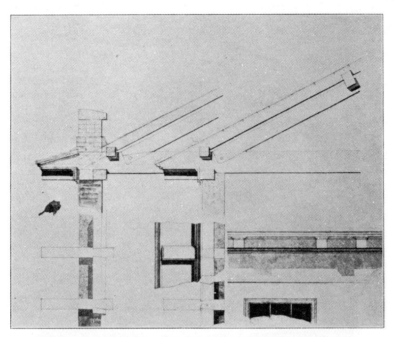

Figure 189. Cornice details. Benjamin Henry Latrobe
From an original drawing in the possession of Ferdinand C. Latrobe

spired by his plates may be found scattered from the Hudson westward through central New York and Michigan (figure 188).

For the external cornice of the house, the academic tendency in Colonial times, with its increasing use of orders for wall treatment, had been toward a full entablature all around. This had been attained, to be sure, only in two examples; far more commonly the lower members of the entablature existed only as fragments over the pilasters. The puristic functional tendency after the Revolution left the walls of a great number of fine houses without an order, and these, almost universally down to 1820, had a cornice only. Where some form of order treatment was used, a continuous entablature became gradually more common. Only a few houses have the old fragments of frieze and cornice, and these are mostly before 1800. An exceptional reversion to the scheme occurs in the side portico of the John Andrew house in Salem, raised 1819, in which frieze and cornice are cut away between supports. More usually the entablature ran continuously as far along as the order extended on portico or pavilion, the cornice only being carried around the rest of the house. In an increasing number of houses, beginning with those destined for the President in New York, Philadelphia, and Washington, the full entablature extended completely around. Jefferson had always preferred this scheme, and followed it whenever he could, as in his designs for Edgehill and Poplar Forest. His houses for the University insured its final triumph: every building has a complete entablature even though there is no order rising to it. The Greek houses which followed show scarcely an exception.

Figure 190. Cornice from the William Gray house, Salem. 1801
Now in the museum of the Essex Institute

Cornices after the Revolution and before the adoption of Greek forms, tended to grow lighter in proportion to the total height of the building (figure 177). Cornices of extreme thinness may be seen in McComb's designs about 1800 (figures 125 and 163), and, still more, in Latrobe's for the Van Ness house (figure 130), 1813, and others (figure 189). This lightness was, in origin, merely a consequence of Adam and Soane influence, but Benjamin rationalized it in "The American Builder's Companion" (1806), by a rather specious train of reasoning, in which he maintained that the height of cornices could be decreased considerably without substantially affecting their appearance, provided the projection remained the same.

The profiles of cornices remained of ordinary academic character until 1800, and beyond that date in the work of such designers as Bulfinch and McIntire, to say nothing of Jefferson. The only essentially novel feature at first was the use, in minor cornices, of dentils split at the top, giving a fret-like effect. This detail, common in England at the time, appears here as early as 1787 in the door-cornice of

From a photograph by Frank Cousins

Figure 191. Porch of the Joseph Peabody house, Salem

the John Reynolds house in Philadelphia. With the turn of the century other designers adopted modifications, sometimes of a fanciful character. In the Octagon Thornton used vertical consoles rising from the frieze into the cornice; at Homewood the brackets in the cornice itself are of fantastic outline. In the William

231

Gray house, Salem, begun in 1801, there are very flat modillions, a row of trumpet-shaped guttae in place of dentils, and a line of little spheres strung on a rod (figure 190). Benjamin, in the "American Builder's Companion," besides giving his individual mouldings greater projection for their height, employed many of these elements. His profiles were followed by many New England craftsmen after its

Figure 192. Oval saloon of the Barrell house, Charlestown. Charles Bulfinch, 1792
Courtesy of Ogden Codman

date. In Salem they were adopted in the main cornices and porch cornices of the Forrester house (1818), the Joseph Peabody house (1819–1820, figure 191),[1] and many others.

For the eaves-balustrade new forms likewise became current. The old scheme, of relatively narrow posts or pedestals with long, open rows of balusters between, was retained, to be sure, in many cases, but from 1800 a new scheme became increasingly popular: with short stretches of baluster openings only over the windows below, and long, solid panels between. This arrangement, which is shown in Pain's "Practical House Carpenter," republished in Philadelphia in 1797, was

[1] For the date see R. S. Rantoul in *Historical Collections of the Essex Institute*, vol. 24 (1887), p. 257.

adopted in the Gore house (figure 178), the Amory (Ticknor) house in Boston (figure 165), 1804, the Samuel Cook house, and, later, the Silsbee house in Salem (figure 173), 1818, and the Nathaniel Russell house in Charleston, finished before

From a photograph by Frank Cousins

Figure 193. Vestibule of the Octagon, Washington. William Thornton, 1798 to 1800

1811—to mention datable examples. In the parapets of other houses these openings above the windows were filled not with balusters but with pierced interlacing circles. Bulfinch introduced this treatment in his design for the houses at the foot of Park Street, Boston, in 1804; it was brought to Portland the following year by Alexander Parris, who used it in the Hunnewell (Shepley) house (figure 112) and others. Benjamin published a detail for it in 1806.[1] In the Swan house, Dorchester (figure 146), the open panels contained Chinese lattice, which Jefferson continued to use in balcony railings until his death in 1826. The John Andrew house, Salem (1818), had fan motives in the parapet, alternating with panels of balusters.

The ambitions of architecture under the republic included the adornment of buildings with figure sculpture, but this was scarcely achieved on the exterior of

Figure 194. Stairs of the Barrell house, Charlestown. Charles Bulfinch, 1792
Courtesy of Ogden Codman

domestic buildings. For his splendid house in Philadelphia Robert Morris brought to America the Italian sculptor Iardella, who carved reliefs of playful allegorical cherubs, in rococo manner, for panels above the windows. On the exterior friezes of some of the pavilions at the University of Virginia Jefferson employed reliefs in composition, garlands with cherubs or ox-skulls.

On the interior the leading features of the style of the early republic were the variety of forms of space, the attenuation of proportions under Adam influence, and the enrichment of members by delicate Pompeian decoration. After 1825,

[1] "American Builder's Companion," pl. 35.

with the victory of Greek forms, came reaction toward rectangular rooms, heavy proportions, and relative absence of ornament.

Novel elements of space, the general composition of which we have discussed, were the circular and elliptical rooms (figures 192 and 193) and stairs, and the interior dome. The stairs, especially, require further individual attention.

Figure 195. Stairs of the Gore house, Waltham. Between 1799 and 1804
Courtesy of Miss N. D. Tupper

Stairs in the Colonial period had been composed exclusively of straight runs of steps. On the eve of the Revolution had appeared a tendency to curve the landings or the hand-rail. The new style involved curving the runs themselves, more or less sharply. Although this brought winders, or wedge-shaped treads, again into use, they did not now, as in the seventeenth century, taper to nothing against

235

a newel post, but surrounded an open well of greater or less size. The first stairs of this sort in America seem to have been those of the Bingham house in Philadelphia, where "the self-supporting broad stairway of fine white marble . . . gave a truly Roman elegance to the passage."[1]

At the Woodlands (figure 109) and in many later houses the staircase has straight runs part-way but makes semicircular turns at the ends. Bulfinch, who

Figure 196. Vestibule of the Woodlands, Philadelphia. 1788
Courtesy of Ogden Codman

had, in the Barrell house, ingeniously fitted a double stair, chiefly with straight runs, in a hall with semicircular ends (figures 120 and 194), used, in the Thomas Russell house, Charlestown, a stair about a broad central well of this form. McIntire sketched it, and imitated it in the Hasket Derby house. Latrobe used it in the Markoe house in Philadelphia and the Van Ness house (figures 111 and 113). In these and other houses the well was kept of regular form, whether steps surrounded it on all sides or landings intervened.

[1] Griswold, "The Republican Court" (1856), p. 262.

A staircase itself semicircular, without any straight portion, and with a semi-circular well, was used by Bulfinch in the Hersey Derby house (1799), and elsewhere. The other side of the well might also be rounded to make a full circle, as in the Manigault house in Charleston, the Gore house (1799–1804, figure 195), the Crafts

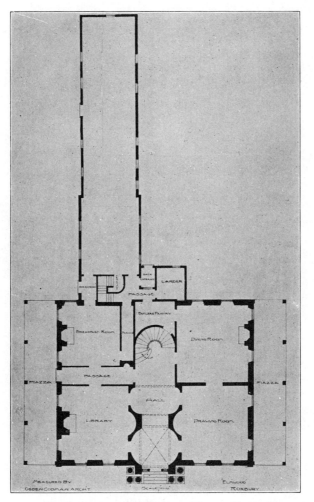

Figure 197.   Crafts house, Roxbury.   Plan.   Peter Banner, 1805
From a measured drawing by Ogden Codman

house (1805), the Wickham house in Richmond (1812), and others.   Both schemes are taken over from Bulfinch in 1806 in Benjamin's "American Builder's Companion."

An elliptical well, wholly or part-way around, was likewise in use at the same dates, in Woodlawn, in the Radcliffe house and the Nathaniel Russell house (figure 126) in Charleston, and in studies by Bulfinch and Parris.

Domed rooms, unknown in Colonial days, were not limited to houses which had a visible exterior dome, such as Monticello and the David Sears house. The great circular saloons of the Swan house in Roxbury (figure 146), and the Jonathan Mason house in Boston, as well as the vestibule of the Woodlands (figure 196), had domes behind vertical exterior walls. Houses with a central circular hall might have a tall dome beneath the roof, lighted by a cupola. This is the case with Brentwood in the city of Washington, where the formal composition of space is

Figure 198. Interior of the John C. Stevens house, College Place and Murray Street New York. Alexander Jackson Davis
From the original drawing in the possession of the New York Historical Society

elaborated by square niches in the diagonal axes of the rotunda. The niche with a semi-dome—large enough, unlike late Colonial niches, to tell in the spatial effect —was not uncommon, especially in the work of Latrobe and his followers. It occurs, for example, in the Markoe house, Philadelphia (1808), the Wickham house, Richmond (1812), and Latrobe's plans for houses at the Pittsburgh arsenal.

Other vault forms, in the plaster ceilings of hall and vestibule, united perhaps with a variety of form in the walls below, prevented a monotony of merely cubical rooms. At Homewood, just in 1800, there was a groin vault in three bays, running transversely in the lateral passage where it intersects the hall. In Parris's design for the Hunnewell house in Portland (figure 112), 1805, such a vault runs back in the hall itself. A more ambitious but less consistent scheme of groined arches supported by pilasters and columns surrounds the large rectangular hall of the Hollister house at Greenfield, where Benjamin published his first book. The Crafts and Sears houses (figures 197 and 127) in Boston have each a groin-vaulted bay in the vestibule, flanked by niches. Most ambitious of all in form is the entrance hall of

From a photograph, copyright 1913, by Frank Cousins

Figure 199.   East parlor of the Jerathmeel Peirce (Nichols) house, Salem
Samuel McIntire

Latrobe's house for Stephen Decatur in Washington, with its segmental vaults: a square bay with pendentives in the centre, a short barrel vault in front, and a great niche, itself with minor niches, as the culminating feature.

The new interest in composition of space, coupled with structural purism, tended to reduce the elaboration of wall surface, and to concentrate attention on individual members, chiefly of a functional character: doorways, windows, chimneypieces, cornices, the centrepieces of ceilings, the strings and hand-rails of stairs.

Panelling, which had been getting less common before the Revolution, soon disappeared entirely in favor of plain surfaces of plaster. In a few houses strip panels were applied to the plastered walls in the Adam manner. McIntire sketched

239

such a treatment in the Barrell house and employed it in the oval room of the Derby mansion. The profiles of the mouldings he derived from Pain's "Practical House Carpenter," recently issued. The pedestal-like dado, generally plain, of late Colonial times, persisted very generally down to 1820. Often, however, the plaster was carried down to the baseboard, leaving the dado cap or "surbase" as an isolated band, decorated in many cases with reedings, dentils, interlaces, floral or

Figure 200. Ballroom, Lyman house, Waltham

wave motives. No one of these has any general priority in time, and many of them appear simultaneously in a single building, as in the Morton house, 1796. Even the surbase was omitted with increasing frequency as the Greek influence gathered strength. Wall-paper continued much in use and silk was occasionally employed; but, as on the eve of the Revolution, the most advanced practice eschewed them. Among houses building in 1800, Monticello, the Octagon, Homewood, and others have none. In the elegant interior of about 1830—as we see it in a water-color by Alexander Jackson Davis for the Stevens house at College Place and Murray Street, New York (figure 198),[1] perfectly plain wall surfaces

[1] In the gallery of the New York Historical Society, and reproduced by kind permission of the Society.

provide a foil for the stately architectural members and for rich furniture, pictures, mirrors, and carpet.

Architectonic treatment of the walls by an order, which had been already falling into disuse under rococo influence, was now generally abjured, and persisted only in exceptional cases. Some of these were essentially survivals of Colonial pilaster treatment, translated into Adam proportions and detail. Thus, in finish-

Figure 201. Interior from the Barrell house, Charlestown. Charles Bulfinch, 1792
Courtesy of Ogden Codman

ing the Adam parlor of the Jerathmeel Peirce house (figure 199), some score of years later than the building, McIntire used pilasters to support an entablature spanning the recesses at either side of the chimney-breast. The most characteristic examples, however, now made use of the column, with its greater functional and monumental quality. The Williams house at 1234 Washington Street, Boston, had Adam Corinthian columns in the same relations as the pilasters of the Peirce house: in the recesses beside the fireplace, resting on a dado. The ballroom of the Lyman house, an addition, has similar columns rising from the floor, very tall and slender, with a screen of columns also at the other end of the room (figure 200).

The vestibule of the Woodlands (1788) is unique in having a unified columnar treatment throughout (figure 196). Its circular cornice is supported by eight columns equally spaced. In the interiors of Greek inspiration, columns were used only in open screens, sometimes double, as the one in the Stevens house in New York.

From a photograph, copyright, 1912, by William K. Semple

Figure 202. The saloon, Monticello. Thomas Jefferson, 1771 to 1809

The form of interior cornices varied much at any given time with the means of the owner and the relative importance of the room, but an evolution may be traced in several respects. Cornices of academic proportions and profile persisted for some time in fine houses, and may even be found in rooms of the Barrell house in 1792, where Adam forms were first introduced into New England (figure 201). Meanwhile lighter cornices, often with a frieze—both usually with enrichment in composition, if they were not entirely of stucco—came in favor. Such cornices and friezes had appeared just before the Revolution at Kenmore and Mount Vernon; they now were adopted at Solitude (figure 204), 1784, in the Otis house of 1795 and other works of Bulfinch such as the Hersey Derby house, in the Octagon (figures 193 and 207), the Lyman house (figure 200), and others down to 1810.

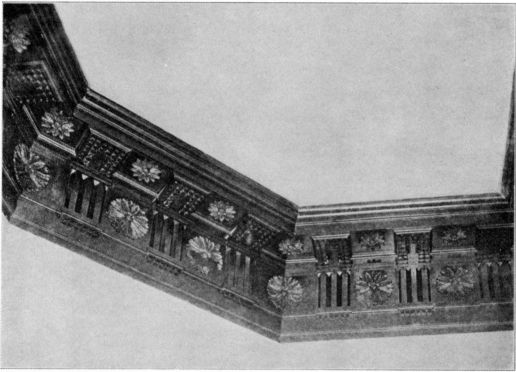

From a photograph by R. W. Holsinger

Figure 203.   Cornice in the North Bow, Monticello.   Thomas Jefferson, about 1805

The examples enumerated have simple classic profiles, often with dentils, plain or fanciful, and with relatively slight projection.   About 1800 shallow, flat blocks, mutules or modillions began to be introduced, the projection of the cornice tended to be increased, and the under side or "planceer" ornamented.   An early cornice of this sort is in the hall at Upsala, 1798, others are at Homewood, in the John Gardner house at Salem, 1805, and the Radcliffe house in Charleston, finished 1806.   Benjamin, in his "Country Builder's Assistant" (1797), had shown no room cornices with modillions, but in "The American Builder's Companion," published 1806, in which he had the collaboration of the stucco worker, Daniel Raynerd,

Figure 204.   Ceiling at Solitude.   1784 to 1785

Figure 205.   Ceiling of the stair hall in the Nathaniel Russell
house, Charleston.   Finished before 1811

mutules frequently occur in the plates engraved by both men, and it is stated that one of the embellishments "ought always to be in the plancere." Scrolls rising below the overhang, which were shown by Benjamin as early as 1797, were also used in the Gardner house. A detail of a stucco cornice having as its main member a hollow adorned with leaves, much like one given by Raynerd in 1806, is preserved among the Tucker papers at the Essex Institute, the Tucker house having

From a photograph by Frank Cousins

Figure 206. John Andrew (Safford) house, Salem. 1818 to 1819

been built in 1809. In the Andrew house in Salem, 1818–1819, finally, the stucco cornice is of plain mouldings of rounded section (figure 206).

A cove cornice, frequent enough in Colonial days, continued in use for a brief time only. The banquet room at Mount Vernon (about 1778) has one, festooned with Adam husks. The oval saloon of the Barrell house (figure 192) likewise had a cove, which was imitated in the similar room of the Hasket Derby house (1795). Latest, perhaps, was the ballroom of the Lyman house.

A full entablature as a room cornice, which had been rather common before the Revolution, was used, for a long time after it, only in Jefferson's work (figures 202 and 203). His entablatures were proportioned to the rooms exactly as if sup-

From a photograph by Frank Cousins

Figure 207. Mantel and cornice in the drawing-room at the Octagon
William Thornton, 1798 to 1800

ported by an order, so that the Tuscan ones in minor rooms at the University are of enormous size. With the supremacy of Greek forms a full entablature once more became the general rule.

Adam sunbursts were adopted in the ceilings at Mount Vernon, as we have seen, just as the Revolution broke out. A richer ceiling of the same sort distinguished Solitude (figure 204), built immediately after the war for John Penn, fresh from England. "The Practical House Carpenter," which seems to have been the work of William Pain mentioned in McIntire's inventory,[1] showed ceilings of this character, and McIntire drew on its plates 92 and 93 for his ceiling in the oval

From a photograph by Frank Cousins

Figure 208. Mantel in the dining-room at the Octagon. William Thornton, 1798 to 1800

room of the Hasket Derby house. Until 1812 or later such ceilings remained in vogue for rooms of special importance, being used in the Hersey Derby, Nathaniel Russell (figure 205), and Wickham houses, among others. Raynerd drew a plate of them for the "American Builder's Companion," in 1806. As time went on ornament tended to be limited to a central rosette. This was the case in the Radcliffe house in Charleston, from 1806. The Andrew house in Salem has one, with four quarter-rosettes in the corners of the ceiling (figure 206). In spite of the forms of

[1] *Essex Probate Records*, vol. 380, p. 367.

the leaves here, their increasing weight and the smooth border-mouldings portend the coming of Victorianism.

The chief feature of the interiors, even more than in Colonial days, was the chimneypiece. Until after 1790 it generally conformed to late Colonial types, having a heavy architrave with ears, and perhaps a similar architrave as an overmantel, which might be flanked by pilasters and crowned by a broken pediment. The characteristic republican type was quite different, being similar to the marble mantels imported on the eve of the Revolution. Like them, it placed less emphasis on a surrounding architrave than on flanking supports, above which, in a frieze, were projecting end blocks. The more elaborate examples had also a centre block or panel, and were richly ornamented with Adam motives in composition.

Marble mantels continued to be imported, as well as marble facings. Solitude, just after the Revolution, has a mantelpiece of gray marble, flanked by half-pilasters like the one in the parlor of the Chase house, just before the war. Its frieze has vertical flutings with special centre and end motives. A splendid marble mantelpiece, the gift of Samuel Vaughan to Washington, reached Mount Vernon in February, 1785.[1] Precisely during the period of Adam supremacy, however, marble mantels were less used in America than either in the late Colonial period or after 1820. The very rich ornament in fashion tended to make them prohibitively expensive, and even in England, although the Adams used many mantels of marble, in their later work they generally gave preference to cast cement. Whole mantels of this, very closely imitated from authentic designs of the brothers, were imported by Thornton for the Octagon (figures 207 and 208). They bear the date 1799 and the name of Coade, whose "manufactory in the Borough of London" Thornton recommended to Jefferson in 1817.[2] More usually ornamental motives of composition were applied to wooden mantels in general accordance with the designs shown in books.

Models for the design of these mantels were furnished especially in Pain's "British Palladio" (1788 ff.),[3] and "Practical House Carpenter" (1792 ff.),[4] the latter soon republished in America. Of native works, Benjamin's first book, "The Country Builder's Assistant" (1797) contained several of a similar character.

The earliest existing mantel of the sort made in this country is one from McIntire's Nathan Read house in Salem, 1793, now removed to The Lindens, Danvers (figure 209). As the Read house was so largely inspired by Bulfinch's Barrell house, built the previous year, we may doubtless assume that it contained similar mantels,

[1] Wilstach, "Mount Vernon," p. 174.   [2] Glenn Brown, "The Octagon" (1916), p. 14.
[3] E. g., pls. 16 and 17.   [4] E. g., pls. 80–82.

although these were later replaced by uninteresting ones of marble. Others, which may show us what Bulfinch's early mantels were like, are still preserved in the Otis house on Cambridge Street (figure 210), 1795, and in the Gore house (figure 211).

From a photograph by Frank Cousins

Figure 209. Mantel from the Nathan Read house, Salem, now in the Hooper house, Danvers. Samuel McIntire, 1793

Several mantels likewise remain in the Hersey Derby house, an authenticated work by Bulfinch from after 1799. Many examples of generally similar character and date to these from New England may be found in other regions.

No special priority seems to have subsisted in the employment, as mantel supports, of engaged columns, pilasters, half-pilasters, or panels of a pilaster-like character. All alike are shown in handbooks of the 'nineties. Free-standing columns or pairs of slender columns, however, did not come into use in American Adam mantels until 1800. The first dated instances come, respectively, from Homewood and from the William Gray house (Essex House) at Salem. Both these show in

Figure 210.   Mantel from the Harrison Gray Otis house, Cambridge Street, Boston.   1795
Courtesy of the Society for the Preservation of New England Antiquities

different ways the beginnings of a tendency to modify the forms of the orders in a fanciful and capricious manner. The mantel in the southwest room at Homewood has a colonnette rising directly to the under side of its cornice. The Gray mantel has colonnettes of quatrefoil plan—of "Gothic architecture improved by rules and proportions"—although arrangement, mouldings, and ornament remain the same as in thoroughly classic examples. Raynerd in the "American Builder's Companion" (1806) shows a colonnette of this sort, as well as slender coupled colonnettes. A tall and very flat console reaching to the floor, which had been used at Woodlawn about 1800, also appears there.

Figure 211.   Mantels from the Gore house, Waltham.   Between 1799 and 1804
Courtesy of Miss N. D. Tupper

The mantel cornices underwent a transformation in profiles similar to that of room cornices. The first fanciful examples are at Homewood, where there is a wide-spreading shelf supported by modillions. The wide shelf may be found also at Woodlawn and in many later mantels in Salem. These last seem to be under the influence of the mantel and cornice designs of the "American Builder's Companion" (1806). Thus the mantels of the Kimball house and the Woman's Bureau have guttae in place of dentils like its plates 12 and 13, and the Kimball mantel has also a line of spheres let into the edge of the mantel-shelf, as in plate 28.

An overmantel was retained in a few instances even after the adoption of Adam forms. Pain's "Practical Builder," of which an edition was published in Boston in 1792, shows one (plate 50); his later works, the "British Palladio" and "Practical House Carpenter" have none. The Adam parlor at the Jerathmeel Peirce house (figure 199) and two rooms at Oak Hill (1800–1801) have overmantels which represent essentially the Colonial scheme with Adam detail. The Williams house at 1234 Washington Street, Boston, had a feature over the mantel more in consonance with the work of the Adams themselves: a medallion with a figure in relief. In the fanciful work under the influence of Benjamin and others, which succeeded the Adam work proper, the scheme of an overmantel flanked by an order still persisted in outlying regions. This seems to have been specially the case in Portsmouth and its sphere of influence. The Haven house in Portsmouth has several chimneypieces with pairs of slender colonnettes both below and above the mantel, and a suggestion of interlaces and festoons made with the drill (figure 212). A very beautiful mantel and overmantel of similar style, from the "Eagle house," Haverhill, is owned by the Metropolitan Museum (figure 213).

The composition of doorways was generally similar to that of mantelpieces, except that a regular architrave was more often retained. Ears were soon abandoned. Whether with an architrave, or with pilasters, half-pilasters, or panels, it was almost universal in the finer doorways after 1790 to have a frieze with end blocks. The first example, and a very rich and characteristic one, is at the Woodlands (figure 214). Modillions, with a wide projection to the cornice, first appear at Homewood; they were characteristic of the houses in Salem about 1818. In the Forrester house and the Andrew house (figure 206) there at this time, and in the Decatur house, Washington, just before, we find the first examples of doors framed, not by a mitred architrave, but by moulded bands with corner blocks, which remained characteristic through the middle of the century.

Stairways in their general, spatial form we have already discussed. It remains only to treat of the details of hand-rails and strings. The open string, with the ends of the treads showing, remained universal. Many of the curved flights, even at the very foot, had no wall below the string: they appeared self-supporting. Besides the customary forms of scroll ends, it became common to find applied scrolls formed merely of a thin sawn strip, often of fantastic outline. The earliest of these

Figure 212.   Mantel in the Haven house, Portsmouth
From Corner and Soderholtz: *Colonial Architecture in New England*

are in the Reynolds house in Philadelphia and in the Barrell house (figure 194). At the Woodlands and in the Gore house (figure 195) the strings for the first time are wholly devoid of enrichment.

Twisted balusters quickly disappeared after the Revolution, and even the simpler turned profiles tended to give way to plain sticks, square or round, as in the Barrell house, the Octagon, Woodlawn, the Gore house, and many others. Balusters sawn in interlacing patterns were occasionally used by McIntire, in the John

253

Gardner house (1805) and in the Jerathmeel Peirce house as completed. In the Peirce house interlacing motives alternate with groups of plain square balusters.

The decorative treatment of the characteristic style of the republic was initially

Figure 213. Mantel from the Eagle house, Haverhill
In the Metropolitan Museum

derived from the artistic fashion of the time in England and France—the style of the brothers Adam and of Louis XVI. Instead of the luxuriant curves of shell-work which had preceded, it employed classical motives, such as mythological figures, griffins, urns, medallions, and slender garlands of husks or of drapery.

This elaborate and tenuous plastic decoration made demands beyond the skill of most of the native craftsmen. The books which popularized the new style in America, such as the later works of William Pain, gave models for the general

Figure 214.   Interior door at the Woodlands.   1788
Courtesy of Ogden Codman

treatment of mantels and other features, but not such full-size details as would enable men unfamiliar with the style to carve the ornament successfully. The cement stucco and plaster compositions developed by the Adams and others in London, however, were reproduced in moulds for application as needed, and the wide diffusion of many elaborate motives, absolutely identical, shows that these ornaments were shipped to all parts of America. As one example among many, we may cite the small baskets of fruit and flowers, of which identical examples may be found in Germantown and in the Barton Myers house in Norfolk. Such ornaments were occasionally mentioned in inventories or offered for sale. Thus among the contents of the great house of Elias Hasket Derby, who died in 1799, is listed: "One box Composition Ornaments broken sets $20";[1] and, among the effects of Samuel McIntire, its designer and carver: "A lot composition ornaments and Draws $35."[2] With other property of McIntire these ornaments were sold April 30, 1811.

From a photograph by R. W. Holsinger

Figure 215. Wedgwood plaque from the dining-room mantel at Monticello

Figure subjects from classical mythology were frequently used in mantels, on the central panels and end blocks. Among the most popular were the muses. Flaxman had modelled these for Wedgwood after 1775 from the "Apotheosis of Homer" relief in the British Museum and from the famous sarcophagus in the Louvre. A Wedgwood plaque (figure 215) with four figures from the latter: Urania, Terpsichore, Euterpe, and Polyhymnia, is the central ornament of the frieze in the dining-room mantel at Monticello, which has also oval medallions of muses at the ends. Figures of single muses cast in composition were favorite ornaments for end blocks. For instance, a muse with a lyre (Terpsichore?) is found in identical form in mantels of McIntire's Jerathmeel Peirce[3] and Felt houses in Salem, of Ver-

[1] *Essex Probate Records*, vol. 372, p. 333.   [2] *Ib.*, vol. 380, p. 367.
[3] Cousins and Riley, "The Woodcarver of Salem," pl. 106.

non and the Lilacs in Philadelphia,[1] and of a house at 74 Prospect Street, Newport.[2] Polyhymnia appears in the William Gray mantel from Salem and in one in the Diller house, Lancaster, Pennsylvania. Many other figures were of wide distribution. The same pair of subjects is found on the end blocks of a mantel in the Otis house, Boston (figure 210), and on those of one at Vernon. A favorite motive

From a photograph by Frank Cousins

Figure 216. Mantel from the Registry of Deeds, Salem. Samuel McIntire, 1807
In the possession of the Essex Institute

for central panels was a reclining figure of Plenty with a cornucopia. This is found in mantels of the Jerathmeel Peirce and Hersey Derby houses in Salem,[3] in the house of L. M. Blackford, Fairfax County, Virginia,[4] and others. Subjects with numerous figures are found in Bulfinch's Otis and Hersey Derby houses, in McIntire's work at Oak Hill and elsewhere, in the Gore house (figure 211), in Vernon, and in other houses of the period from 1795 to 1805.

[1] Wise and Beidleman, "Colonial Architecture," pp. 243, 245.
[2] *American Architect*, vol. 55 (1897), no. 1098.
[3] "Woodcarver of Salem," pls. 106, 61.   [4] "Georgian Period," part 1, pl. 10.

257

A few exceptional craftsmen, above all Samuel McIntire, had skill to carve motives in the style of those imported, scarcely yielding to them in mastery and having the flavor inherent only in original work. McIntire's bill for carving on the Hasket Derby house, dated June 18, 1798, is preserved at the Essex Institute. In spite of the use of a great deal of composition ornament, the work on the interior includes—besides capitals, modillions, and roses—festoons for three doors in one room, forty draperies for the frieze in another, "some carving on a chimneypiece" in a third. Most notable of McIntire's decorative carvings were his eagles, of which a characteristic example is that of a mantel from the Registry of Deeds, built in 1807 (figure 216).

The embargo of 1807 and the War of 1812 tended to cut off the foreign supply of composition ornaments and stimulated not only carving but domestic manufacture. As early as 1798 McIntire had made for Derby "a pattern to cast some roses from." Among the first of the later products were small medallion reliefs of leading men. Those of Hamilton, whose tragic death occurred in 1804, are specially numerous in Salem, a Federalist stronghold, where the Essex Institute also possesses two unused examples. Later, more elaborate motives were attempted. Two mantels from the Beltzhoover house, Carlisle, Pennsylvania, now in the Metropolitan Museum, show, respectively, the Battle of Lake Erie (figure 217), and a sarcophagus surmounted by an eagle with the inscription: "To the Memory of Departed Heroes," and the name of the maker: "R. Wellford, Phila. delit."[1] Robert Wellford appears in the Philadelphia directories from 1801 to 1839 as "ornamental composition manufacturer," and in 1807 he calls his product the "original American composition ornament."[2]

Embargo and war may also have had their part in developing a substitute for composition ornament, although its beginnings fall somewhat earlier. This was the ingenious suggestion of similar motives by the aid of the simplest tools, in local vernacular adaptations of much interest and beauty. Festoons and rosettes indicated in flutings with a gouge may be found at Upsala in 1798, and other festoons of auger holes in gradated sizes were used at Woodlawn in 1800. In the Haven house, Portsmouth, the ornament is outlined by triangular incisions made with the gouge. Another motive was the interlace of narrow bands multiplied, shown in plate 32 of Pain's "Practical Builder," in the Boston edition of 1792 (figure 218).

---

[1] These are discussed by A. L. Kocher, their discoverer, in the *Architectural Record*, vol. 50 (1921), pp. 225–226. To assign to Wellford, as Kocher does, *all* the ornament of these two mantels, and then all those of other mantels having ornaments identical with some of these, and so forth, even to Salem in 1799, is to carry inference too far.

[2] *Bulletin of the Metropolitan Museum of Art*, vol. 14 (1919), pp. 36–37.

It occurs in substantially the same form in the cornice of a room from Haverhill belonging to the Metropolitan Museum (figure 219).

Summarizing the development of style in interior detail, we may distinguish several successive phases. First, a transitional or "post-Colonial" phase, represented by the Langdon, John Reynolds, and John Brown houses, in which certain minor elements of novelty appear in houses fundamentally Colonial in style. Secondly, the phase of Adam inspiration proper, beginning with isolated houses in the 'eighties, but dominating from around 1792 to about the time of the Embargo of

Figure 217. Mantel with ornament by Robert Wellford, after 1813
In the Metropolitan Museum

1807. Then followed the era of free modification of Adam forms exemplified by Benjamin's book of 1806 and the Salem houses after the peace of 1815. Finally, about 1825, begins the supremacy of Greek forms.

A word may be permitted in conclusion on the forces which ultimately put the classic style in eclipse. Romanticism and rationalism combined to overshadow it. Beginning with Latrobe's design for Sedgley near Philadelphia (1797), and stimulated by Irving's romantic Sunnyside (1835), the Gothic revival began in domestic architecture. As the "English cottage style" it won the support of H. W. S. Cleveland in his rationalistic article of 1836 in the *North American Review*, and was championed in the works of Andrew Jackson Downing from 1842. By 1848 Mrs. Louisa Carolina Tuthill, in her sketch of the condition of architecture in the United States, could speak of the "Greek mania" as having passed by.

In spite of the variety of suggestions which it followed, and the disparity of its work in different phases, the architecture of the republic during its first half-century was made essentially one by its ultimate inspiration from the classic. The triumph of literal classicism in 1825, with its ideal formal schemes of temple and rotunda, had been prepared by Jefferson's prophetic insistence on these very types, from the time of the Revolution itself. It is in its classical essence, moreover,

Figure 218. Interlace from Pain's *Practical Builder*

rather than in the less austere phases of transition and compromise, that American domestic architecture made its independent contribution to universal development. The houses of the second quarter of the century, from "Arlington" and "Andalusia" to obscure dwellings of the Northwest, represent an extreme of classicism which has no counterpart abroad.

Criticism of such buildings from a functional view-point is irrelevant to historical consideration, which is concerned only with determining and understanding the actual course of evolution. Whatever be thought of them, there can be no doubt that they endowed America with an architectural tradition unsurpassed in the qualities of monumentality and dignity.

It is only this unequalled heritage of classical monuments from the formative period of the nation which can explain America's leadership in the new classical revival of the present. When this began in the 'nineties, the characteristic striving elsewhere was toward differentiation, toward original forms expressive of the novel elements in modern life, rather than toward unity and emphasis on the elements of continuity with the past. Its vitality in America, as well as the distinguishing austerity of its work, are due to the familiarity and to the special character of the early buildings of the republic, to the effort of the founders to establish classic architecture as a permanent national style.

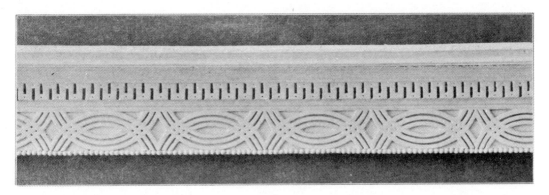

Figure 219. Cornice with interlace, from the Eagle house, Haverhill
In the Metropolitan Museum

NOTES ON INDIVIDUAL HOUSES

DATE, AUTHORSHIP, AND ORIGINAL FORM

NOTES ON INDIVIDUAL HOUSES

DATE, AUTHORSHIP, AND ORIGINAL FORM

Towns and plantations are arranged alphabetically, with houses under a given town alphabetically by the name of the original owner (in most cases), with references from other names commonly used.

Houses designed by Samuel McIntire are reserved for discussion in the writer's forthcoming work on McIntire. For houses by Jefferson, see "Thomas Jefferson, Architect" (1916).

ALBANY, NEW YORK.—SCHUYLER HOUSE. The bills of mechanics, from 1761 and 1762, are listed and reproduced in facsimile in "The Schuyler Mansion" (1911), by Georgiana Schuyler, pp. 5–8.

VAN RENSSELAER MANOR-HOUSE (fig. 50). It bore the date 1765 in conspicuous letters of wrought iron on one of the outer walls, having been erected by Stephen Van Rensselaer, who married Catherine Livingston in 1764. T. A. Glenn, "Some Colonial Mansions," p. 156. The house was drastically remodelled by Richard Upjohn in 1840–1843, as described by M. T. Reynolds, "The Colonial Buildings of Rensselaerwyck," *Architectural Record*, vol. 4 (1895), p. 425, and ultimately torn down in 1893. Reynolds shows a plan and exterior of the house as remodelled, and interior views of the old work.

AMPTHILL, CHESTERFIELD COUNTY, VIRGINIA. The traditional date of the house, 1732, is not contradicted by public records. Fairfax Harrison, the discriminating historian of the Carys, writes us: "Henry Cary moved from Williamsburg to Henrico in 1727 and established himself on the south side of the James at the place to which he gave the name 'Warwick,' where later he built his mill. He then and until 1732 described himself in deeds, etc., as of 'Warwick' in Henrico, as shown by the county records. After 1732 he described himself as of the parish of Dale. He never used the name Ampthill as did his son, not even in his will, 1748. In 1730 he sold his inherited lands in Warwick County and was then in funds to build a new house."

ANDALUSIA, BENSALEM TOWNSHIP, BUCKS COUNTY, PENNSYLVANIA. The original house, with octagonal ends, was built by John Craig after 1794. The front to the Delaware (fig. 139), with its portico, was added by Nicholas Biddle in 1834–1836, under the supervision of Thomas U. Walter, according to bills in the possession of Edward Biddle. The library wing was added at the same period.

ANNAPOLIS, MARYLAND.—CHASE HOUSE. The documents which justify the attribution of the house to the years 1769–1771, between the purchase of the land by Samuel Chase and its sale with improvements to Edward Lloyd, are given by J. M. Hammond, "Colonial Mansions of Maryland and Delaware" (1914), pp. 18–19. Measured drawings and photographs are published by Coffin and Holden, "Brick Architecture of the Colonial Period in Maryland and Virginia" (1919), plates 13–19. A plan is shown there, p. 12; a more accurate one, by T. H. Randall, in the *Architectural Record*, vol. 1 (1891), p. 328 (*cf.* figs. 46 and 103).

AMERICAN DOMESTIC ARCHITECTURE

ARLINGTON, ALEXANDRIA COUNTY, VIRGINIA (fig. 138). Although George Washington Parke Custis may have erected some building on the Arlington estate as early as 1802 the mansion as it stands to-day was built much later. His daughter, the wife of Robert E. Lee, writes that at first he "lived in a small cottage on the Potomac. . . . He then built the two wings now at Arlington; married in Alexandria and brought his bride . . . there, and we lived in them many years. I can just remember when the middle house was built, but do not recollect the date. It was never completed until just before the war, as . . . the means were not at hand for finishing it." This is quoted by Laura Carter Holloway, "The Ladies of the White House" (1886), pp. 58–60. As Mrs. Lee was born October 1, 1808, the "middle house" must have been occupied by 1820 at latest. The portico was doubtless the last exterior element to be finished, although it was apparently complete in 1830, when it was described by Jonathan Elliot in his "Historical Sketches of . . . the District of Columbia," pp. 290–291, and drawn by him for the "Washington Guide" of that year. William Dunlap, "History of the Arts of Design" (1834), vol. 1, p. 336, gives the name of the architect, George Hadfield, who died in 1826.

ASHLAND, KENTUCKY. The home of Henry Clay was originally built in 1813 and following years, from designs of Latrobe, as is indicated by a letter of Latrobe, dated August 13, 1813, in the possession of Ferdinand C. Latrobe. It was gutted by fire in the middle of the century, and only the general form was preserved in the rebuilding.

BACON'S CASTLE, SURRY COUNTY, VIRGINIA, so called from its having served as the stronghold of those concerned in Bacon's Rebellion in 1676, when it is spoken of as "Allen's brick house." It was then the property of Major Arthur Allen, who had received the estate as an inheritance from his father, Arthur Allen, a justice of the peace for the county, who came from England in 1649 and died in 1670. See R. A. Lancaster, "Historic Virginia Homes" (1915), p. 50. See also "Old Places in Surry County" in *William and Mary Quarterly*, vol. 5 (1897), pp. 189–190, and vol. 8 (1900), p. 151. A woodcut of it was published in *Frank Leslie's Illustrated Weekly* before 1860 (fig. 21). A measured survey of the existing house made in 1919 by Donald Millar, under a grant from the Foundation for Research in American Art, will shortly be published in the *Architectural Record*. We are fortunate to be able to show three of the principal drawings here (fig. 20).

BERRY HILL, HALIFAX COUNTY, VIRGINIA (fig. 140). The plain house built by Edward Carrington on the plantation was, writes Philip Alexander Bruce, "bought by my uncle (James Coles Bruce) sometime between 1835 and 1840, and my impression is that he completely remodelled it." The present owner of the estate, Malcolm G. Bruce, and other members of the family, name the same period as that of the rebuilding of the house.

BEVERLY, MASSACHUSETTS.—WILLIAM BROWNE HOUSE, FOLLY HILL. Doctor Alexander Hamilton described this in his "Itinerarium" (1907) on his visit to it in 1744, and wrote "it is not yet quite finished" (p. 147). Captain Francis Goelet's "Journal" for October 20, 1750, in its description says: "Nor is the Building yet Compleat, wants a Considerable workman Ship to Compleat it, so as the design is." *New England Historical and Genealogical Register*, vol. 24 (1870), p. 57. The house has long been demolished; a reservoir now occupies its site. A portrait of Browne's wife, Mary Burnet, now in Baltimore, shows the house in the background. The *Historical Collections of the Essex Institute*, vol. 31 (1895), has an article on it, and gives, p. 312, a plan made from the foundations then existing.

BOSTON, MASSACHUSETTS. SEE ALSO CHARLESTOWN, DORCHESTER, JAMAICA PLAIN, AND ROXBURY.

NOTES ON INDIVIDUAL HOUSES

THOMAS AMORY (TICKNOR) HOUSE, Park and Beacon Streets (fig. 165). The deed of the land to Thomas Amory was recorded on November 22, 1803. In a conveyance of 1804 a building on this lot was mentioned, and in 1807, in a conveyance from Amory to Samuel Dexter, a dwelling-house is mentioned. Close analogies with other dwellings designed by Bulfinch would indicate that he was the architect, as he is known to have been of the adjacent houses on Park Street. The house was later subdivided, and a separate entrance made on Beacon Street. It has since been remodelled into offices, but the porch is substantially intact. Old photographs, both of the exterior and of the interior, are among those lent to the Metropolitan Museum by Ogden Codman.

HENRY BRIDGHAM HOUSE. Deacon Henry Bridgham, who died March 12, 1670-1, in his will, executed November 8, 1670, provided: "The new house that I have raised & proceeding in the building of itt, my will is that out of the estate it be finished, made habitable." It became Julien's restaurant by deed of July, 1794, and was taken down in July, 1824. See N. B. Shurtleff, "Topographical and Historical Description of Boston" (1871), pp. 654–660; C. Shaw, "Description of Boston" (1817), pp. 289–290, with a cut which we reproduce (fig. 7).

COLONNADE ROW. This block of houses, nineteen in all, on Tremont Street, facing the Common, was designed by Bulfinch in 1810, according to E. S. Bulfinch, "Charles Bulfinch," p. 122.

JOHN SINGLETON COPLEY HOUSE. The letters quoted in our text, and many others in the "Copley-Pelham Letters," *Collections of the Massachusetts Historical Society*, vol. 71, show that the house was in course of erection in 1771, and that Copley was his own architect. Some of his drawings are reproduced there, facing pp. 136 and 232.

"THE OLD FEATHER STORE," formerly standing on Dock Square at the corner of Ann or North Street. Demolished July, 1860. See N. B. Shurtleff, "Topographical and Historical Description of Boston" (1871), p. 648. C. H. Snow, "History of Boston," second edition (1828), quoted in the text, gives a woodcut, p. 166, and says further: "The peaks of the roof remain precisely as they were first erected, the frame and external appearance never having been altered. The timber used in the building was principally oak. . . ." A woodcut from a painting of 1817 at the Massachusetts Historical Society is given in J. Winsor, "Memorial History of Boston," vol. 1 (1880), p. 547. None of these views reveals substantial differences from the building as shown by photographs.

FOSTER (HUTCHINSON) HOUSE. "In some family memorandums of Thomas (Hutchinson), he . . . writes of himself: 'Thomas Hutchinson . . . was born in Boston, Sunday, September 9th, 1711 . . . and was the first person born in the house which had been built between twenty and thirty years, and which afterwards came to him by inheritance.'" P. O. Hutchinson, "Diary of Thomas Hutchinson" (1884), vol. 1, pp. 46–47. The house had been built by John Foster, his mother's father. In 1748 the roof and lantern at least suffered from fire. *Ib.*, p. 54. August 26, 1765, it was sacked by a mob. An officer, addressing the Lords of Trade, wrote: "As for the house, which from the structure and inside finishing seemed to be from a design of Inigo Jones or his successor, it appears they were a long time resolved to level it to the ground. They worked three hours at the cupola before they could get it down, and they uncovered part of the roof; but I suppose, that the thickness of the walls, which were of very fine brickwork, adorned with Ionic pilasters worked into the wall, prevented their completing their purpose." C. H. Snow, "History of Boston," second edition (1828). The house was repaired and stood until 1833, when it was demolished, one of the pilaster capitals going to the Massachusetts Historical Society (fig. 37). A view (fig. 36) is published in the *American Magazine of Useful and Entertaining Knowledge*, February, 1836; a description of the interior, in Lydia Maria Child's novel, "The Rebels."

FRANKLIN CRESCENT. A full account of this enterprise of Bulfinch, 1793 to 1796, is given by E. S. Bulfinch, "Charles Bulfinch," pp. 98–102. Bulfinch's original drawing for the central pavilion, preserved at the Massachusetts Institute of Technology, is reproduced there, facing p. 100, as well as the contemporary engraving from the *Massachusetts Magazine*, 1794 (fig. 150).

HANCOCK HOUSE. The contract for freestone work, between Thomas Hancock and Thomas Johnson, of Middletown, Connecticut, dated in the "tenth year of the reign of . . . George the Second" (1737), is published with many other documents by Arthur Gilman in "The Hancock House," *Atlantic Monthly*, vol. 11 (1863), pp. 692–707. Hancock's first letter from the new house is dated: "At my house in Beacon Street, Boston yᵉ 22ᵈ Mar, 1739–40" (*i. e.*, 1740). The Boston Public Library has the bills to Hancock from William More, the joiner who panelled the "Loer Rume" and the "Chamber" in 1745–1746. Two large wings shown in old views, the one on the east side containing a ballroom, the other a kitchen and other offices, had disappeared long prior to 1863, when the house itself was torn down. Photographs of the exterior exist (fig. 34), as well as a unique series of measured drawings, which we are privileged to reproduce through the very great kindness of R. Clipston Sturgis (figs. 40, 58, and 100); there are also front and rear elevations. Three interior photographs, too faint to reproduce successfully, are in the Hancock Collection of the Bostonian Society at the Old State House. The main staircase is incorporated in a house at Manchester, Massachusetts (fig. 101). A baluster from the same stair and one from the roof railing are at the Essex Institute (nos. 2086 and 102937 respectively), together with two capitals (no. 2038, fig. 78). A larger capital, evidently from the "Loer Rume," is in the National Museum, Independence Hall, Philadelphia. The Massachusetts Historical Society has one of the carved modillions from the cornice (fig. 62).

HARRIS HOUSE. William Bentley wrote in his Diary, November 2, 1797, when on a visit to Boston, of "the new & lofty House of Mr. Harris which is erected on the south side of Fort Hill. This Building is of five Stories, a height unknown in the town, is plain, of Brick, & is not yet finished within. . . ." An elevation and a sketch of the house are preserved by the Bostonian Society.

HARRISON GRAY OTIS HOUSE, Cambridge Street (fig. 161). The date of building is given as 1795 by S. E. Morrison in his detailed and circumstantial account of Otis in the *Bulletin of the Society for the Preservation of New England Antiquities*, no. 16 (1916), p. 193. *Cf.* also his "Harrison Gray Otis" (1913), vol. I, p. 44. The house was purchased by the Society in 1916, and an account of its condition at that time and of the restorations undertaken may be found in that and subsequent *Bulletins*. A crude engraving of the front in its original condition is given as the frontispiece of "The Ladies' Medical Oracle" (1834). Relying on this, the Society has placed a semicircular porch in front of the doorway, although it cannot be certain that the engraver did not mean to indicate merely an elliptical fanlight over columnar mullions. An elevation generally similar to the façade of this house, by Charles Bulfinch, the architect of Otis's house on Mount Vernon Street, is preserved at the Massachusetts Institute of Technology (fig. 172). As the doorway in this is based on one in Plaw's "Rural Architecture" (pl. 24), which appeared in 1796, it would seem that it cannot be the design for this very house, but in view of its similarity, of Bulfinch's known relation with Otis, and of the fact that the Adam detail found in the house had but just been introduced into New England by Bulfinch, there can be little doubt that Bulfinch was the architect of the house on Cambridge Street (*cf.* fig. 210).

HARRISON GRAY OTIS HOUSE, 85 Mount Vernon Street (fig. 161). The date is given as 1801 in Mr. Morrison's "Otis," p. 229. Miss Bulfinch states that Bulfinch was the architect. E. S. Bulfinch, "Charles Bulfinch," p. 127.

NOTES ON INDIVIDUAL HOUSES

HARRISON GRAY OTIS HOUSE, 45 Beacon Street. Mr. Morrison's account, p. 229, fixes the date
as 1807. Otis's connection with Bulfinch, as well as the style of the house itself, suggests that
this building also was his work. Until 1831 the house stood free on the east. The interior has
been somewhat modified, especially the mantels and stairs. Measured drawings by Ogden
Codman show its original form. A fine photograph of the exterior is in J. M. Corner and E. E.
Soderholtz, "Colonial Architecture in New England," plate 50.

NOS. 1 TO 4 PARK STREET. In "The Life of John Collins Warren . . . compiled chiefly from his
autobiography and journals" by Edward Warren (1860), Dr. Warren states under date of
August 6, 1849 (vol. 2, p. 23): "Mr. Davis lent me a copy of the original deed of land of my
house in Park Street, given by Arnold Welles to him. He (Davis) built both houses: the one,
for Mr. Welles; the other, for himself. The latter he sold to Francis C. Lowell, who after finishing it off, sold it. The date of the deed was August 5, 1805; but the land was sold by the
town to Mr. Welles in March, 1801. I inhabited the house in October, 1805,—two months
after the deed was given." The deed from Davis to Lowell was also of August 5, 1805. Three
plans of this pair of houses, with an "Elevation of four houses proposed to be built on Park
Street," signed by Charles Bulfinch, are preserved by the present Dr. John Collins Warren
(figs. 151 and 152). Fine old photographs of the houses are preserved by the Bostonian Society.

PARKMAN HOUSES, Bowdoin Square (fig. 166). The original design for these houses, a story
less in height, is preserved among Bulfinch's drawings at the Massachusetts Institute of Technology. The paper is watermarked 1806, which would place the date of the houses probably
two or three years later. The houses, which stood between Green Street and Cambridge Street,
were built by Samuel Parkman for his two daughters, Mrs. Edward Blake and Mrs. Edward
Tuckerman.

PROVINCE HOUSE. SEE PETER SERGEANT HOUSE.

DAVID SEARS HOUSE, Beacon Street. The date, 1816, and the name of the architect, Alexander
Parris, are inscribed on a stone in the basement, reproduced in the history of the Somerset
Club, which has long occupied the house. Extensive remodellings were made when it took
possession, including the addition of an upper story and the lengthening of the façade, with
the duplication of its projecting bay. A perspective view of the house restored to its original
condition, by Ogden Codman, is reproduced in the history of the club, facing p. 6 (cf. fig. 127).

PETER SERGEANT HOUSE (fig. 24). Sergeant bought the land October 21, 1676. In the iron railing crowning a small portico of two columns over the door were interwoven: 16 PS 79. The
house was purchased from Sergeant's heirs by the province by deeds of April 11th and 12th,
1716, and was known henceforth as the "Province House." Apparently it was not radically
remodelled just at that time, for in June, 1716, the sum of £20 was appropriated for the purchase of ornamental hangings for decorating the house. A view of the house is shown by S. A.
Drake, "Old Landmarks and Historic Personages of Boston" (1873), p. 235. Hawthorne gives
in "Twice-Told Tales" some description of the interior as it was about 1840: "A wide door
with double leaves admitted me to the hall or entry." In the room to the right he mentions
"the panelled wainscot . . . a chimney-piece set round with Dutch tiles of blue-figured China,
representing scenes from Scripture." "The great staircase . . . winds through the midst of
the house by flights of broad steps, each flight terminating in a square landing-place. . . . A
carved balustrade . . . borders the staircase with its quaintly twisted and intertwined pillars,
from top to bottom." In 1851 the interior was radically remodelled; in 1864 it was gutted by
fire. See N. B. Shurtleff, "Topographical and Historical Description of Boston" (1871), pp.

594 ff. Some of the panelling is incorporated in the Indian Hill house at West Newbury. A banister is preserved in the Essex Institute Museum, No. 1612. The carved arms of England, as well as the weather-vane, which adorned the house when it belonged to the province, are in the museum of the Massachusetts Historical Society.

CAMBRIDGE, MASSACHUSETTS.—APTHORP HOUSE. East Apthorp was appointed to the mission in Cambridge in 1759. Christ Church was built 1759–1761. Meanwhile Apthorp had married, "and in 1761 there was erected for him, and apparently by him . . . a spacious and splendid mansion." S. A. Drake, "History of Middlesex County," vol. 1 (1880), p. 335. Apthorp returned to England in 1764. The house has had an attic story added, and has been moved and otherwise modified, but the exterior is substantially intact.

JOHN VASSALL (LONGFELLOW) HOUSE (figs. 46 and 68). S. F. Batchelder, the painstaking student of the Vassall family records, states that it was built, "all of a piece," in 1759. "Notes on Colonel Henry Vassall" (1917), p. 14. The additions made by Andrew Craigie after the Revolution are brought out in the very complete measured drawings by Donald Millar, "Some Colonial and Georgian Houses," vol. 2, plates 52–62.

CARTER'S CREEK. SEE FAIRFIELD.

CARTER'S GROVE, JAMES CITY COUNTY, VIRGINIA (figs. 47, 53, and 54). An old plantation account-book of Carter Burwell, the owner, shows that the house was begun in June and finished in September, 1751; also that a "master workman," David Minitree, was brought from England especially for the work. These facts and many additional items are given by R. A. Lancaster, "Historic Virginia Homes" (1915), p. 54.

CHARLESTON, SOUTH CAROLINA.—WILLIAM BRANDFORD (HORRY) HOUSE, Meeting and Tradd Streets. Legal documents make clear that the house was built between the marriage of William Brandford with Elizabeth Savage in 1751 and his death in 1767. Smith, "Dwelling Houses of Charleston," pp. 104 ff., where plans, views, and details are given.

MILES BREWTON (PRINGLE) HOUSE, King Street (fig. 46). The account of the house in Alice R. Huger Smith's "The Pringle House" (1914) makes clear that Miles Brewton began the house soon after 1765. An advertisement of "Ezra Waite, Civil Architect, Housebuilder in general, and Carver, from London," published in the *South Carolina Gazette* for August 22, 1769, makes clear the substantial completeness of the house at that time, and the extent of Waite's connection with it. This is republished, with plans and many drawings and views, in Smith, "Dwelling Houses of Charleston," pp. 93–110. Other fine photographs may be found especially in E. A. Crane and E. E. Soderholtz, "Colonial Architecture in South Carolina and Georgia" (1898) (fig. 80).

COLONEL ROBERT BREWTON'S HOUSE, Brewton's Corner. The house is mentioned in a deed of 1733. Smith, "Dwelling Houses of Charleston," p. 43.

GEORGE EVELEIGH HOUSE, Meeting Street. Eveleigh purchased the land in 1743, and on January 12, 1753, ordered the sale of "the dwelling house on White Point late in my occupation," which must meanwhile have been erected on it. Smith, "Dwelling Houses of Charleston," p. 66. Plans, with a sketch and a photograph, are there published.

WILSON GLOVER HOUSE (CHARLESTON CLUB). The lot was purchased by Wilson Glover in 1800. Smith, "Dwelling Houses of Charleston," p. 196.

RALPH IZARD HOUSE, Broad Street. This is mentioned in the will of Izard, September 13, 1757. Smith, "Dwelling Houses of Charleston," p. 249. Plans and views are there given.

NOTES ON INDIVIDUAL HOUSES

MIDDLETON-PINCKNEY HOUSE, George Street. Frances Middleton only acquired in 1796 the second of the two lots on which it was built, but $10,000 of its total cash cost of $45,000 had been expended on it before her marriage to Thomas Pinckney, October 19, 1797. Smith, "Dwelling Houses of Charleston," p. 132. It is now occupied by the Water Company, which has removed or altered the partitions of the lower story.

CHARLES PINCKNEY HOUSE, Colleton Square. Estimates, accounts, and specifications from 1745 and 1746 are published at length in Smith, "Dwelling Houses of Charleston," pp. 361–371, where an old photograph of the house, after the bombardment and fire of 1861, is reproduced (fig. 66). The same photograph, with another, is published by F. T. Miller, "Photographic History of the Civil War" (1911), vol. 9, pp. 319, 321.

THOMAS RADCLIFFE HOUSE, George and Meeting Streets. Thomas Radcliffe acquired the lots in 1800. He "died in 1806, leaving to his wife a life interest in the house, which he had just finished building." Smith, "Dwelling Houses of Charleston," p. 141, where a plan is published. In recent years the house has been used as the High School. In 1916 the interior woodwork was acquired by the Metropolitan Museum.

NATHANIEL RUSSELL HOUSE. The Charleston *Times* of September 11, 1811, describes damage done by a tornado: "The new and large house of Nathaniel Russell . . . entirely unroofed. . . ." Smith, "Dwelling Houses of Charleston," p. 155, where a plan (fig. 126) and views of the house are given (*cf.* fig. 204).

COLONEL JOHN STUART HOUSE, Tradd and Orange Streets. Sir John Stuart, son of the builder, in a memorial to the British government, stated that his father built the house about 1772. Smith, "Dwelling Houses of Charleston," p. 240, where plans, views, and details are given.

CHARLESTOWN, MASSACHUSETTS.—JOSEPH BARRELL HOUSE. William Bentley wrote in his diary, September 19, 1792 (vol. 1, p. 395): "Barrell's house advanced to the second story upon Lechmere's point & Cobble Hill." It was designed by Bulfinch and is described and illustrated by E. S. Bulfinch, "Charles Bulfinch" (1896), pp. 193–195. The estate was purchased for the McLean Asylum for the Insane, which was opened for patients in 1818. A drawing by Bulfinch preserved at the Massachusetts Institute of Technology shows the two wings erected for the asylum. After the removal of the asylum to Waverly about 1900 the house was torn down and rebuilt in Wayland, Massachusetts, with some modifications. Messrs. Little and Brown, architects for the rebuilding, made a plan of the old house before its destruction, and photographs of several rooms are extant (figs. 192, 194, and 201). With the aid of all these evidences Ogden Codman has prepared drawings which accurately represent the original form of the house, and which we are privileged to reproduce (figs. 120 and 145).

COCUMSCUSSUC, RHODE ISLAND.—RICHARD SMITH HOUSE. This house, built by Richard Smith, Jr., replaced one burned after the Great Swamp Fight of 1675. It is described in his inventory, 1692, although there is some doubt as to how much of the existing house belongs to the original fabric. Isham and Brown, "Rhode Island Houses," pp. 62–64, and plate 52.

CONCORD, MICHIGAN.—ST. CLAIR BEAN HOUSE. According to information furnished by St. Clair Bean, Jr., the present owner, the house was built for his father in 1857, by Houghton Butler and Son, and by one Mr. Gladen. The parapet of the west wing was removed in 1919.

DEERFIELD, MASSACHUSETTS.—JOHN SHELDON ("INDIAN") HOUSE. Sheldon purchased lot no. 12 in Deerfield some time after 1687, and built here "about 1696," according to G. Sheldon, "History of Deerfield," vol. 1 (1895), pp. 277 and 601, which states that "the exact date of purchase or building is not found." In 1698, the last year of King William's War, he bargained with the town for about one-fourth of an acre out of the training-field, that he might build his house within the stockade. *Ib.*, p. 601. On this evidence, doubtless, is based the date of 1698 given for its building on the memorial tablet which marks the site. The house, as revealed by contemporary documents (*ib.*, p. 304), survived the attack on the town in 1704 and stood until 1848. A view of it, reproduced by Sheldon as the frontispiece of volume 2, is apparently derived from a woodcut in Barber's "Historical Collections" (1838). The door (fig. 12) and brackets of the overhang are preserved by the Pocumtuck Valley Memorial Association. All these remains and views are reproduced conveniently in *Old-Time New England*, vol. 12 (1922), pp. 99–108, where there are also detailed drawings of the door hardware.

JOHN WILLIAMS HOUSE. "January 9, 1706-7. Att a Legall Town meeting in Deerfield, It was y^n agreed and voted y^t ye Towne would build a house for Mr. Jno. Williams in Derfield as big as Ens. John Sheldon's a back room as big as may be thought convenient." G. Sheldon, "History of Deerfield," vol. 1 (1895), p. 360. On October 17, "y^t is nerly bilt." The house replaced one built soon after 1686 and destroyed in the Indian attack of 1704. The new house in its original form is shown in an old painting, after a pen sketch of about 1729, reproduced by M. Harland, "Some Colonial Homesteads" (1897), facing p. 404. This shows the building with a framed overhang in front, a clustered central chimney, a plain doorway, and a single pair of casements to either side of it. The lean-to appears in much the same proportions as at present. In 1756 Captain Elijah Williams, according to his books in the hands of the Pocumtuck Valley Memorial Association, rebuilt the house, giving it its present form. G. and J. M. A. Sheldon, "The Rev. John Williams House" (1918), esp. pp. 10, 29. On passing into the hands of the Deerfield Academy in 1875 the house was moved and modified in some respects; in 1916 and 1917 it was restored. *Ib.*, p. 31.

DEXTER, MICHIGAN.—DEXTER HOUSE (fig. 142), "was built between 1840 and '43," writes Mrs. Julia Dexter Stannard, daughter of Samuel Dexter, the original owner.

DRAYTON HALL, ASHLEY RIVER, SOUTH CAROLINA.—An advertisement in the *South Carolina Gazette*, December 22, 1758, quoted by H. A. M. Smith in the *South Carolina Hictorical Magazine*, vol. 20 (1919), p. 11, says: "From this House you have the agreeable Prospect of the Honourable John Drayton, Esqr's Palace and Gardens. . . ." A photograph of it is reproduced in "The Georgian Period," part 10, plate 39.

EAST WINDSOR, CONNECTICUT.—EBENEZER GRANT HOUSE. Contemporary building accounts, still extant, fix its building in 1757 and 1758. Isham and Brown, "Early Connecticut Houses," p. 87, where drawings and a full discussion are given.

ELSING GREEN, KING WILLIAM COUNTY, VIRGINIA. The house was rebuilt in 1758 by Carter Braxton, as his initials and the date over the west door attest. Lancaster, "Historic Virginia Homes," p. 268. The interior has been radically modified as a result of several fires.

FAIRFIELD, OR CARTER'S CREEK, GLOUCESTER COUNTY, VIRGINIA (fig. 22). "Upon one of its gables was in iron figures the date 1692 and, also in iron, the letters L. A. B.—the initials of Lewis and Abigail Burwell." See R. A. Lancaster, "Historic Virginia Homes" (1915), pp. 225–230. "It consisted of a main building with a wing extending back at right angles at each end. One of these wings was burned, or torn away, long ago, though the foundation can still be traced; the other contained a very large room known traditionally as the 'ballroom.'" For many years before its destruction it was in a state of ruin, and it was finally burned a few years prior to 1915.

NOTES ON INDIVIDUAL HOUSES

GERMANTOWN, PENNSYLVANIA.—CLIVEDEN (fig. 33). Chief-Justice Benjamin Chew purchased the land July 17, 1763. A measured plan and details are published by J. P. Sims and C. Willing, "Old Philadelphia Colonial Details" (1914), plates 49–55.

JOHNSON HOUSE, 6305 Germantown Road. "Dirck Jansen . . . began the house in 1765 and finished it in 1768, which is the date on the stone in the peak." Eberlein and Lippincott, "Colonial Homes of Philadelphia," p. 240.

DANIEL PASTORIUS HOUSE, 6019 Germantown Road. There is a date-stone with the initials of Daniel and Sarah Pastorius and the date, 1748. Wise and Beidleman, "Colonial Architecture," p. 110.

STENTON (figs. 47 and 60). J. F. Watson, who was familiar with Logan's papers, gives the date of its erection as 1727 to 1728, "Annals of Philadelphia," second edition (1844), vol. 2, p. 39. A fireback in the house has the inscription, "I. L. 1728." "It is certain that James Logan was residing there in 1732, although it is probable that the main dwelling was not entirely finished until 1734." "In deeds made prior to 1730 he describes himself as 'James Logan of Philadelphia,' but in 1732 he began to style himself 'James Logan of Stenton.'" N. H. Keyser, "History of Old Germantown" (1907), pp. 135, 140.

UPSALA. "One of the copper rain-conductor-heads bears the date of 1798, and family records show that John Johnson, Jr., moved into the house in 1800." Wise and Beidleman, "Colonial Architecture," p. 149.

GRAEME PARK, HORSHAM, PENNSYLVANIA (figs. 44, 58, and 96). Governor William Keith made the contract for erecting the house, December 12, 1721, with John Kirk, mason. T. A. Glenn, "Some Colonial Mansions" (1899), p. 374. An old weather-vane formerly on the building has the inscription: "W. K. 1722." A fireback with the date 1728 is reproduced by Eberlein and Lippincott, "Colonial Homes of Philadelphia," facing p. 300. Measured drawings of the house are published by Donald Millar, "Some Colonial and Georgian Houses," plates 35–40.

GRASS LAKE, MICHIGAN.—SMITH HOUSE (fig. 188). C. W. Smith, the present owner, writes that the house was built in 1840 by his father, Sydney Smith, who came to Michigan in 1839; that Silas Winchester was head carpenter and Levi Babbitt mason.

GUILFORD, CONNECTICUT.—HENRY WHITFIELD HOUSE. There is sufficient evidence to establish the identity of the house with that built by Reverend Henry Whitfield, who came to Guilford at its foundation in 1639 and died in 1657. W. G. Andrews, in "Historical Papers relating to the Henry Whitfield House" (1911). The contention that the house must have been built immediately, 1639 to 1640, is not substantiated. Whitfield's will, published in the *New England Historical and Genealogical Register*, vol. 51 (1897), p. 417, merely leaves all to his wife; and the first documentary mention is in a deed of 1659, "when Whitfield's son Nathaniel sold what had been his father's New England residence . . . proving identity of that with the 'old stone house' of Guilford." Andrews, *op. cit.*, p. 7. The house has undergone many transformations. Those down to the close of the nineteenth century are detailed by Isham and Brown, "Early Connecticut Houses" (1900), pp. 112–124, where plans at different periods are reproduced. In 1903 the house was transformed to contain the State Historical Museum, the front part being treated as a single hall running through two stories. The finding of an old fireplace opening at the second story level leaves the authenticity of this treatment in doubt. The wainscoting of the lower walls was supplied *a priori*. The fireplace at the north end, however, is an original feature. A plan and section of it may be found with Andrews's paper, after p. 23, where there are also photographs of the house in its present condition.

AMERICAN DOMESTIC ARCHITECTURE

GUNSTON HALL, FAIRFAX COUNTY, VIRGINIA (fig. 46). A documentary account of its building is given by K. M. Rowland, "George Mason" (1892), p. 57. After suffering some defacements, the house has recently been restored by Glenn Brown. An elevation, a plan, and photographs are reproduced in "The Georgian Period," vol. 2, p. 50; others, since the restoration, are in Coffin and Holden, "Brick Colonial Architecture in Maryland and Virginia," p. 14, plates 38–40.

HACKENSACK, NEW JERSEY.—ZABRISKIE (BOARD) HOUSE, Paramus Road. The lintel of one of the cellar windows, with the inscription "A. C. Z. 1790," is reproduced by J. T. Boyd, "Some Early Dutch Houses of New Jersey," *Architectural Record*, vol. 36 (1914), p. 44. Other views are shown on pp. 37 and 151.

THE HERMITAGE, NEAR NASHVILLE, TENNESSEE. In the Jackson Papers, Division of Manuscripts, Library of Congress, are a number of documents bearing on the rebuilding of the house. Receipts by Joseph Rieff and William C. Hume for carpenter's work range from July, 1835, to June, 1836. Rieff's proposal for doing the carpenter's work, vol. 97, no. 20350, speaks of "rebuilding the Hermitage as it was before it burned down," with alterations the chief of which is "the roof to be maid of a lower pitch then it was before." "Porches back and front as before . . . East wing to be finished as before."

HOMEWOOD, BALTIMORE COUNTY, MARYLAND. In a letter in the possession of Johns Hopkins University, kindly communicated by Professor John H. Latané, former Governor John Lee Carroll, of Maryland, writes from Doughoragan Manor under date of October 7, 1907: "About the year 1798 the construction of the House was begun by Charles Carroll of Carrollton, as a residence for his son 'Charles fourth of Homewood,' to be conveyed to him after his marriage in 1800. The marriage took place in that year and my father was born there in July, 1801." Since the acquisition of Homewood by the Johns Hopkins University, the house has been restored, but with little modification of the original work. The fullest publication of the house, with a plan, measured drawings, and photographs, is in the *Architectural Record*, vol. 41 (1917), pp. 435–447 and 525–535.

IPSWICH, MASSACHUSETTS.—JOHN WHIPPLE HOUSE (fig. 4). The fullest publication of the documents concerning it is in the monograph by Thomas F. Waters, which constitutes no. 20 in the *Publications of the Ipswich Historical Society* (1915). They make it clear that the main house in its full extent was standing at the death of Captain John Whipple in 1682. As structural examination discloses that the eastern and western ends were built at different periods, the latter being less elaborate and expensive, the conclusion is that it was the house in the town mentioned in the inventory of Elder John Whipple, who died in 1669. Earlier documents show that John Fawn built a house on the lot before 1638. Regarding the identity of this house with the western part of the Whipple house, Mr. Waters grew more sanguine as time went on. In no. 6 of the Society *Publications* (1898) he wrote, pp. 35–36: "I cannot believe that even the oldest part of this venerable house could have been in existence then (1638)." In 1901, when reprinting this as no. 10, he modified this statement to read, p. 34: "It is not beyond the bounds of possibility that this western end of the old mansion may have been erected by Mr. Fawne." In "Ipswich in the Massachusetts Bay Colony" (1905), p. 325, he wrote: "The house built by John Fawn is undoubtedly the western part of the House of the Historical Society," and this remained his final opinion. During all this time he was considering the same evidence, but gradually gave greater weight to analogy with Deputy Governor Symonds's description of his intended house in 1638, as indicating that such a house could have been built at that time. Fawn, however, was an obscure private citizen whose dwelling, as Waters himself originally inferred, would have been far inferior to that of Symonds. The later history of the house is traced in the monograph referred to above, especially pp. 32 and 43. Photographs of the interior are there given.

JAMESTOWN, VIRGINIA.—"COUNTRY HOUSE" AND PHILIP LUDWELL HOUSES. Documents which establish that these were built between 1662 and 1666 are published by their discoverer, S. H. Yonge, "James Towne" (1907), pp. 85, 95. They were burned in 1676, partially rebuilt 1685–1686, excavated 1903 (fig. 17).

LONGMEADOW, MASSACHUSETTS.—SAMUEL COLTON HOUSE. "To Mrs. George E. Brewer of Longmeadow we owe the following information, based on contemporary documents: Samuel Colton 'built the finest mansion in town, John Steele being the builder. The entries in his ledger during its construction begin in 1753 . . . and in June, 1754, five days' work was done on the fore door. The last reference is not until 1755 and reads: "Stepstones for my fore door £29."'" E. J. Hipkiss in (Boston) *Museum of Fine Arts Bulletin*, vol. 19 (1921), p. 57.
    Some drawings of this doorway appear in "The Georgian Period," vol. 2, p. 63.

LOWER YONKERS. SEE NEW YORK CITY.

MARBLEHEAD, MASSACHUSETTS.—JEREMIAH LEE HOUSE (figs. 64, 89, 90, and 99). The date of 1768 on the house is confirmed by Thomas Amory Lee, "The Lee Family," *Historical Collections of the Essex Institute*, vol. 42 (1916), p. 331. *Cf.* also the pamphlet issued by its present owner, the Marblehead Historical Society.

MEDFORD, MASSACHUSETTS.—PETER TUFTS HOUSE, long erroneously known as the "Cradock house" (fig. 25). The documents which establish the date and original ownership of this house are given and discussed by John H. Hooper in the *Medford Historical Register*, vol. 7 (1904), pp. 50–56. The house has been much modified in fairly recent years. Drawings made before these modifications appeared in the *American Architect and Building News*, vol. 6 (1881), no. 296; and others with a valuable text in *Carpentry and Building*, vol. 6 (1884), pp. 145–146.

USHER (ROYALL) HOUSE (fig. 61). In the building of this house there were no less than four periods, as has been pointed out by J. H. Hooper, *Medford Historical Register*, vol. 3 (1900), pp. 133–153, where the legal documents bearing on the matter are cited, and the drawings are published which we reproduce as figure 19. Hooper supposes that the part A was built "very likely during the ownership of the Winthrops," *i. e.*, prior to 1677; but as for many years before this time the estate was occupied by tenants, it seems more reasonable to suppose that it was built by Colonel Charles Lidgett, who owned it from 1677 to about 1692, and apparently occupied it until 1689, or by Lieutenant-Governor John Usher, who succeeded to its ownership and occupied it from 1697 to his death in 1726. All we know of this certainly is that the house, as "the brick house in which the said John Usher now dwells," is mentioned in a mortgage deed of 1707. Hooper, *op. cit.*, p. 138, and Wyman, "Genealogies and Estates of Charlestown," 1879, vol. 2, p. 980. The part B, as Hooper suggests, may have been added during the occupancy of the Ushers, or after the purchase of the place in February, 1732–3, by Isaac Royall, who seems to have raised and modified the east front prior to taking up his residence in the house, 1737. The part D, which Hooper proves by structural analysis to be not contemporary with C, would then have been added some time between the death of Royall in 1738 and his son's flight to England in 1775. This son Isaac, born in 1719, married in 1738; his mother died in 1747. *New England Historical and Genealogical Register*, vol. 39 (1885), pp. 356–357. These dates suggest that the final remodelling may have taken place after 1747, and it may well have been completed by 1750, when Captain Francis Goelet described it as "one of the grandest in the colonies." *Ib.*, vol. 24 (1870), p. 58. This coincides well with the date for the interior finish resulting from our discussion in the text. Measured details of the house are published in "The Georgian Period," plates 3–6. These make clear that the present east door and some of the present sash are restorations in the old frames.

MIDDLETOWN, CONNECTICUT.—RUSSEL HOUSE, HIGH STREET. An engraving of this house faces page 482 of volume 2 in J. H. Hinton, "History and Topography of the United States" (1832). George Dudley Seymour, in his notice of David Hoadley in the catalogue of the Third Annual Exhibition of the Architectural Club of New Haven (1922), says: "The Russell mansion on High Street, Middletown, was, as I judge, Hoadley's last important design. This house, completed in 1828, has happily escaped alterations and is to-day perhaps the most notable piece of domestic architecture in its locality."

MILL GROVE, LOWER PROVIDENCE TOWNSHIP, PENNSYLVANIA. The house, built by James Morgan, has a date-stone in the gable with the date 1762. Eberlein and Lippincott, "Colonial Homes of Philadelphia," p. 200.

MONTICELLO, ALBEMARLE COUNTY, VIRGINIA (figs. 52, 147, 202, 203, and 215). For discussion of this and other houses designed by Jefferson see the writer's work, "Thomas Jefferson, Architect" (1916).

MONTPELLIER, ORANGE COUNTY, VIRGINIA (fig. 186). The central portion of the house seems to have been built by the father of James Madison; the portico was added in 1793; the wings later, originally one story in height. *Cf.* Kimball, "Thomas Jefferson, Architect," p. 57 and note. In recent years the wings have been raised to the height of the main house.

MOUNT AIRY, RICHMOND COUNTY, VIRGINIA (figs. 35, 50, 53). The date of 1758 for its erection is given in the volume "In Memoriam: Benjamin Ogle Tayloe" (1872), compiled by one who had known the family papers before their destruction in the fire of 1844. This gutted the interior and destroyed the old cornice, but the original stonework is still intact. A plan and other measured drawings are given, with photographs, by Coffin and Holden, "Brick Colonial Architecture of Maryland and Virginia," page 18, and plates 60–64. A more correct plan of the house, with the gardens, is published by F. C. Baldwin, with other photographs, in the *Journal of the American Institute of Architects*, vol. 4 (1916), pp. 448–454.

MOUNT VERNON, FAIRFAX COUNTY, VIRGINIA (fig. 53). The fullest account of its vicissitudes is given by Paul Wilstach: "Mount Vernon" (1916), supplemented for the earlier period by Warren D. Brush in *The House Beautiful*, vol. 51 (1922), pp. 130 ff. Brush establishes that the central portion, originally of one story and a half, was raised to two stories 1758–9. Wilstach makes clear that the addition which forms the south end of the house was erected between October, 1773, and the end of 1775 (pp. 126–127), and that the north end, with the finishing of the entrance front, falls in the years 1776 to 1778 (p. 141). He would seem, however, to be in error in supposing (p. 141) that the portico on the river front was built at this time. The entries in Washington's diary for 1786: "May 22, Began to take up the pavement of the piazza," and "May 23, Began to lay the flags of my piazza," do not imply that the portico in its present form had been built for some time, or even that there had previously been a covered portico at all. On the contrary, it would seem that the new flags were laid before the erection of the columns. If so it would closely limit the date of raising the portico, for this appears on the "Sketch Plan of Mt. Vernon by Samuel Vaughan, Aug. 1787," preserved at the house.

NOTES ON INDIVIDUAL HOUSES

THE MULBERRY ("MULBERRY CASTLE"), COOPER RIVER, SOUTH CAROLINA (fig. 43). The major part of the plantation was conveyed to Thomas Broughton, January 20, 1708. On May 17, 1712, the three hundred acres on which the house stands were brought into the plantation by exchange, Broughton having lately set up some erections and buildings on it, mistakenly supposing it to be included in his property. See H. A. M. Smith, "The Fairlawn Barony," in *South Carolina Historical Magazine*, vol. 11 (1910), pp. 196–197. By his will, dated July 22, 1725, he left to his wife "the Capitoll Messuage Tenement Mansion or Dwelling House called the Mulberry." See D. E. Huger Smith, "The Broughton Letters," *ib.*, vol. 15 (1914), p. 171. An old weather-vane on the house bears the date 1714, but it has not proved feasible to examine it to determine at what period it was placed there and to what degree reliance may be placed on it. A plan, elevations, and other drawings appear in "The Georgian Period," part 10, plate 38.

NEWBERN, NORTH CAROLINA.—TRYON'S PALACE. The construction of the building was provided for by Chapter II of the Laws of 1766. Governor Tryon wrote to the Earl of Shelburne, January 31, 1767: "I have emploved Mr. Hawks, who came with me out of England to superintend this work in all its branches. He was in the service of Mr. Leadbeater. Mr. Hawks has contracted to finish the whole in three years from the laying of the first brick which I guess will be in May next." *Colonial Records of North Carolina*, vol. 7 (1890), p. 431. Complete estimates signed by John Hawks are published there, pp. 542–543. On January 12, 1769, Tryon writes that it is covered and roofed, giving also other information. B. J. Lossing, "Pictorial Field Book of the Revolution," vol. 2 (1852), p. 570, publishes a view of the entrance front, saying: "This picture of the *palace* I made from the original drawings of the plan and elevation, by John Hawks, Esq., the architect. These drawings, with others of minor details, such as sections of the drawing room, chimney-breasts for the council-chamber and dining-hall, sewers, &c., are in the present possession of a grandson of the architect, the Reverend Francis L. Hawks, D.D., LL.D., rector of Calvary Church, in the City of New York." Lossing gives additional details, descriptions, etc., and states the house was destroyed by fire about fifty years previously, leaving only the two outbuildings. When he states that "the rear of the building was finished in the style of the mansion house in London," the implication is that it had a pedimented frontispiece above a basement.

NEWBURY, MASSACHUSETTS.—(SPENCER) PIERCE HOUSE. J. J. Currier, in his "Ould Newbury" (1896), pp. 25–41, has an exhaustive study of the many documents relating to this property, with its important early stone and brick house, but wisely concludes, regarding the date of its building, that they do "not furnish sufficient evidence to determine the question beyond a reasonable doubt." There is no doubt that there was "housing" on the land in the time of John Spencer, Jr., who sold the farm in 1651, and housing is mentioned also in the will of Daniel Pierce, who died in 1677, but in neither case can we affirm that it was identical with the stone house now standing. The same must be said of the house mentioned by Samuel Sewall in his "Commonplace Book," *Collections of the Massachusetts Historical Society*, series 5, vol. 6, p. 17: "May 7, 1681, there was a Hurrican at Newbury which . . . uncover'd Capt. Pierce's new house at the ũper end of Chandler's Lane, blew down the Chimneys," quoted by Currier, "History of Newbury" (1902), p. 671, and the first certain reference to the house is in the will of this Daniel Pierce, dated August 12, 1701, which gives to his wife, among other things, "the Parlor in the Stone house."

NEWBURYPORT, MASSACHUSETTS.—JONATHAN MULLIKEN (CUTLER-BARTLETT) HOUSE. "In 1782, this house, then in process of construction, was bought from the estate of Jonathan Mulliken by John Babson and completed by him." Albert Hale, "Old Newburyport Houses" (1912), p. 27. It was restored in 1915.

ENOCH THURSTON (LUNT-SHEPARD) HOUSE, 79 High Street. "This house was in process of construction by Enoch Thurston at the time of his death, in 1805, and was completed by Edward St. Loe Livermore." Albert Hale, "Old Newburyport Houses" (1912), p. 50.

BENAIAH TITCOMB HOUSE. Benaiah Titcomb purchased the land in 1695. See J. J. Currier, "History of Newburyport" (1909), vol. 2, p. 54. The house is now re-erected, considerably modified, in the town of Essex. See *Bulletin of the Society for the Preservation of New England Antiquities*, no. 18 (1918), pp. 29–30.

NEWCASTLE, DELAWARE.—KENSEY JOHNS HOUSE, 2 Orange Street. The bills for this house are preserved, placing the date of erection in 1790. A letter of Peter Justis, which suggests his agency in its design, is published by H. C. Wise and H. F. Beidleman, "Colonial Architecture" (1913), p. 123.

GEORGE READ II HOUSE, on the Strand. The names of the contractors, with the dates of building, 1791 to 1801, are given from the original papers in Wise and Beidleman, "Colonial Architecture," p. 129, together with several photographs.

NEW HAVEN, CONNECTICUT.—GOVERNOR EATON HOUSE. The evidence as to this house is given in full by Isham and Brown, "Early Connecticut Houses," pp. 97–111. A revaluation and reinterpretation of this evidence, however, leads us to different conclusions. The sole basis for the E form shown in the restoration by these writers is the statement of E. R. Lambert, "History of the Colony of New Haven" (1838), p. 52, with the accompanying cut. The house, however, was destroyed before 1730, and Lambert's account in other respects is not such as to inspire confidence in its accuracy. The inventory taken "in the twelfth moneth: 1657," published in full by Isham and Brown, *ib.*, pp. 287–296, requires much forcing to make it fit the assumption of an E plan. The pantry or buttery shown by them is an addition to the accommodations listed in the inventory. The counting-house, which they incorporate as a room of the mansion, is mentioned in such a connection—after the garret and before the brew-house—and with such contents—a grindstone, a wheelbarrow, and 228 pounds of old iron—that it must almost certainly have been an outbuilding. Taking these away, it is possible to account for the eight rooms surely forming part of the house as parts of an ordinary narrow rectangular house with additions at the ends and rear. Messrs. Isham and Brown rightly conclude that Lambert and Stiles are fantastic in their report of twenty-one or nineteen fireplaces, but in invoking the mention of ten sets of fire-irons in the inventory to justify their own assumption of ten fireplaces they count separately the "andirons," "small andirons," and "doggs," which are in reality supplementary, and are grouped in four rooms only, so that only a single chimney is absolutely needed to account for them. The discrepancy between Lambert and the house shown on a map of 1724 may thus be explained as due to the imaginary character of Lambert's view.

JAMES HILLHOUSE, JR., HOUSE (SACHEM'S WOOD). This is listed in William Dunlap's "History of the Arts of Design in the United States" (1833), as one of the works done by Ithiel Town and Alexander Jackson Davis, since the formation of their partnership in 1829 (1918 edition, pp. 212–213). It is still standing, somewhat remodelled in recent years, but with the façade little changed.

A. N. SKINNER HOUSE, 46 Hillhouse Avenue. This is also mentioned by Dunlap, "Arts of Design" (1918 edition), vol. 3, p. 213, as one of the works of Town and Davis between 1829 and the date of the work, 1833. It is still preserved, slight modifications by the present owner, Mrs. Rutherford Trowbridge, not having affected the front.

NOTES ON INDIVIDUAL HOUSES

NEWPORT, RHODE ISLAND.—DANIEL AYRAULT HOUSE, Thames and Anne Streets. The contract between Ayrault and "Richard Monday and Benjamin Wyatt both of Newport . . . House Carpenters," dated 1739, is published by George C. Mason in the *American Architect*, vol. 10 (1880), pp. 83–84, together with other estimates and records of payments running from May, 1739, to April, 1741. The original plan, with legends in a handwriting not Wyatt's, and thus presumably Munday's, is preserved by Mr. Mason, and published here by his kind permission (fig. 45). A photograph of the doorway is published by Corner and Soderholtz, "Colonial Architecture in New England," plate 4; and one of the whole house is among those lent to the Metropolitan Museum by Ogden Codman.

NINYON CHALLONER HOUSE, long destroyed. The original drawing by Benjamin Wyatt (fig. 32), now in the possession of George C. Mason, bears the date, March.13, 1735.

NEW YORK CITY.—COLONNADE ROW (LA GRANGE TERRACE), Lafayette Place. The *Ladies' Companion* of November, 1836, speaks of the block as recently completed. Photographs and measured drawings by C. M. Price were published in the *American Architect*, vol. 99 (1911), pp. 245–250. One-half the row was pulled down about 1900, the other was remodelled in 1917, but leaving the exterior intact.

DYCKMAN HOUSE, Broadway and 204th Street (fig. 148). In the detailed and circumstantial history of the Dyckman family in the official guide-book, "The Dyckman House" (1916), by Bashford Dean and Alexander M. Welch, the statement is made (p. 23) that the house was rebuilt immediately after the return of William Dyckman at the close of the Revolutionary War, about 1783, and that he died here in 1787.

GOVERNMENT HOUSE, Lower Broadway, erected as a house for the President of the United States, when it was hoped the capital would remain in New York. Designs were invited by competition and a selection had been made prior to April 26, 1790, according to I. N. P. Stokes, "The Iconography of Manhattan Island," vol. 1 (1917), p. 418. Three old views are reproduced there as plates 55, 63, and 66. Several studies for the building by John McComb are preserved at the New York Historical Society, and these seem to have had an influence on the executed design, although the *New York Magazine* for 1795, which printed the earliest engraving of the building, says its "stile . . . reflects much credit on the professional abilities of those who had the direction of it, Messrs. Robinson, Moore, and Smith" (p. 1). After being used as a residence for the governors of New York, as a Custom House, and for other purposes, it was torn down in 1818.

THE GRANGE, 142d Street and Tenth Avenue. A. M. Hamilton, in his "Life of Alexander Hamilton," pp. 336–356, prints a number of documents regarding the building of this house, which was designed by John McComb, and built largely in 1801. Other bills, etc., regarding it are among the Hamilton Papers, Division of Manuscripts, Library of Congress. The house, now moved so that it adjoins St. Luke's Episcopal Church, has been shorn of its side verandas. A photograph taken about 1864 is reproduced in A. M. Hamilton's "Life," facing p. 340.

ROGER MORRIS (JUMEL) HOUSE (fig. 74). The documents bearing on its building are fully set forth by Rawson W. Haddon in the *Architectural Record*, vol. 42 (1917), pp. 47–62, 126–139, where the date is established as 1765. In view of the history of the house from the outbreak of the Revolution, the long description of 1791, published there, p. 61, must apply equally to its condition before 1775. A full series of measured drawings with this article may be compared with an equally elaborate set by Donald Millar, "Some Colonial and Georgian Houses," vol. 2, plates 45–51.

VAN CORTLANDT HOUSE. "The declaration 'Whereas, I am about finishing a large stone dwelling house on the plantation in which I now live,' in Jacobus Van Cortlandt's will, dated 1749, confirms beyond any doubt the figures '1748' on the date stone of the Van Cortlandt Mansion in Van Cortlandt Park, New York City." E. H. Hall, "Philipse Manor Hall" (1912), p. 233. Jacobus, above, is apparently an error for Frederick. The will is dated October 2. Measured drawings of the house are published by Donald Millar, "Some Colonial and Georgian Houses," plates 26–34.

NORTHAMPTON, MASSACHUSETTS.—JOSEPH BOWERS HOUSE. An engraving of this house faces page 475 of volume 2 in J. H. Hinton, "History and Topography of the United States" (1832).

ODESSA, DELAWARE.—CORBIT HOUSE. The accounts of its building, extending from 1772 to 1774, are summarized by Wise and Beidleman, "Colonial Architecture," p. 130, where exterior and interior photographs are given.

PHILADELPHIA. SEE ALSO GERMANTOWN.

JOHN BARTRAM HOUSE. "In September, 1728, he bought at sheriff's sale a piece of ground. . . . Upon a stone built in the walls is this inscription: JOHN AND ANN BARTRAM, 1731." T. Westcott, "Historic Mansions of Philadelphia," p. 182. Over the cut-stone architrave of the study window is the inscription:

> IT IS GOD ALONE ALMYTY LORD
> THE HOLY ONE BY ME ADORED
> JOHN BARTRAM 1770

WILLIAM BINGHAM HOUSE. The earliest reference to the house seems to be one in Peter Markoe's poem, "The Times," published in 1788, and reprinted by Westcott, "Historic Mansions of Philadelphia," p. 338. Bulfinch dined there in April, 1789, according to a letter published by E. S. Bulfinch, "Charles Bulfinch," p. 75. Griswold's "Republican Court" (1856), pp. 259–260, 262, gives the fullest description, supplemented by others in Westcott. An engraving of the house was published by William Birch in 1799 (fig. 170).

BURD HOUSE, Chestnut Street, corner of Ninth Street. Latrobe, in listing his work in a letter of January 12, 1816, in possession of Ferdinand C. Latrobe, mentions as from 1801 or 1802 "Mr. Burd's building." Several photographs of this house, long demolished, are preserved at the Ridgway Library, in the scrap-book, "Miscellaneous Views" (vol. 6), pp. 27 (fig. 167), 49, 55, 187, and 211.

LANSDOWNE, FAIRMOUNT PARK. The Honorable John Penn bought the land in 1773; "the house must have been finished before 1777, because it appears on Faden's map of that year." Westcott, "Historic Mansions of Philadelphia," p. 334, where there is a woodcut of the exterior. It was burned July 4, 1854, and the walls were pulled down after 1866.

LETITIA HOUSE. SEE WILLIAM PENN HOUSE.

MARKOE HOUSE, 293 Chestnut Street. Latrobe's original "Sketch of a design for the house of John Markoe, Esq.," dated "Columbia, Jan. 14, 1808," exists in one of his sketch-books, preserved by Ferdinand C. Latrobe (fig. 113). After John Markoe's death in 1835, the height was increased by additional stories; and in 1880 the house was demolished. Photographs and an early view are preserved by the Historical Society of Pennsylvania.

ROBERT MORRIS HOUSE, Chestnut Street. The data concerning its building are given by Westcott, "Historic Mansions of Philadelphia," p. 363: "The first entry on account of this building is dated March 9, 1793, and records a survey of the ground. The last charge . . .

is made July 9, 1801." The house and land had meanwhile, on December 11, 1797, been sold to satisfy Morris's creditors. Birch's engraving of the unfinished house (fig. 128) is well known. A sketch plan of it by Latrobe, showing merely the outline of the exterior walls, is preserved in one of his note-books, belonging to Ferdinand C. Latrobe. One of the reliefs in marble carved by the sculptor Iardella for the panels above the windows, together with two Ionic capitals, remains near the quarry at Consohocken from which they came. They are illustrated in "The Georgian Period," vol. 3, p. 23. Another relief of the series may be recognized as adorning one of the Drayton tombs in South Carolina, of which there is a photograph in the same work, part 11, plate 20.

MOUNT PLEASANT, FAIRMOUNT PARK (figs. 39, 50, 53, and 98). John Macpherson, who built the house, bought the land in September, 1761. Westcott, "Historic Mansions of Philadelphia," p. 214. Measured plans, elevations, and details are published in "The Georgian Period," part 4, plates 30, 32, 33, 35, 36.

HOUSES ON NINTH STREET, BETWEEN WALNUT AND LOCUST STREETS. The original design for this block by Robert Mills, dated 1809, is preserved by Alexander Dimitry, and will shortly be published by Mrs. Austin Gallagher in her forthcoming study of Mills.

WILLIAM PENN ("LETITIA") HOUSE (fig. 27). The house seems to have been begun before Penn's arrival in October, 1682, but was not occupied by him that winter. It was apparently completed in 1683. Penn returned to England June 12, 1684, leaving the occupancy of "my house in Philadelphia" to Thomas Markham. See Westcott, "Historic Mansions of Philadelphia," pp. 14–19, 21. *Cf.* J. F. Watson, "Annals of Philadelphia" (1830), pp. 145–149. It was removed in 1883 from its original position on what is now Letitia Street to Fairmount Park, and restored in accordance with old views. The hood and the chimneypiece are original features. The cove cornice of wood is a restoration.

PRESIDENT'S HOUSE, Ninth Street South of Market Street. In furtherance of a law passed in 1791 this building was erected for the use of the President of the United States. The corner-stone was laid on May 10, 1792, and the house was nearly completed when tendered March 3, 1793, for the use of John Adams. Westcott, "Historic Mansions of Philadelphia," p. 270. Engravings of it were made by William Birch (fig. 158) and others. Weld, the English traveller, an inaccurate observer in architectural matters, says: "The original plan of this building was drawn by a private gentleman in the neighborhood of Philadelphia," which, however, may not deserve more credence than Weld's other statements in regard to the house. In 1800 it was sold to the University of Pennsylvania, and has long been demolished.

JOHN REYNOLDS (MORRIS) HOUSE, 225 South Eighth Street (fig. 108). This house was built in 1786 by John Reynolds, and has the date 1787 on the old conductor-heads. It soon came into possession of Luke Wistar Morris. In recent years it has been restored by Effingham B. Morris, who removed the adjacent houses and raised the iron fences at either side. An elevation and details are given in "The Georgian Period," part 3, plates 21 and 22; a plan, in the table of contents of part 3.

SANSOM'S BUILDINGS. Scharff and Westcott, "History of Philadelphia," vol. 1 (1884), p. 511, mention among the "various improvements of 1800 and 1801," "the first row of houses on a uniform plan . . . erected by or for Mr. Sansom . . . on Walnut street, north side, between Seventh and Eighth and in the street between Walnut and Chestnut, from Seventh to Eighth, afterwards called Sansom Street." "The Plan and Elevation of the South Buildings in Sansom Street . . ." (fig. 153), with the signature of Thomas Carstairs, is preserved at the Ridgway

Library in a folio scrap-book on Philadelphia, numbered N. Y. 8.5659 F. Latrobe, in a letter of January 12, 1816, in the possession of Ferdinand C. Latrobe, lists among his works, from 1800–1801: "Mr. Sansom's building . . . in Walnut Street."

SEDGLEY. The land was purchased by William Cramond, March 25, 1799; the house was immediately built and occupied by him until his bankruptcy in 1806. Westcott, "Historic Mansions of Philadelphia," pp. 449–451. Westcott states that Latrobe was the architect of this "Gothic" villa, and Latrobe's pioneer position in the Gothic revival, in America generally, confirms this. The house, then in disrepair, was pulled down after 1857. An early engraving forms one of Birch's series of American country-seats.

THE "SLATE HOUSE" OR "SLATE ROOF HOUSE" (fig. 23). This house, one of several built by Samuel Carpenter on part of the lot purchased by him at the founding of Philadelphia, was occupied by William Penn during the greater part of his second stay in Philadelphia. He took up his residence here some time in January, 1700. See Westcott, "Historic Mansions of Philadelphia," p. 42. A manuscript description of 1828 states that a narrow entry separated the principal rooms, from which those in the wings were reached, and says: "It is not many years since the diamond shaped sash remained in some of the windows." See E. and L. H. Carpenter, "Samuel Carpenter" (1912), pp. 17–24, where the description is quoted in full. The house was pulled down in 1867.

SOLITUDE, FAIRMOUNT PARK. The house was built for John Penn, who came to America in 1783. He writes of purchasing the land early in 1784, and of taking possession, while the house was still unfinished, in 1785. Westcott, "Historic Mansions of Philadelphia," pp. 437–441. Plans, elevations, and details are published in "The Georgian Period," part 6, plates 10 and 11 (cf. fig. 204).

WALN HOUSE. Latrobe, in a letter of January 10, 1808, mentions the house as under construction from his designs.

WHITBY HALL, KINGSESSING, WEST PHILADELPHIA. A date-stone has the date, 1754. Wise and Beidleman, "Colonial Architecture," p. 41. Sims and Willing, "Old Philadelphia Colonial Details," shows measured drawings, plate 43.

WOODFORD, FAIRMOUNT PARK. William Coleman, who built the house, purchased the land in 1756. Eberlein and Lippincott, "Colonial Homes of Philadelphia," p. 134. A plan, an elevation, and interior details are in "The Georgian Period," part 6, plates 4 and 5.

THE WOODLANDS (figs. 155 and 185). The property came by will in 1741 to Andrew Hamilton, the second, and was left by him in 1747 to his son, William Hamilton. "Shortly after it went into the possession of the Hamiltons (1735) a mansion was built there which the second Andrew occupied and his son William after him. It is supposed to have been a comfortable house, but not near so handsome in style and appearance as the mansion which succeeded it, and which it is supposed was erected about the time of the Revolution"—thus Westcott, "Historic Mansions," p. 424. Just when the rebuilding took place seems to be indicated in some letters of William Hamilton published in the *Pennsylvania Magazine*, vol. 29 (1905), especially pp. 146–158. These make clear that from early in 1788 until the end of 1789, at least, radical building operations were going on at the Woodlands, under the direction of a Mr. Child. There can be little doubt that it was at this time that the house assumed its present form, with the curved rooms, the portico, etc. A letter of 1802 mentions the portico as under repair at that date. The house is still little changed. We reproduce some measured drawings of it made by Ogden Codman (fig. 109).

NOTES ON INDIVIDUAL HOUSES

PORTLAND, MAINE.—RICHARD HUNNEWELL (SHEPLEY) HOUSE. The date of building is given in the contemporary "Journals of Smith and Deane" (1849) as 1805 (p. 416). The original drawings for the house (figs. 112 and 177) are preserved in the sketch-book of Alexander Parris, now in the Boston Athenæum, from which a selection of designs is shortly to be published by Mrs. George F. Lord.

PORTSMOUTH, NEW HAMPSHIRE.—LANGDON HOUSE. The date generally assigned to this house is 1784, but in 1782 the Marquis de Chastellux wrote, "Mr. Langdon . . . his house is elegant and well finished and the apartments well wainscoted," and it is obviously to this house which he refers. The best photographs of it are those published by Corner and Soderholtz, "Colonial Architecture in New England" (1892), plate 35, and G. H. Polley, "Architecture . . . of the American Colonies in the Eighteenth Century" (1914), plates 3–6 (cf. fig. 182).

LARKIN (HENRY LADD) HOUSE, Middle Street (fig. 168). Samuel Larkin, who built the house, wrote in his diary August 31, 1829: "This day I moved into the house (next on the east) from which I moved in 1817, November 30, having lived in the brick house almost twelve years." C. S. Gurney, "Portsmouth" (1902), p. 134.

ARCHIBALD MCPHEDRIS (WARNER) HOUSE (fig. 56). The earliest published account of this house, in the Concord (N. H.) *Statesman*, in July, 1857, is republished in J. Wentworth: "The Wentworth Genealogy" (1878), vol. 1, p. 302 n., and its statements vouched for by a careful student of the records: "Capt. McPhedris married Sarah Wentworth. . . . He occupied the mansion but six years, and died in 1728." In the text, pp. 301–302, is the information that Sarah Wentworth's father gave her land as Mrs. McPhedris, June 5, 1718, and that McPhedris made his will May 18, 1728. These facts confirm the statement of C. W. Brewster, "Rambles in Portsmouth," vol. 1 (1859), p. 138, that "the work was commenced in 1718 and finished in 1723." The present owner of the house, Miss Sherburne, formerly had a number of papers dealing with its building, but these were destroyed by fire, and she now retains only a bill of lading for furniture, dated 1716. It is doubtless by a misinterpretation of this that Gurney, "Portsmouth," p. 119, reached the conclusion that the house was built in 1712–1715, and occupied in 1716. The best interior photographs of the house are published in G. H. Polley, "Architecture of the American Colonies during the Eighteenth Century," plates 34 and 35.

PROVIDENCE, RHODE ISLAND.—JOHN BROWN HOUSE. Believed to have been erected in 1786. John Quincy Adams wrote in his diary September 9, 1789: "Mr. John Brown's house is . . . the most magnificent and elegant private mansion that I have ever seen on this continent." *Collections of the Massachusetts Historical Society*, second series, vol. 16 (1902), p. 456. A number of sketches of interior detail first published in the *American Architect*, January 15, 1887, are reprinted in "The Georgian Period," part 12, plates 37, 38.

RICHMOND, VIRGINIA.—BROCKENBROUGH HOUSE ("WHITE HOUSE OF THE CONFEDERACY"), Clay and Twelfth Streets. A letter of Brockenbrough to Robert Mills, May 20, 1813, in the possession of Alexander Dimitry, establishes the date and authorship of this house. "Not long before the war . . . Mr. Lewis D. Crenshaw . . . occupied it for a brief period, during which he added the top story." R. A. Lancaster, "Historic Virginia Homes" (1915), p. 134.

MARSHALL HOUSE, Ninth and Marshall Streets. The deed of the lot to John Marshall, preserved at the house, is dated July 7, 1789.

WICKHAM HOUSE (VALENTINE MUSEUM), Eleventh and Clay Streets. On the second story of the bow toward the garden is the date in figures of the period: 1812. The tradition of Mills's authorship is unbroken.

ROSEWELL, GLOUCESTER COUNTY, VIRGINIA (figs. 49 and 65). Rosewell was built by Mann Page I, who was born in 1691 and died in 1730, leaving the house to be finished by his widow and son. An act of 1744, authorizing Mann Page II to sell certain entailed lands, recites that his father "devised to his wife Judith, his dwelling house, with all out houses thereto belonging, where he then lived, and the mansion house then building." Hening, "Statutes at Large," vol. 5 (1819), p. 278. Bishop Meade in his "Old Churches, Ministers, and Families of Virginia" (1857), vol. 1, facing p. 332, gives a woodcut of the house prior to its dismantling by Thomas B. Booth between the years 1838 and 1855. This shows a flat roof with a parapet, and a lantern rising at either end. According to R. C. M. Page, "Genealogy of the Page Family in Virginia," second edition (1893), p. 60, "Mr. Booth changed the original flat roof to its present shape, covering it with galvanized iron instead of the lead, which he sold. . . . The mahogany wainscoting was detached from the walls of the hall and sold." After standing in partial decay for many years, the house was burned about 1919, but the massive walls are still erect.

ROXBURY, MASSACHUSETTS.—EBEN CRAFTS HOUSE. The date of this house, 1805, and the name of the architect, Peter Banner, are given by W. W. Wheildon in his "Memoir of Solomon Willard" (1865), pp. 29, 30, n. Measured drawings of the house were made by Ogden Codman in 1892 (figs. 157 and 197).

MORTON (TAYLOR) HOUSE. William Bentley wrote in his diary, October 12, 1796, when on a visit to Roxbury (vol. 2, p. 201): "Mrs. Morton is building a new house upon the Road." As Bulfinch was Mrs. Perez Morton's first cousin, it is reasonable to suppose that he was the architect. Measured drawings of plan, elevation, and details first published in the *American Architect* for June 20, 1891, are reprinted in "The Georgian Period," part 6, plates 19, 20. Many photographs, both of the exterior (fig. 156) and of the interior, are in the collection lent by Ogden Codman to the Metropolitan Museum.

SHIRLEY PLACE. Governor William Shirley purchased from General Samuel Waldo on November 22, 1746, a dwelling-house and thirty-three acres, including the site of the house. F. S. Drake, "The Town of Roxbury" (1875, reprint 1905), p. 123. "A lawn of considerable extent fronted the house. It was said to have been levelled by soldiers returned from the Louisburg expedition (1745). Mr. Aaron D. Williams often heard his father speak of having seen the soldiers at work there." The interior of the house was much modified by a later owner, Governor Eustis, and the whole building was later moved to a different site and shorn of its end porches. A fine photograph of the exterior, on the original site (fig. 67), is in the Museum of the Society for the Preservation of New England Antiquities. Measured drawings by Ogden Codman show the house before its removal, and drawings showing a restoration to the original form, prepared by William Wade Cordingley, are published by him, with his conclusions, in *Old-Time New England*, vol. 12 (1921), pp. 51–63.

SALEM, MASSACHUSETTS. Houses designed by Samuel McIntire are reserved for discussion in the writer's forthcoming work on McIntire.

JOHN ANDREW (SAFFORD) HOUSE, 13 Washington Square, West. William Bentley chronicles the progress of the house, July 13, 1818: "The foundation of Andrew's house, west of the Square, is laid" ("Diary," vol. 4, p. 533); October 21, 1819: "This week Capt. John Andrews is raising his four large columns on the south side of his house" (623). The present doorway is a restoration based on that of the Forrester house (*cf.* fig. 206).

BOARDMAN HOUSE, 82 Washington Square, East. "Capt. Boardman bought the land of John Hodges in 1782." B. F. Browne, in *Historical Collections of the Essex Institute*, vol. 4 (1861), p. 4. The house was commented on by Washington during his visit to Salem in 1789.

NOTES ON INDIVIDUAL HOUSES

JONATHAN CORWIN HOUSE, 310 Essex Street. Purchased of Captain Nathaniel Davenport by Jonathan Corwin and considerably rebuilt by him, according to his contract with Daniel Andrews, February 19, 1674–5, for "filling, plastering and finishing," published by S. Perley in the *Essex Antiquarian*, vol. 7 (1903), pp. 169–171. The inventory of George Curwin in 1746 showed the house still of the same accommodations as in 1674. "It is said the porch was removed in that year and with it of course the entry chamber." *Ib., id.* "In 1746 the peaked roof was taken off and a gambrel-roof built," *Salem Gazette*, December 8, 1826, quoted in *Historical Collections of the Essex Institute*, vol. 42 (1906), p. 311. A banister from the staircase built on the eastern side at this time, removed in the modern reconstruction of this side for commercial purposes, is preserved in the Essex Institute Museum. A drawing of the original stair in Millar, "Some Colonial and Georgian Houses," vol. 1, plate 25.

EZEKIEL HERSEY DERBY HOUSE (MAYNES BLOCK), 202½ Essex Street. The original drawings for this house, hitherto erroneously ascribed to McIntire, are preserved at the Essex Institute, and have been published by Cousins and Riley, "The Woodcarver of Salem," facing p. 68, along with photographs of the building. The legends on the drawings are unmistakably in Bulfinch's handwriting. Two of the drawings are watermarked with the date 1798, and must fall after this time. The land on which the house stood, "with all the buildings thereon," had been conveyed to Elias Hasket Derby by John Saunders December 10, 1795. Essex Deeds, 159 : 206. Elias Hasket Derby left by will to his son Ezekiel Hersey: "the house and land in Essex street . . . which I purchased of John Saunders in which the said Ezekiel Hersey now lives." Essex Probate Records, 367 : 93. It would seem, then, that the new house had not been built prior to the death of the father in 1799, but was undertaken by the son immediately afterward. After a number of changes of ownership, it was finally remodelled into shops and offices, but some of the original finish remains, both on the exterior and on the interior.

PICKERING DODGE (SHREVE) HOUSE, 29 Chestnut Street (fig. 176). U. G. Spofford states in a letter to Francis H. Lee, dated May 21, 1884: "The Dodge Place was built by Mr. David Lord, the Barn was Erected in the fall of 22. All the woodwork for the house was . . . got out in the Winter. . . . Mr. Lord was the Architect of the House. He made and drew us several patterns of fancy Architraves . . . and we young Carpenters would profit by it. . . . I assisted in building the Barn in the fall and worked through the winter till April in getting out finish for the House." F. H. Lee's "Scrap Book" at the Essex Institute. Measured drawings of the central motive are in "The Georgian Period," part 7, plate 17; photographs in Cousins, "Fifty Salem Doorways" (1912), plates 39 and 40.

PHILIP ENGLISH HOUSE, formerly standing at Essex Street and English Street. An old house on the site was conveyed to the great merchant, Philip English, January 3, 1682–3, at a price of sixty pounds. He shortly took it down and erected his "great house," raised in 1690 according to Bentley, and plundered during the witchcraft delusion of 1692. See S. Perley, "Salem in 1700," *Essex Antiquarian*, vol. 9 (1905), pp. 168–169. It was demolished in 1833. An old view is preserved at the Essex Institute. William Bentley, who described the house in 1791 and 1793, stated that "Two gable ends in the west part (front), another in the east have been taken down." See his "Diary," vol. 1 (1905), p. 248; vol. 2 (1907), pp. 22–26. When the house passed by will in 1785, it had to the west a "great porch" and a "porch chamber" not shown in the view. Perley, *loc. cit.*

DANIEL EPES ("GOVERNOR ENDECOTT") HOUSE, formerly standing near what is now 53 Washington Street. This house has been mistakenly identified as that of Governor John Endecott, and has even been supposed to have been the house erected in 1624 for the Dorchester Adventurers at Cape Ann, removed thence in 1628. See *Historical Collections of the Essex Institute*, vol. 1 (1859), p. 156, and vol. 2 (1860), pp. 39–42, where the later history of the house is also traced, and an old drawing is reproduced, "representing it as it appeared in 1775, before any alteration in its style of architecture had taken place." The inadequacies of the argument for its identification with the houses named need not be pointed out in detail, since we find that the small lot where it stands was conveyed to Daniel Epes in April, 1679, without any buildings on it. He purchased the surrounding land in 1681, and died possessed of the land and house in 1722. See S. Perley, "Salem in 1700," *Essex Antiquarian*, vol. 8 (1904), pp. 34–35, where the same cut is again reproduced. In 1792 the house was raised a story and otherwise remodelled out of recognition, but it stood until after 1850. A part of one of its oak timbers is in the museum of the Essex Institute.

JOHN FORRESTER HOUSE (SALEM CLUB), 29 Washington Square. The progress of this house may be traced in William Bentley's "Diary": July 3, 1818, cellar (vol. 4, p. 530); July 24 "not yet above the first story" (534); October 21, 1919, "Forrester is now preparing the front of his house . . . which will soon be ready for him" (624); December 9, "Forrester is moving into his new house" (634). When, after being long in the Peabody family, the house was sold to the Salem Club in 1893, a fine white marble mantelpiece was removed from the right front parlor, and the present wooden mantelpiece, a modern reproduction of the mantel in the Kimball house, Pickman Street, was substituted. Measured drawings and details of the front are published in "The Georgian Period," part 7, plate 15.

WILLIAM GRAY HOUSE (ESSEX HOUSE), 176½ Essex Street. The date of this house, which stood on the site of the Sun Tavern, is fixed by a reference by Bentley to the removal of the tavern, February 12, 1801 ("Diary," vol. 2, p. 365). On October 9, 1804, Margaret Holyoke wrote in her diary (p. 145): "Mr. Gray's three chimneys were blown down." After Gray's removal from Salem in 1809 his house became the Essex House. In 1896 the hotel was enlarged and remodelled, and it was again remodelled after a severe fire in 1915. An old lithograph and later photographs of the old house are preserved, and from these Ralph W. Gray has made a drawing reproduced by Edward Gray, "William Gray of Salem, Merchant" (1914), facing p. 30. Sections of the cornice (fig. 190) and of the roof balustrade are preserved in the museum of the Essex Institute. Of the mantel formerly in the hotel office a photograph is reproduced by J. E. Chandler, "The Colonial House" (1916), p. 228, and measured drawings by Frank E. Wallis in the *American Architect*, September 4, 1886.

BENJAMIN HOOPER HOUSE, also called the Hathaway house and the "Old Bakery." This stood originally at 23 Washington Street. Benjamin Hooper acquired this lot October 27, 1682, and died in possession of lot and house in or before 1693. See S. Perley, "Salem in 1700," *Essex Antiquarian*, pp. 32–33, which also shows details of the framing. The house originally extended only for the length of the overhanging portion, the part beyond the chimney being in the style of the eighteenth century. The house was removed to the grounds at 54 Turner Street and restored in 1911. The size and position of the restored casement frames and the former existence of the restored front gable were determined by indications in the framing. The wide board about the base of the house is an authentic feature. The upper part of the "drops" remained in place, the lower part being restored on the basis of examples elsewhere, as is the case with the doorway and door. The entire chimney with its fireplaces is new. See J. E. Chandler, "The Colonial House" (1916), pp. 86–90, with measured elevations and photographs; also *Visitor's Guide to Salem* (1916), p. 35.

JOSEPH HOSMER (WATERS) HOUSE. William Bentley wrote in his diary, May 2, 1795 (vol. 2, p. 135): "Saw the raising of Hosmer's House."

NOTES ON INDIVIDUAL HOUSES

LEWIS HUNT HOUSE, formerly standing on the northwest corner of Washington and Lynde Streets. The lot was conveyed to Lewis Hunt, September 15, 1698; he constructed the house and occupied it until his death in 1717. S. Perley, "Salem in 1700," *Essex Antiquarian*, vol. 2 (1898), p. 173. It was taken down in 1863, but several photographs of it are extant.

NARBONNE HOUSE, 71 Essex Street, also known as the Simon Willard house. The lot belonged to Paul Mansfield in 1661, and to Thomas Ives, with the house thereon, about 1671. See S. Perley, "Salem in 1700," *Essex Antiquarian*, vol. 10 (1906), p. 126.

NICHOLS HOUSE, 37 Chestnut Street. In a letter to Francis H. Lee, dated January, 1884, John H. Nichols writes: "My first recollection of Chestnut Street was in 1816 (when I was five years of age) the foundation on my father's house (No. 37) being then laid. Prior to its erection I remember that Jabez Smith the master carpenter, came to the house then occupied by the family . . . and submitted plans no architect having been employed." F. H. Lee's Scrap Book I, p. 222, Essex Institute. A photograph of the doorway and porch is reproduced in Cousins, "Fifty Salem Doorways," plate 32.

TIMOTHY ORNE HOUSE, 266 Essex Street. Colonel Benjamin Pickman speaks in 1793 of this house, now destroyed, as belonging to his sister-in-law, "daughter to Mr. Timothy Orne . . . who built it in 1761." *Historical Collections of the Essex Institute*, vol. 6 (1864), p. 106. Photographs of the exterior and the stairway still exist.

DELIVERANCE PARKMAN HOUSE, formerly standing on the northeast corner of Essex and North Streets. The lot came into the possession of Deliverance Parkman through Sarah Veren, whom he married "9: 10 mo: 1673," and the house was doubtless built before her death "14: 11: 1681-2." See S. Perley, "Salem in 1700," *Essex Antiquarian*, vol. 2 (1898), p. 171. A view of it early in the nineteenth century, preserved at the Essex Institute, is reproduced, redrawn, *ib.*, facing p. 178.

JOHN PICKERING HOUSE, 18 Broad Street. Speaking of some alterations made in the house, Timothy Pickering writes: "I remember hearing my father say, that when he made the alterations and repairs above mentioned, the Eastern End of the house was one hundred years old, and the western end Eighty years old. Consequently the Eastern End is now (December 3, 1828) 177 years old. For I am 83, and was but six years old in July, 1751, the year when the alterations and repairs took place." This would place the older part about 1651, the newer about 1671, with a reasonable margin for the use of round numbers by the father. The ground on which the house stands was conveyed June 10, 1659, to John and Jonathan Pickering, "successors to their father John," who had owned the adjoining lot for some years prior to his death in 1657. See S. Perley, "Salem in 1700," *Essex Antiquarian*, vol. 4 (1900), p. 169. From the reference to the elder John in the deed we must assume that he had himself some connection with the lot, perhaps a lease, so that it is not impossible that the house was built prior to the deed. An iron fireback from the house, reproduced in "The Pickering Genealogy" (1897), vol. 1, p. 23, with the initials I P A for John and Alice Pickering has the date 1660, but this may well be some years after the erection of the house. A lean-to was added later, and its roof was raised to give a second story at the rear in 1751, as Colonel Pickering relates in connection with the passage quoted above, cited from the transcript in F. H. Lee's Scrap Book I at the Essex Institute. The house was remodelled in 1841, when the present exterior finish was added.

BENJAMIN PICKMAN HOUSE, 165 Essex Street, Salem (fig. 63). Colonel Benjamin Pickman, the owner, born in 1740, wrote in 1793 that it "was built in 1750 by Benjamin Pickman, Esq., father of the writer." *Historical Collections of the Essex Institute*, vol. 6 (1864), p. 95. After the marriage of Anstis Derby to Benjamin Pickman, Jr., a circular bow was added at the rear, with finish by Samuel McIntire now preserved at the Essex Institute and the Peabody Museum. An interior sketch is shown by Arthur Little, "Early New England Interiors" (1878). The house has been much damaged by remodelling. The carved and gilded codfish which adorned the block ends of the stairs are now mostly incorporated in a house at Newport, although the Essex Institute has two of them.

BENJAMIN PICKMAN (DERBY) HOUSE, 70 Washington Street. Colonel Benjamin Pickman, son of the builder, wrote in 1793: "The house was built in 1764." *Historical Collections of the Essex Institute*, vol. 6 (1864), p. 102. This house was refronted, during the occupancy of Elias Hasket Derby, from a design by McIntire on paper watermarked 1786. A view of the Salem Court House, published in the *Massachusetts Magazine* for March, 1790, still shows the old front. A view in the early nineteenth century "M.J.D. del." was reproduced by "Pendleton's Litho." The house was torn down in 1915. Photographs of the exterior and of the stairs are preserved. The cupola of the house is in the gardens of the Essex Institute.

DUDLEY L. PICKMAN (SHREVE-LITTLE) HOUSE, 27 Chestnut Street. Bentley writes, December 9, 1819 ("Diary," vol. 4, p. 634): "D. Pickman's house on the Pickering farm is covered." The porch and doorway have been frequently reproduced, for instance in Cousins, "Fifty Salem Doorways," plate 36.

NATHANIEL SILSBEE HOUSE, 94 Washington Square (fig. 173). Silsbee writes in his autobiography, published in the *Historical Collections of the Essex Institute*, vol. 35 (1899), p. 36: "On my return to Salem in May, 1818, at the close of my first congressional session, I purchased . . . a site . . . on the east side of Pleasant Street and opposite Washington Square, and commenced to build thereon a new brick dwelling house. . . . The nineteenth day of October, 1819 . . . my family took possession of it as their future residence." Bentley chronicles the same events. ("Diary," vol. 4, pp. 533, 588, 624.) The Essex Institute has photographs of the house taken in 1855, before considerable modifications were made in it.

TURNER HOUSE ("HOUSE OF THE SEVEN GABLES"), 54 Turner Street. We may hope for a full publication of the documents regarding this house in a forthcoming book by Donald Millar. Meanwhile the principal facts may be summarized with his aid and that of George Francis Dow. The lot and "one old dwelling house" were sold by Ann More to John Turner, April 17, 1668. This house, on the east side of what is now Turner Street, seems to have been still standing in 1745, for John Turner III entered a claim (in town records) for common rights on account of his mansion, built before 1702, and Widow More's cottage, built before 1661, and in the division of his property in 1745 is mentioned "Land on east side of the lane, old house and barn, £250." The claim for common rights, just mentioned, published by H. F. Waters in a newspaper letter of 1879, disposes of the contention of Sidney Perley in the *Essex Antiquarian*, vol. 10 (1906), pp. 62–65, that John Turner I removed the widow's house and erected one of his own on its site. Perley contended that the present house was erected by John Turner III after the division of the estate of his father in 1696, but this is refuted by the inventory of John Turner II, who died in 1692, which lists the rooms of the existing house, including those of the unique south wing. Unfortunately the goods of John I, who died in 1680, were not listed by rooms, so that, although it is probable he built the main body of the house, and his son the south wing, this is not definitely established. The belief of H. F. Waters and others that the house was built in 1669, immediately after the purchase of the land, would seem to be merely *a priori*. The existence of the old More house would have permitted a delay of some years. The later history of the house is traced by Donald Millar in his "Colonial and Georgian Houses," where full measured drawings and details are given, plates 10–14.

NOTES ON INDIVIDUAL HOUSES

JOHN WARD HOUSE (figs. 6 and 9). The house originally stood at 38 St. Peter Street, with the overhanging end to the west, instead of to the south, as now. The lot on which the house itself stood was conveyed to John Ward November 13, 1684. See S. Perley, "Salem in 1700," *Essex Antiquarian*, vol. 8 (1904), p. 70. The house at first consisted only of the entry and the two western rooms, which are framed of pine, the rooms on the other side of the chimney being framed of oak. The lean-to represents a third period of building, prior to Ward's death in 1732, when it appears in his inventory. The house was removed to the grounds of the Essex Institute and restored about 1911. The chimney, the wainscot sheathing, and the sash are entirely new, as is the stair, copied from that of the Capen house, Topsfield. The front gables and the casement window-frames are restored in accordance with the indications of the framing. Millar, "Colonial and Georgian Houses," vol. 1, intro. and plates 4 and 5, with plans, etc.

"WITCH HOUSE," SEE JONATHAN CORWIN HOUSE.

SANDSTONE TOWNSHIP, MICHIGAN.—CHAPEL HOUSE. This interesting stone house, with its bas-relief, "Diana," in the gable, bears the carved inscription on the lintel of the doorway: "Caleb M. Chapel June 1850." In 1918 the porches were widened and their detail was much damaged.

SAUGUS, MASSACHUSETTS.—"SCOTCH HOUSE," purchased February 4, 1686–7, by William Boardman (fig. 3). Painstaking investigations by Walter Kendall Watkins have established the fact that this was built for the Undertakers of the Ironworks there in 1651, to house some of the prisoners captured at the Battle of Dunbar and sent to America as indentured servants. The mass of documents found by Mr. Watkins has not yet been published, but he writes us: "The legal troubles incident to the erection of the 'Scotch House' and the fact of its mention on the boundary line of Boston and Saugus in the town perambulations of the 17th and 18th century makes its identity unquestioned." Originally there were two rooms each up-stairs and down, the lean-to being an addition. The second-story rooms still have the original unplastered ceilings; the original chimney, many original doors, and much original sheathing remain in place. The stair to the garret is the original one, but the lower stair is later in date. The house was acquired by the Society for the Preservation of New England Antiquities in 1913–1914, and some repairs have been made. See its *Bulletin*, especially no. 12 (1915), p. 7; no. 18 (1918), pp. 18–23; and no. 20 (1919), p. 7. Millar, "Colonial and Georgian Houses," vol. 1, intro. and plates 1–3, with plans, etc.

SMITH'S FORT, GRAY'S CREEK, SURRY COUNTY, VIRGINIA.—THOMAS WARREN HOUSE (fig. 18). A deposition of March, 1677, stating that "about five or six and twenty years since," Thomas Warren "did begin to build that fifty foot Brick house which now stands" on Smith's Fort plantation, sets the date as 1651 or 1652. See *William and Mary College Quarterly*, vol. 8 (1900), pp. 151–152. The interior has panelling with pilasters on pedestals, apparently of the early eighteenth century, and the exterior has been much modernized.

STRATFORD, WESTMORELAND COUNTY, VIRGINIA (figs. 38, 41, 53, and 84). The date of the house is convincingly discussed, on the basis of contemporary documents, and fixed as 1725–1730, by F. W. Alexander, "Stratford Hall and the Lees" (1912), pp. 47, 59.

TARRYTOWN, NEW YORK.—SUNNYSIDE. The stone cottage on the site was remodelled for Washington Irving in 1835 by the architect George Harvey, according to documents published by P. M. Irving, "Life and Letters of Irving" (1882), pp. 276–283. The house has since been greatly enlarged, but in a direction which does not modify the most familiar aspect.

THOMASTON, MAINE.—HENRY KNOX HOUSE. In Easton's "History of Thomaston" (1865), vol. 1, chapter 11 is devoted to "Knox and his Home in Thomaston." On page 209 it is stated that the house was begun in 1793 "under the superintendence of Ebenezer Denton, the architect." Photographs of the house, now demolished, still exist, and on the back of a piece of wall-paper from it, preserved at the Maine Historical Society, is a pencil-sketch of the plan. This is so closely identical with the plan of the Barrell house, begun the year before, as to lead to the supposition that Denton erected the house from a design by Bulfinch.

TOPSFIELD, MASSACHUSETTS.—CAPEN HOUSE (figs. 5, 8, 13, and 14). The date of raising, "JUN Ye 8 1683" (Millar) or "JULY Ye 8 1683" (Dow), was found during restoration inscribed on the frame in two places. The land was granted by the town to Reverend Joseph Capen and laid out by him February 28, 1682–3. See S. Perley, "Topsfield in 1700," *Essex Antiquarian*, vol. 5, 1901, p. 100. The house was acquired by the Topsfield Historical Society and restored in 1913. The fireplaces, the stair railing and newel, and the middle bracket of one gable, as well as the size and position of the window openings, are original; the sash, door, sheathing, chimney-top, and pendills are restored on analogy with examples elsewhere. D. Millar, in *Architectural Record*, vol. 38 (1915), pp. 349–361, with photographs and measured drawings, including plans; in "Colonial and Georgian Houses," intro. and plates 6 and 7; and in *Old-Time New England*, vol. 11 (1920), pp. 3–8, with photographs. G. F. Dow, in *Historical Collections of the Topsfield Historical Society*, vol. 19 (1914).

TUCKAHOE, GOOCHLAND COUNTY, VIRGINIA (figs. 41, 42, 83, and 97). The plantation was established by Thomas Randolph "of Tuckahoe," who was born in 1683, married Judith Churchill about 1710, and died in 1730. William Byrd describes a visit to it in 1732 in his "Progress to the Mines," and although he does not describe the house, it is clear that it was a considerable one. J. S. Bassett, "Writings of William Byrd" (1901), pp. 337–342. The son, William Randolph, born in 1712, married about 1735, and may have enlarged it.

WALTHAM, MASSACHUSETTS.—GORE HOUSE (figs. 124, 178, 179, 195, and 211). The present house is the successor of one built very shortly previous, of which Bentley writes in September, 1793 ("Diary," vol. 2, p. 60): "We saw rising on our right the splendid seat belonging to Gore, the right wing was not completed but the whole formed a fine object." A writer quoted in the *Proceedings of the Massachusetts Historical Society*, vol. 13, p. 420, says: "The house he built there was burnt down March 19, 1799, while I lived there," and states that Mr. and Mrs. Gore arrived from England April 12, 1804, after the rebuilding.

LYMAN HOUSE (figs. 162 and 200). With other works by Samuel McIntire, this is reserved for discussion in the writer's forthcoming work on this artist.

WASHINGTON, DISTRICT OF COLUMBIA.—BELLEVIEW. The portico of Belleview was added by Latrobe in 1813, according to a letter of his dated July 7, in the possession of Ferdinand C. Latrobe.

STEPHEN DECATUR HOUSE, LAFAYETTE SQUARE. Latrobe was the architect, as is revealed by letters in the possession of Ferdinand C. Latrobe. Proposals were received June 4, 1817. The house has been much injured by remodelling. Measured drawings of the vestibule are published by H. F. Cunningham, "Georgian Architecture in the District of Columbia," 1914, plates 26 and 27.

THE OCTAGON, 1741 New York Avenue (figs. 129, 193, 207, and 208). The land was purchased April 19, 1797; construction was begun in 1798 and completed in 1800. Glenn Brown, "The Octagon" (1916), p. 5. This folio work contains old views of the house, photographs, and complete measured drawings.

NOTES ON INDIVIDUAL HOUSES

Tudor Place, Georgetown.   The studies for the plan of the house, by Thornton, are on paper watermarked 1810. They are preserved in the Division of Manuscripts, Library of Congress, Thornton Papers, and will shortly be published by Wells Bennett. Another study for the plan is reproduced by Glenn Brown in the *Architectural Record*, vol. 6 (1896), p. 64. Studies for the elevation are at the Octagon House. A plan of the house as it stands is published in "The Georgian Period," part 3, in the table of contents.

Van Ness House.   This house, which stood until 1907 on the site of the Pan-American Union, was begun in 1813 on designs by Latrobe. Witness his letter to General John P. Van Ness, September 26, 1813. Measured drawings (figs. 111 and 130) were made of it for Ogden Codman before its destruction, and photographs also exist. An early description of the house and grounds is given by Jonathan Elliot, "Historical Sketches of . . . the District of Columbia" (1830), pp. 270–272. *Cf.* Allen C. Clark, "General John Peter Van Ness," *Records of the Columbia Historical Society*, vol. 22 (1919), pp. 125–204, with illustrations.

The White House.   The competition programme was dated March 14, 1792, and the first premium was awarded to James Hoban on July 17. His elevation (fig. 159) was first published in "The Restoration of the White House" (1903), after p. 47; his plan (fig. 119) in Kimball: "Thomas Jefferson, Architect," fig. 179, where the later modifications of the design are also discussed.

Watertown, Massachusetts.—Oakley.   In 1809, according to the circumstantial account by S. E. Morrison, "Harrison Gray Otis" (1913), vol. 1, p. 230, Otis completely transformed a farmhouse at Watertown into the country-seat of Oakley. On its conversion into the Oakley Country Club, in 1898, it was radically remodelled. A photograph of the interior of its oval drawing-room is among those lent to the Metropolitan Museum by Ogden Codman.

Westover, Charles City County, Virginia (figs. 46 and 59).   J. S. Bassett, editor of "The Writings of William Byrd" (1901), from an intimate knowledge of Byrd's movements and financial affairs, fixes (p. lxxxi) the period shortly after 1726 as the time of the building of the mansion-house. A plat of 1735 shows all the largest buildings. Byrd had then finished his grounds. On p. lxxxviii, n., Bassett quotes notes of Miss Elizabeth Byrd Nicholas to the effect that the house was twice burned, the last fire being on the occasion of the christening of that William Byrd who was born August 2, 1749. Besides the outbuilding to the left in our photograph there was one on the other side, which appears in a sketch reproduced in "Battles and Leaders of the Civil War," vol. 2 (1887), p. 425. After the purchase of the estate by Mrs. W. M. Ramsay in 1901 this wing was "restored" with modifications, and both wings were connected with the house by brick passages. Some changes also were made in the interior. Very full publications of photographs may be found in *House and Garden*, vol. 11 (1907), pp. 231–235, and *Country Life in America*, vol. 4 (1907), pp. 414–418, with a plan, and vol. 30 (1916), pp. 25–27.

Whitehall, Anne Arundel County, Maryland (fig. 50).   Governor Horatio Sharpe secured the tract by act of the legislature in 1763 and by virtue of a power of attorney of 1764. J. D. Warfield, "The Founders of Anne Arundel and Howard Counties" (1905), p. 213. The first mention of the house is a letter of Lord Baltimore to Sharpe, February 29, 1764: "Captain Love having hinted to me of your desire for some English Hares he informs me you have a villa and grounds to keep them in." Love had left Maryland in September, 1763. *Archives of Maryland*, vol. 3 (1895), p. 142. A French traveller who visited Sharpe on June 22, 1765, wrote, "He has bought a farm and is building a pretty box of a house on the Bay side, which he Calls white hall," *American Historical Review*, vol. 27 (1921), p. 72. William Eddis wrote under date of October 1, 1769: "Colonel Sharpe . . . his house is on a large scale, the design is excellent, the apartments well fitted up, and perfectly convenient. The adjacent grounds are so judiciously disposed, that utility and taste are everywhere happily united; and when the worthy owner has completed his extensive plan, Whitehall will be one of the most desirable situations in this, or in any of the neighboring provinces." "Letters from America" (1792). A structural examination of Whitehall, September 26, 1916, before the repointing of the walls, revealed that the several parts of the whole house must have been constructed successively, that the rooms over parlor and dining-room, with the stairs leading to them, were additions subsequent to the first construction; that the portico (the cornice of which is of wholly different profile from the main cornice and intersects most awkwardly with it) was added still later.

WILLIAMSBURG, VIRGINIA.—GOVERNOR'S PALACE (figs. 47, 53, and 114). The legislative act of 1705 providing for its building, with other documents, is cited by Kimball, "Thomas Jefferson, Architect," where the sketch plan made by Jefferson about 1779 is reproduced as figure 95. The later history of the house, destroyed in 1781, is also traced there.

WOODLAWN, FAIRFAX COUNTY, VIRGINIA. The land was left to Eleanor Parke Lewis and her husband by Washington's will, drawn in July, 1799. Mrs. William Thornton wrote in her diary, August 4, 1800, during a visit to Mount Vernon: "Mrs. Lewis . . . and I went in Mrs. Washington's carriage to see Mr. Lewis's Hill where he is going to build. Dr. T. has given him a plan for his house." ' Library of Congress, Division of Manuscripts. Whether the house as executed followed Thornton's plan cannot be determined, although in the absence of other evidence the presumption is that it had some influence. Measured drawings of the house may be found in "The Georgian Period," part 6, plates 20–23.

WORCESTER, MASSACHUSETTS. SIMEON BURT HOUSE, Chestnut and Elm Streets. "Madam Salisbury writes on February 20, 1833:—'I saw the plan of his house (Mr. Burt's) yesterday at Mr. Carter's.'" Harriette M. Forbes, "Elias Carter, Architect," in *Old-Time New England*, vol. 11 (1920), p. 64.

STEPHEN SALISBURY HOUSE, Highland Street. The house was nearly completed at the date of a letter of June 19, 1837, referring to Elias Carter as the designer, and quoted by Mrs. Forbes, p. 69, in connection with photographs of the house.

DANIEL WALDO HOUSE, Main Street. Several letters quoted by Mrs. Forbes (p. 62) make clear that the house was built in the years 1829 and 1830, for Daniel Waldo, a patron of Elias Carter, architect. The house has long been demolished, but an old view of it is published by Mrs. Forbes.

CHRONOLOGICAL CHART

CHRONOLOGICAL CHART

HOUSES OF WHICH THE DATE AND AUTHORSHIP ARE ESTABLISHED BY DOCUMENTS

COLONIAL HOUSES

	1651		"Scotch House," Saugus, Massachusetts
Begun	1651 or	1652	Warren house, Smith's Fort, Gray's Creek, Surry County, Virginia
Between 1651 and 1660			Eastern part of Pickering house, Salem, Massachusetts
Between 1662 and 1666			"Country House" and Philip Ludwell house, Jamestown, Virginia
Before	1669		Western part of Whipple house, Ipswich, Massachusetts
Between 1661 and 1671			Narbonne house, Salem
	1670		Henry Bridgham house ("Julien's"), Boston
About	1671		Western part of Pickering house, Salem
Finished	1675		Jonathan Corwin ("Witch") house, Salem
Before	1676		"Bacon's Castle," Surry County, Virginia
	1676 to	1679	Peter Sergeant house ("Province House"), Boston
Between 1673 and 1682			Deliverance Parkman house, Salem
Between 1677 and 1680			Peter Tufts ("Cradock") house, Medford, Massachusetts
Before	1680		Main body of Turner house ("House of the Seven Gables"), Salem
After	1679		Daniel Epes house, Salem
	1680		"Old Feather Store," Boston
Before	1682		Eastern part of Whipple house, Ipswich
	1682 to	1683	William Penn ("Letitia") house, Philadelphia
	1683		Capen house, Topsfield, Massachusetts
Between 1681 and 1691			John Foster (Hutchinson) house, Boston
Between 1683 and 1692			Philip English house, Salem
Between 1682 and 1693			Benjamin Hooper house ("Old Bakery"), Salem
After	1684		John Ward house, Salem
Before	1692		South wing of Turner house, Salem
	1692		Fairfield (Carter's Creek), Gloucester County, Virginia
Before	1697		Usher house (nucleus of Royall house), Medford
After	1695		Benaiah Titcomb house, Newburyport, Massachusetts
After	1698		Hunt house, Salem
Before	1700		"Slate House," Philadelphia
	1705 to	1706	Governor's Palace, Williamsburg, Virginia
	1707		John Williams house, Deerfield, Massachusetts, in its original form
Between 1708 and 1725			The Mulberry, Goose Creek, South Carolina
	1721 to	1722	Graeme Park, Horsham, Pennsylvania. *John Kirk*

Before	1728	McPhedris (Warner) house, Portsmouth, New Hampshire
1728		Stenton, Germantown, Pennsylvania
Before	1730	Tuckahoe, Goochland County, Virginia
1730		Rosewell, Gloucester County, Virginia
Between 1725 and 1730		Stratford, Westmoreland County, Virginia
After 1726		Westover, Charles City County, Virginia
1730 to 1731		John Bartram house, Philadelphia, in its original form
About 1732		Ampthill, Chesterfield County, Virginia
Before 1733		Col. Robert Brewton's house, Charleston
Between 1733 and 1737		Second enlargement of Royall house, Medford, establishing present east façade
1735		Challoner house, Newport, Rhode Island. *Benjamin Wyatt*
1737 to 1740		Hancock house, Boston
1739 to 1741		Ayrault house, Newport. *Richard Munday*
Unfinished 1744, 1750		William Browne house, Beverly, Massachusetts
1745 to 1746		Pinckney house, Colleton Square, Charleston
After 1746		Shirley Place, Roxbury, Massachusetts
1748		Van Cortlandt house, Lower Yonkers, New York
1748		Daniel Pastorius house, Germantown, Pennsylvania
Between 1743 and 1753		Eveleigh house, Charleston
1750		Benjamin Pickman house, Essex Street, Salem
1751		Carter's Grove, James City County, Virginia. *David Minitree*
1753 to 1755		Samuel Colton house, Longmeadow, Massachusetts. *John Steele*
1754		Whitby Hall, Philadelphia
1756		Remodelling of John Williams house, Deerfield
Before 1757		Izard house, Charleston
After 1756		Woodford, Philadelphia
Before 1758		Drayton Hall, Ashley River, South Carolina
1757 to 1758		Ebenezer Grant house, East Windsor, Connecticut
1758		Gunston Hall, Fairfax County, Virginia
1758		Mount Airy, Richmond County, Virginia
1758		Elsing Green, King William County, Virginia
1759		John Vassall (Longfellow) house, Cambridge
1761		Timothy Orne house, Salem
1761 to 1762		Schuyler house, Albany
Between 1761 and 1764		Apthorp house, Cambridge
After 1761		Mount Pleasant, Philadelphia
1762		Mill Grove, Lower Providence, Pennsylvania
After 1763		Cliveden, Germantown
1764		Pickman house, Washington Street, Salem, in its original form
Begun 1763		Whitehall, Anne Arundel County, Maryland
1765		Roger Morris (Jumel) house, New York
1765 to 1768		Van Rensselaer Manor House, Albany
1765 to 1769		Miles Brewton house, Charleston. *Ezra Waite*
1767 to 1770		Tryon's Palace, Newbern, North Carolina. *John Hawks*
1768		Jeremiah Lee house, Marblehead, Massachusetts
1768		Johnson house, Germantown
1769 to 1771		Chase house, Annapolis
1771		Copley house, Boston. *John Singleton Copley*

CHRONOLOGICAL CHART

	1771 to	1775	Monticello, Albemarle County, Virginia, in its original form. *Thomas Jefferson*
About	1772		John Stuart house, Charleston
	1772 to	1774	Corbit house, Odessa, Delaware
	1773 ff.		Additions to Mount Vernon
	1773 to	1777	Lansdowne, Philadelphia

HOUSES OF THE EARLY REPUBLIC

	1779		Designs for remodelling the Governor's Palace, Williamsburg, and for the Governor's house, Richmond. *Jefferson*
After	1779		Jerathmeel Peirce (Nichols) house, Salem. *Samuel McIntire*
	1780		Derby house near Derby Wharf, Salem. *McIntire*
Before	1782		Langdon house, Portsmouth
	1782		Jonathan Mulliken (Cutler-Bartlett) house, Newburyport
About	1783		Rotonda study for Governor's house, Richmond. *Jefferson*
After	1783		Dyckman house, New York
	1784 to	1785	Solitude, Philadelphia
Between	1786 and	1787	Portico of Mount Vernon
	1786 to	1787	John Reynolds (Morris) house, Philadelphia
Between	1782 and	1789	Boardman house, Salem
	1787 to	1790	Kensey Johns house, Newcastle, Delaware. *Peter Justis?*
Before		1788	Bingham house, Philadelphia
	1788		Remodelling of the Woodlands, Philadelphia
Before		1789	John Brown house, Providence, Rhode Island
After	1789		John Marshall house, Richmond
About	1790		Remodelling of Pickman house, Washington Street, Salem. *McIntire*
	1790		Board-Zabriskie house, Hackensack, New Jersey
	1790 to	1791	Government House, New York. *John McComb and John Robinson*
	1791 to	1801	George Read II house, Newcastle, Delaware
	1792		Joseph Barrell house, Charlestown, Massachusetts. *Charles Bulfinch*
	1792 to	1797	President's house, Philadelphia
	1792 to	1829	The White House, Washington. *James Hoban*
	1793		Nathan Read house, Salem. *McIntire*
	1793		Remodelling of the Assembly House, Salem. *McIntire*
	1793		Portico of Montpellier, Orange County, Virginia
	1793 to	1795	Knox house, Thomaston, Maine
	1793 to	1796	Franklin Crescent, Boston. *Bulfinch*
	1793 to	1801	Robert Morris house, Philadelphia. *Pierre Charles L'Enfant*
After	1793		Lyman house, Waltham, Massachusetts. *McIntire*
	1795		Joseph Hosmer house, Salem
	1795		Harrison Gray Otis house, Cambridge Street, Boston
	1795 to	1798	Elias Hasket Derby house, Salem. *McIntire*
	1796		Morton (Taylor) house, Roxbury
	1796 ff.		Middleton (Pinckney) house, Charleston
	1796 to	1808	Remodelling of Monticello. *Jefferson*
	1798		Upsala, Germantown
Before		1799	Ezekiel Hersey Derby house, Salem. *Bulfinch*
	1798 to	1800	The Octagon, Washington. *William Thornton*

1798 to	1800	Homewood, Baltimore
1798 ff.		Edgehill, Albemarle County, Virginia, in its original form. *Jefferson*
1799		Bulfinch house, Bulfinch Place, Boston. *Bulfinch*
1799 to	1800	Sedgley, Philadelphia. *Benjamin Henry Latrobe*
Between 1799 and	1804	Rebuilding of Gore house, Waltham
1800 ff.		Woodlawn, Fairfax County, Virginia
1800 to	1801	Oak Hill, Danvers, Massachusetts
1800 to	1801	Harrison Gray Otis house, Mount Vernon Street, Boston. *Bulfinch*
1800 to	1801	Sansom's Buildings, Philadelphia. *Latrobe* and *Thomas Carstairs*
After 1800		Wilson Glover house (Charleston Club), Charleston
1801		The Grange, New York. *McComb*
1801		William Gray house, Salem
1801 to	1802	Burd house, Philadelphia. *Latrobe*
1802 to	1803	Remodelling of Farmington, Albemarle County, Virginia. *Jefferson*
Between 1803 and	1804	Thomas Amory (Ticknor) house, Boston
Before	1804	Plan for Pantops, executed at Poplar Forest, Bedford County, Virginia, 1806–1809. *Jefferson*
1804 to	1805	Houses nos. 1–4 Park Street, Boston. *Bulfinch*
After 1804		Samuel Cook (Oliver) house, Salem. *McIntire*
1805		Crafts house, Roxbury. *Peter Banner*
1805		Enoch Thurston (Shepard) house, Newburyport
1805		John Gardner (Pingree) house, Salem. *McIntire*
1805		Hunnewell (Shepley) house, Portland, Maine. *Alexander Parris*
Finished	1806	Radcliffe (King) house, Charleston
After 1806		Parkman houses, Bowdoin Square, Boston. *Bulfinch*
Between 1806 and	1811	Enoch Dow house, Salem. *McIntire*
1807		House of the Registrar of Deeds, Salem. *McIntire*
1807		Harrison Gray Otis house, Beacon Street, Boston
1807 to	1808	Waln house, Philadelphia. *Latrobe*
1808 to	1811	Markoe house, Philadelphia. *Latrobe*
1809		Gideon Tucker (Rice) house, Salem. *McIntire*
1809		Remodelling of Oakley, Watertown, Massachusetts
1809		Buildings on 9th Street, between Walnut and Locust, Philadelphia. *Robert Mills*
Between 1808 and	1811	Joseph Felt (Chapman) house, Salem. *McIntire*
Before	1811	Nathaniel Russell house, Charleston
1810		Colonnade Row, Boston. *Bulfinch*
After 1810		Tudor Place, Georgetown. *Thornton*
1812		Wickham house (Valentine Museum), Richmond. *Mills*
1812 to	1813	Brockenbrough house, Richmond. *Mills*
1813		Portico of Belleview, Washington. *Latrobe*
1813 ff.		Ashland, Kentucky. *Latrobe*
1813 to	1819	Van Ness house, Washington. *Latrobe*
1815 to	1817	Ampthill, Cumberland County, Virginia. *Jefferson*
1816		Nichols house, Chestnut Street, Salem. *Jabez Smith*
1816		David Sears house (nucleus of Somerset Club), Boston. *Parris*
Finished	1817	Larkin house, Portsmouth
1817		Barboursville, Orange County, Virginia. *Jefferson*
1817 to	1819	Decatur house, Washington. *Latrobe*

CHRONOLOGICAL CHART

1817 to	1824	Pavilions of the University of Virginia. *Jefferson*
1818 to	1819	Forrester house (Salem Club), Salem
1818 to	1819	John Andrew (Safford) house, Salem
1818 to	1819	Nathaniel Silsbee house, Salem
1819		Dudley L. Pickman (Shreve-Little) house, Salem
1822 to	1823	Pickering Dodge house, Salem. *David Lord*
Before	1826	Arlington, Alexandria County, Virginia. *George Hadfield*
1829 to	1830	Daniel Waldo house, Worcester, Massachusetts. *Elias Carter*
Before	1832	Russel house, Middletown, Connecticut
Before	1832	Joseph Bowers house, Northampton, Massachusetts
Between 1829 and 1833		Hillhouse house, New Haven. *Ithiel Town* and *Alexander Jackson Davis*
Between 1829 and 1833		Skinner (Trowbridge) house, New Haven. *Town* and *Davis*
1833 to	1834	Simeon Burt house, Worcester. *Carter*
1833 to	1836	Colonnade Row, New York
1834 to	1836	Andalusia, Bucks County, Pennsylvania
1835		Remodelling of Sunnyside, Tarrytown, New York. *George Harvey*
1835 to	1836	Rebuilding of The Hermitage, Nashville, Tennessee. *Joseph Rieff*
1835 to	1840	Berry Hill, Halifax County, Virginia
1836 to	1837	Stephen Salisbury house, Worcester
1840		Smith house, Grass Lake, Michigan
1840 to	1843	Dexter house, Dexter, Michigan
1850		Chapel house, Sandstone Township, Michigan
1857		Bean house, Concord, Michigan

INDEX

INDEX

The index covers references in the text and illustrations, the presence of an illustration being indicated by a page reference in *Italic* type. Towns, county seats, and plantations are listed alphabetically, with houses under a given town alphabetically by the name of the original owner (in most cases), with references from other names commonly used.

INDEX

INDEX

INDEX

INDEX

INDEX

INDEX

313

INDEX

Dover Books on Art

ANIMALS IN MOTION, Eadweard Muybridge. The largest collection of animal action photos in print. 34 different animals (horses, mules, oxen, goats, camels, pigs, cats, lions, gnus, deer, monkeys, eagles—and 22 others) in 132 characteristic actions. All 3919 photographs are taken in series at speeds up to 1/1600th of a second, offering artists, biologists, cartoonists a remarkable opportunity to see exactly how an ostrich's head bobs when running, how a lion puts his foot down, how an elephant's knee bends, how a bird flaps his wings, thousands of other hard-to-catch details. "A really marvellous series of plates," NATURE. 380 full-page plates. Heavy glossy stock, reinforced binding with headbands. 7⅞ x 10¾. T203 Clothbound $10.00

THE BOOK OF SIGNS, R. Koch. 493 symbols—crosses, monograms, astrological, biological symbols, runes, etc.—from ancient manuscripts, cathedrals, coins, catacombs, pottery. May be reproduced permission-free. 493 illustrations by Fritz Kredel. 104pp. 6⅛ x 9¼. T162 Paperbound $1.00

A HANDBOOK OF EARLY ADVERTISING ART, C. P. Hornung. The largest collection of copyright-free early advertising art ever compiled. Vol. I: 2,000 illustrations of animals, old automobiles, buildings, allegorical figures, fire engines, Indians, ships, trains, more than 33 other categories! Vol. II: Over 4,000 typographical specimens; 600 Roman, Gothic, Barnum, Old English faces; 630 ornamental type faces; hundreds of scrolls, initials, flourishes, etc. "A remarkable collection," PRINTERS' INK.
Vol. I: Pictorial Volume. Over 2000 illustrations. 256pp. 9 x 12.
  T122 Clothbound $10.00
Vol. II: Typographical Volume. Over 4000 specimens. 319pp.
9 x 12. T123 Clothbound $10.00
  Two volume set, Clothbound, only $18.50

THE UNIVERSAL PENMAN, George Bickham. Exact reproduction of beautiful 18th-century book of handwriting. 22 complete alphabets in finest English roundhand, other scripts, over 2000 elaborate flourishes, 122 calligraphic illustrations, etc. Material is copyright-free. "An essential part of any art library, and a book of permanent value," AMERICAN ARTIST. 212 plates. 224pp. 9 x 13¾. T20 Clothbound $10.00

AN ATLAS OF ANATOMY FOR ARTISTS, F. Schider. This standard work contains 189 full-page plates, more than 647 illustrations of all aspects of the human skeleton, musculature, cutaway portions of the body, each part of the anatomy, hand forms, eyelids, breasts, location of muscles under the flesh, etc. 59 plates illustrate how Michelangelo, da Vinci, Goya, 15 others, drew human anatomy. New 3rd edition enlarged by 52 new illustrations by Cloquet, Barcsay. "The standard reference tool," AMERICAN LIBRARY ASSOCIATION. "Excellent," AMERICAN ARTIST. 189 plates, 647 illustrations. xxvi + 192pp. 7⅞ x 10⅝. T241 Clothbound $6.00

GREEK REVIVAL ARCHITECTURE IN AMERICA, T. Hamlin. A comprehensive study of the American Classical Revival, its regional variations, reasons for its success and eventual decline. Profusely illustrated with photos, sketches, floor plans and sections, displaying the work of almost every important architect of the time. 2 appendices. 39 figures, 94 plates containing 221 photos, 62 architectural designs, drawings, etc. 324-item classified bibliography. Index. xi + 439pp. 5⅜ x 8½.

T1148 Paperbound $3.00

CREATIVE LITHOGRAPHY AND HOW TO DO IT, Grant Arnold. Written by a man who practiced and taught lithography for many years, this highly useful volume explains all the steps of the lithographic process from tracing the drawings on the stone to printing the lithograph, with helpful hints for solving special problems. Index. 16 reproductions of lithographs. 11 drawings. xv + 214pp. of text. 5⅜ x 8½.

T1208 Paperbound $1.65

TEACH YOURSELF ANTIQUE COLLECTING, E. Bradford. An excellent, brief guide to collecting British furniture, silver, pictures and prints, pewter, pottery and porcelain, Victoriana, enamels, clocks or other antiques. Much background information difficult to find elsewhere. 15pp. of illus. 215pp. 7 x 4¼.

Clothbound $2.00

PAINTING IN THE FAR EAST, L. Binyon. A study of over 1500 years of Oriental art by one of the world's outstanding authorities. The author chooses the most important masters in each period—Wu Tao-tzu, Toba Sojo, Kanaoka, Li Lung-mien, Masanobu, Okio, etc.—and examines the works, schools, and influence of each within their cultural context. 42 photographs. Sources of original works and selected bibliography. Notes including list of principal painters by periods. xx + 297pp. 6⅛ x 9¼.

T520 Paperbound $2.25

THE ALPHABET AND ELEMENTS OF LETTERING, F. W. Goudy. A beautifully illustrated volume on the aesthetics of letters and type faces and their history and development. Each plate consists of 15 forms of a single letter with the last plate devoted to the ampersand and the numerals. "A sound guide for all persons engaged in printing or drawing," Saturday Review. 27 full-page plates. 48 additional figures. xii + 131pp. 7⅞ x 10¾.

T792 Paperbound $2.00

THE COMPLETE BOOK OF SILK SCREEN PRINTING PRODUCTION, J. I. Biegeleisen. Here is a clear and complete picture of every aspect of silk screen technique and press operation—from individually operated manual presses to modern automatic ones. Unsurpassed as a guidebook for setting up shop, making shop operation more efficient, finding out about latest methods and equipment; or as a textbook for use in teaching, studying, or learning all aspects of the profession. 124 figures. Index. Bibliography. List of Supply Sources. xi + 253pp. 5⅜ x 8½.

T1100 Paperbound $2.00

AN ATLAS OF ANIMAL ANATOMY FOR ARTISTS, W. Ellenberger, H. Baum, H. Dittrich. The largest, richest animal anatomy for artists in English. Form, musculature, tendons, bone structure, expression, detailed cross sections of head, other features, of the horse, lion, dog, cat, deer, seal, kangaroo, cow, bull, goat, monkey, hare, many other animals. "Highly recommended," DESIGN. Second, revised, enlarged edition with new plates from Cuvier, Stubbs, etc. 288 illustrations. 153pp. 11⅜ x 9.

T82 Clothbound $6.00

ANIMAL DRAWING: ANATOMY AND ACTION FOR ARTISTS, C. R. Knight. 158 studies, with full accompanying text, of such animals as the gorilla, bear, bison, dromedary, camel, vulture, pelican, iguana, shark, etc., by one of the greatest modern masters of animal drawing. Innumerable tips on how to get life expression into your work. "An excellent reference work," SAN FRANCISCO CHRONICLE. 158 illustrations. 156pp. 10½ x 8½.

T426 Paperbound $2.00

ARCHITECTURAL AND PERSPECTIVE DESIGNS, Giuseppe Galli Bibiena. 50 imaginative scenic drawings of Giuseppe Galli Bibiena, principal theatrical engineer and architect to the Viennese court of Charles VI. Aside from its interest to art historians, students, and art lovers, there is a whole Baroque world of material in this book for the commercial artist. Portrait of Charles VI by Martin de Meytens. 1 allegorical plate. 50 additional plates. New introduction. vi + 103pp. 10⅛ x 13¼.

T1263 Paperbound $2.25

HANDBOOK OF DESIGNS AND DEVICES, C. P. Hornung. A remarkable working collection of 1836 basic designs and variations, all copyright-free. Variations of circle, line, cross, diamond, swastika, star, scroll, shield, many more. Notes on symbolism. "A necessity to every designer who would be original without having to labor heavily," ARTIST AND ADVERTISER. 204 plates. 240pp. 5⅜ x 8.

T125 Paperbound $1.90

CHINESE HOUSEHOLD FURNITURE, G. N. Kates. A summary of virtually everything that is known about authentic Chinese furniture before it was contaminated by the influence of the West. The text covers history of styles, materials used, principles of design and craftsmanship, and furniture arrangement—all fully illustrated. xiii + 190pp. 5⅝ x 8½.

T958 Paperbound $1.50

DECORATIVE ART OF THE SOUTHWESTERN INDIANS, D. S. Sides. 300 black and white reproductions from one of the most beautiful art traditions of the primitive world, ranging from the geometric art of the Great Pueblo period of the 13th century to modern folk art. Motives from basketry, beadwork, Zuni masks, Hopi kachina dolls, Navajo sand pictures and blankets, and ceramic ware. Unusual and imaginative designs will inspire craftsmen in all media, and commercial artists may reproduce any of them without permission or payment. xviii + 101pp. 5⅝ x 8⅜.

T139 Paperbound $1.00

200 DECORATIVE TITLE-PAGES, edited by A. Nesbitt. Fascinating and informative from a historical point of view, this beautiful collection of decorated titles will be a great inspiration to students of design, commercial artists, advertising designers, etc. A complete survey of the genre from the first known decorated title to work in the first decades of this century. Bibliography and sources of the plates. 222pp. 8⅜ x 11¼.

T1264 Paperbound $2.75

ON THE LAWS OF JAPANESE PAINTING, H. P. Bowie. This classic work on the philosophy and technique of Japanese art is based on the author's first-hand experiences studying art in Japan. Every aspect of Japanese painting is described: the use of the brush and other materials; laws governing conception and execution; subjects for Japanese paintings, etc. The best possible substitute for a series of lessons from a great Oriental master. Index. xv + 117pp. + 66 plates. 6⅛ x 9¼.

T30 Paperbound $2.00

A HANDBOOK OF ANATOMY FOR ART STUDENTS, Arthur Thomson. This long-popular text teaches any student, regardless of level of technical competence, all the subtleties of human anatomy. Clear photographs, numerous line sketches and diagrams of bones, joints, etc. Use it as a text for home study, as a supplement to life class work, or as a lifelong sourcebook and reference volume. Author's prefaces. 67 plates, containing 40 line drawings, 86 photographs—mostly full page. 211 figures. Appendix. Index. xx + 459pp. 5⅜ x 8⅜. T1163 Paperbound $3.00

WHITTLING AND WOODCARVING, E. J. Tangerman. With this book, a beginner who is moderately handy can whittle or carve scores of useful objects, toys for children, gifts, or simply pass hours creatively and enjoyably. "Easy as well as instructive reading," N. Y. Herald Tribune Books. 464 illustrations, with appendix and index. x + 293pp. 5½ x 8⅛.

T965 Paperbound $1.75

ONE HUNDRED AND ONE PATCHWORK PATTERNS, Ruby Short McKim. Whether you have made a hundred quilts or none at all, you will find this the single most useful book on quiltmaking. There are 101 full patterns (all exact size) with full instructions for cutting and sewing. In addition there is some really choice folklore about the origin of the ingenious pattern names: "Monkey Wrench," "Road to California," "Drunkard's Path," "Crossed Canoes," to name a few. Over 500 illustrations. 124 pp. 7⅞ x 10¾. T773 Paperbound $1.85

ART AND GEOMETRY, W. M. Ivins, Jr. Challenges the idea that the foundations of modern thought were laid in ancient Greece. Pitting Greek tactile-muscular intuitions of space against modern visual intuitions, the author, for 30 years curator of prints, Metropolitan Museum of Art, analyzes the differences between ancient and Renaissance painting and sculpture and tells of the first fruitful investigations of perspective. x + 113pp. 5⅜ x 8⅜. T941 Paperbound $1.00

MASTERPIECES OF FURNITURE, Verna Cook Salomonsky. Photographs and measured drawings of some of the finest examples of Colonial American, 17th century English, Windsor, Sheraton, Hepplewhite, Chippendale, Louis XIV, Queen Anne, and various other furniture styles. The textual matter includes information on traditions, characteristics, background, etc. of various pieces. 101 plates. Bibliography. 224pp. 7⅞ x 10¾.

T1381 Paperbound $2.00

PRIMITIVE ART, Franz Boas. In this exhaustive volume, a great American anthropologist analyzes all the fundamental traits of primitive art, covering the formal element in art, representative art, symbolism, style, literature, music, and the dance. Illustrations of Indian embroidery, paleolithic paintings, woven blankets, wing and tail designs, totem poles, cutlery, earthenware, baskets and many other primitive objects and motifs. Over 900 illustrations. 376pp. 5⅜ x 8.   T25 Paperbound $2.00

AN INTRODUCTION TO A HISTORY OF WOODCUT, A. M. Hind. Nearly all of this authoritative 2-volume set is devoted to the 15th century—the period during which the woodcut came of age as an important art form. It is the most complete compendium of information on this period, the artists who contributed to it, and their technical and artistic accomplishments. Profusely illustrated with cuts by 15th century masters, and later works for comparative purposes. 484 illustrations. 5 indexes. Total of xi + 838pp. 5⅜ x 8½. Two-volume set, T952-3 Paperbound $5.00

A HISTORY OF ENGRAVING AND ETCHING, A. M. Hind. Beginning with the anonymous masters of 15th century engraving, this highly regarded and thorough survey carries you through Italy, Holland, and Germany to the great engravers and beginnings of etching in the 16th century, through the portrait engravers, master etchers, practicioners of mezzotint, crayon manner and stipple, aquatint, color prints, to modern etching in the period just prior to World War I. Beautifully illustrated —sharp clear prints on heavy opaque paper. Author's preface. 3 appendixes. 111 illustrations. xviii + 487 pp. 5⅜ x 8½.

T954 Paperbound $2.75

ART STUDENTS' ANATOMY, E. J. Farris. Teaching anatomy by using chiefly living objects for illustration, this study has enjoyed long popularity and success in art courses and home-study programs. All the basic elements of the human anatomy are illustrated in minute detail, diagrammed and pictured as they pass through common movements and actions. 158 drawings, photographs, and roentgenograms. Glossary of anatomical terms. x + 159pp. 5⅝ x 8⅜.   T744 Paperbound $1.50

COLONIAL LIGHTING, A. H. Hayward. The only book to cover the fascinating story of lamps and other lighting devices in America. Beginning with rush light holders used by the early settlers, it ranges through the elaborate chandeliers of the Federal period, illustrating 647 lamps. Of great value to antique collectors, designers, and historians of arts and crafts. Revised and enlarged by James R. Marsh. xxxi + 198pp. 5⅝ x 8¼.

T975 Paperbound $2.00

PINE FURNITURE OF EARLY NEW ENGLAND, R. H. Kettell. Over 400 illustrations, over 50 working drawings of early New England chairs, benches, beds, cupboards, mirrors, shelves, tables, other furniture esteemed for simple beauty and character. "Rich store of illustrations . . . emphasizes the individuality and varied design," ANTIQUES. 413 illustrations, 55 working drawings. 475pp. 8 x 10¾.   T145 Clothbound $10.00

BASIC BOOKBINDING, A. W. Lewis. Enables both beginners and experts to rebind old books or bind paperbacks in hard covers. Treats materials, tools; gives step-by-step instruction in how to collate a book, sew it, back it, make boards, etc. 261 illus. Appendices. 155pp. 5⅜ x 8.   T169 Paperbound $1.45

DESIGN MOTIFS OF ANCIENT MEXICO, J. Enciso. Nearly 90% of these 766 superb designs from Aztec, Olmec, Totonac, Maya, and Toltec origins are unobtainable elsewhere. Contains plumed serpents, wind gods, animals, demons, dancers, monsters, etc. Excellent applied design source. Originally $17.50. 766 illustrations, thousands of motifs. 192pp. 6⅛ x 9¼.
                    T84 Paperbound $1.85

A DIDEROT PICTORIAL ENCYCLOPEDIA OF TRADES AND INDUSTRY. Manufacturing and the Technical Arts in Plates Selected from "L'Encyclopédie ou Dictionnaire Raisonné des Sciences, des Arts, et des Métiers," of Denis Diderot, edited with text by C. Gillispie. Over 2000 illustrations on 485 full-page plates. Magnificent 18th-century engravings of men, women, and children working at such trades as milling flour, cheesemaking, charcoal burning, mining, silverplating, shoeing horses, making fine glass, printing, hundreds more, showing details of machinery, different steps in sequence, etc. A remarkable art work, but also the largest collection of working figures in print, copyright-free, for art directors, designers, etc. Two vols. 920pp. 9 x 12. Heavy library cloth.   T421 Two volume set $18.50

SILK SCREEN TECHNIQUES, J. Biegeleisen, M. Cohn. A practical step-by-step home course in one of the most versatile, least expensive graphic arts processes. How to build an inexpensive silk screen, prepare stencils, print, achieve special textures, use color, etc. Every step explained, diagrammed. 149 illustrations, 201pp. 6⅛ x 9¼.   T433 Paperbound $1.55

STICKS AND STONES, Lewis Mumford. An examination of forces influencing American architecture: the medieval tradition in early New England, the classical influence in Jefferson's time, the Brown Decades, the imperial facade, the machine age, etc. "A truly remarkable book," SAT. REV. OF LITERATURE. 2nd revised edition. 21 illus. xvii + 240pp. 5⅜ x 8.
                    T202 Paperbound $1.65

THE AUTOBIOGRAPHY OF AN IDEA, Louis Sullivan. The architect whom Frank Lloyd Wright called "the master," records the development of the theories that revolutionized America's skyline. 34 full-page plates of Sullivan's finest work. New introduction by R. M. Line. xiv + 335pp. 5⅜ x 8.
                    T281 Paperbound $2.00

ART ANATOMY, Dr. William Rimmer. One of the few books on art anatomy that are themselves works of art, this is a faithful reproduction (rearranged for handy use) of the extremely rare masterpiece of the famous 19th century anatomist, sculptor, and art teacher. Beautiful, clear line drawings show every part of the body—bony structure, muscles, features, etc. Unusual are the sections on falling bodies, foreshortenings, muscles in tension, grotesque personalities, and Rimmer's remarkable interpretation of emotions and personalities as expressed by facial features. It will supplement every other book on art anatomy you are likely to have. Reproduced clearer than the lithographic original (which sells for $500 on up on the rare book market.) Over 1,200 illustrations. xiii + 153pp. 7¾ x 10¾.

T908 Paperbound $2.00

THE CRAFTSMAN'S HANDBOOK, Cennino Cennini. The finest English translation of IL LIBRO DELL' ARTE, the 15th century introduction to art technique that is both a mirror of Quatrocento life and a source of many useful but nearly forgotten facets of the painter's art. 4 illustrations. xxvii + 142pp. D. V. Thompson, translator. 5⅜ x 8. T54 Paperbound $1.50

THE BROWN DECADES, Lewis Mumford. A picture of the "buried renaissance" of the post-Civil War period, and the founding of modern architecture (Sullivan, Richardson, Root, Roebling), landscape development (Marsh, Olmstead, Eliot), and the graphic arts (Homer, Eakins, Ryder). 2nd revised, enlarged edition. Bibliography. 12 illustrations. xiv + 266 pp. 5⅜ x 8.

T200 Paperbound $1.75

THE STYLES OF ORNAMENT, A. Speltz. The largest collection of line ornament in print, with 3750 numbered illustrations arranged chronologically from Egypt, Assyria, Greeks, Romans, Etruscans, through Medieval, Renaissance, 18th century, and Victorian. No permissions, no fees needed to use or reproduce illustrations. 400 plates with 3750 illustrations. Bibliography. Index. 640pp. 6 x 9. T577 Paperbound $2.50

THE ART OF ETCHING, E. S. Lumsden. Every step of the etching process from essential materials to completed proof is carefully and clearly explained, with 24 annotated plates exemplifying every technique and approach discussed. The book also features a rich survey of the art, with 105 annotated plates by masters. Invaluable for beginner to advanced etcher. 374pp. 5⅜ x 8. T49 Paperbound $2.50

OF THE JUST SHAPING OF LETTERS, Albrecht Dürer. This remarkable volume reveals Albrecht Dürer's rules for the geometric construction of Roman capitals and the formation of Gothic lower case and capital letters, complete with construction diagrams and directions. Of considerable practical interest to the contemporary illustrator, artist, and designer. Translated from the Latin text of the edition of 1535 by R. T. Nichol. Numerous letterform designs, construction diagrams, illustrations. iv + 43pp. 7⅞ x 10¾. T1306 Paperbound $1.25

PRINCIPLES OF ART HISTORY, H. Wölfflin. This remarkably instructive work demonstrates the tremendous change in artistic conception from the 14th to the 18th centuries, by analyzing 164 works by Botticelli, Dürer, Hobbema, Holbein, Hals, Titian, Rembrandt, Vermeer, etc., and pointing out exactly what is meant by "baroque," "classic," "primitive," "picturesque," and other basic terms of art history and criticism. "A remarkable lesson in the art of seeing," SAT. REV. OF LITERATURE. Translated from the 7th German edition. 150 illus. 254pp. 6⅛ x 9¼. T276 Paperbound $2.00

FOUNDATIONS OF MODERN ART, A. Ozenfant. Stimulating discussion of human creativity from paleolithic cave painting to modern painting, architecture, decorative arts. Fully illustrated with works of Gris, Lipchitz, Léger, Picasso, primitive, modern artifacts, architecture, industrial art, much more. 226 illustrations. 368pp. 6⅛ x 9¼. T215 Paperbound $2.00

METALWORK AND ENAMELLING, H. Maryon. Probably the best book ever written on the subject. Tells everything necessary for the home manufacture of jewelry, rings, ear pendants, bowls, etc. Covers materials, tools, soldering, filigree, setting stones, raising patterns, repoussé work, damascening, niello, cloisonné, polishing, assaying, casting, and dozens of other techniques. The best substitute for apprenticeship to a master metalworker. 363 photos and figures. 374pp. 5½ x 8½.
T183 Clothbound $8.50

SHAKER FURNITURE, E. D. and F. Andrews. The most illuminating study of Shaker furniture ever written. Covers chronology, craftsmanship, houses, shops, etc. Includes over 200 photographs of chairs, tables, clocks, beds, benches, etc. "Mr. & Mrs. Andrews know all there is to know about Shaker furniture," Mark Van Doren, NATION. 48 full-page plates. 192pp. 7⅞ x 10¾. T679 Paperbound $2.00

LETTERING AND ALPHABETS, J. A. Cavanagh. An unabridged reissue of "Lettering," containing the full discussion, analysis, illustration of 89 basic hand lettering styles based on Caslon, Bodoni, Gothic, many other types. Hundreds of technical hints on construction, strokes, pens, brushes, etc. 89 alphabets, 72 lettered specimens, which may be reproduced permission-free. 121pp. 9¾ x 8. T53 Paperbound $1.35

THE HUMAN FIGURE IN MOTION, Eadweard Muybridge. The largest collection in print of Muybridge's famous high-speed action photos. 4789 photographs in more than 500 action-strip-sequences (at shutter speeds up to 1/6000th of a second) illustrate men, women, children—mostly undraped—performing such actions as walking, running, getting up, lying down, carrying objects, throwing, etc. "An unparalleled dictionary of action for all artists," AMERICAN ARTIST. 390 full-page plates, with 4789 photographs. Heavy glossy stock, reinforced binding with headbands. 7⅞ x 10¾. T204 Clothbound $10.00

GRAPHIC WORLDS OF PETER BRUEGEL THE ELDER,
H. A. Klein. 64 of the finest etchings and engravings made from
the drawings of the Flemish master Peter Bruegel. Every aspect
of the artist's diversified style and subject matter is represented,
with notes providing biographical and other background information. Excellent reproductions on opaque stock with nothing
on reverse side. 63 engravings, 1 woodcut. Bibliography. xviii +
289pp. 11⅜ x 8¼.   T1132 Paperbound $3.00

THE COMPLETE WOODCUTS OF ALBRECHT DURER,
edited by Dr. Willi Kurth. Albrecht Dürer was a master in various media, but it was in woodcut design that his creative genius
reached its highest expression. Here are all of his extant woodcuts, a collection of over 300 great works, many of which are
not available elsewhere. An indispensable work for the art historian and critic and all art lovers. 346 plates. Index. 285pp.
8½ x 12¼.   T1097 Paperbound $2.50

GRAPHIC REPRODUCTION IN PRINTING, H. Curwen. A
behind-the-scenes account of the various processes of graphic
reproduction—relief, intaglio, stenciling, lithography, line
methods, continuous tone methods, photogravure, collotype—
and the advantages and limitations of each. Invaluable for all
artists, advertising art directors, commercial designers, adver-
tisers, publishers, and all art lovers who buy prints as a hobby.
137 illustrations, including 13 full-page plates, 10 in color. xvi +
171pp. 5¼ x 8½.   T512 Clothbound $6.00

WILD FOWL DECOYS, Joel Barber. Antique dealers, collectors,
craftsmen, hunters, readers of Americana, etc. will find this the
only thorough and reliable guide on the market today to this
unique folk art. It contains the history, cultural significance, regional design variations; unusual decoy lore; working plans for
constructing decoys; and loads of illustrations. 140 full-page
plates, 4 in color. 14 additional plates of drawings and plans by
the author. xxvii + 156pp. 7⅞ x 10¾.   T11 Paperbound $2.75

1800 WOODCUTS BY THOMAS BEWICK AND HIS SCHOOL.
This is the largest collection of first-rate pictorial woodcuts in
print—an indispensable part of the working library of every
commercial artist, art director, production designer, packaging
artist, craftsman, manufacturer, librarian, art collector, and
artist. And best of all, when you buy your copy of Bewick, you
buy the rights to reproduce individual illustrations—no permission needed, no acknowledgments, no clearance fees! Classified
index. Bibliography and sources. xiv + 246pp. 9 x 12.
                    T766 Clothbound $10.00

THE SCRIPT LETTER, Tommy Thompson. Prepared by a noted
authority, this is a thorough, straightforward course of instruction with advice on virtually every facet of the art of script
lettering. Also a brief history of lettering with examples from
early copy books and illustrations from present day advertising
and packaging. Copiously illustrated. Bibliography. 128pp.
6½ x 9⅛.   T1311 Paperbound $1.00

VITRUVIUS: TEN BOOKS ON ARCHITECTURE. The most influential book in the history of architecture. 1st century A.D. Roman classic has influenced such men as Bramante, Palladio, Michelangelo, up to present. Classic principles of design, harmony, etc. Fascinating reading. Definitive English translation by Professor H. Morgan, Harvard. 344pp. 5⅜ x 8.

T645 Paperbound $2.00

HAWTHORNE ON PAINTING. Vivid re-creation, from students' notes, of instructions by Charles Hawthorne at Cape Cod School of Art. Essays, epigrammatic comments on color, form, seeing, techniques, etc. "Excellent," Time. 100pp. 5⅜ x 8.

T653 Paperbound $1.00

THE HANDBOOK OF PLANT AND FLORAL ORNAMENT, R. G. Hatton. 1200 line illustrations, from medieval, Renaissance herbals, of flowering or fruiting plants: garden flowers, wild flowers, medicinal plants, poisons, industrial plants, etc. A unique compilation that probably could not be matched in any library in the world. Formerly "The Craftsman's Plant-Book." Also full text on uses, history as ornament, etc. 548pp. 6⅛ x 9¼.

T649 Paperbound $3.00

DECORATIVE ALPHABETS AND INITIALS, Alexander Nesbitt. 91 complete alphabets, over 3900 ornamental initials, from Middle Ages, Renaissance printing, baroque, rococo, and modern sources. Individual items copyright free, for use in commercial art, crafts, design, packaging, etc. 123 full-page plates. 3924 initials. 129pp. 7¾ x 10¾.   T544 Paperbound $2.25

METHODS AND MATERIALS OF THE GREAT SCHOOLS AND MASTERS, Sir Charles Eastlake. (Formerly titled "Materials for a History of Oil Painting.") Vast, authentic reconstruction of secret techniques of the masters, recreated from ancient manuscripts, contemporary accounts, analysis of paintings, etc. Oils, fresco, tempera, varnishes, encaustics. Both Flemish and Italian schools, also British and French. One of great works for art historians, critics; inexhaustible mine of suggestions, information for practicing artists. Total of 1025pp. 5⅜ x 8.

Two volume set, T718-9 Paperbound $4.50

BYZANTINE ART AND ARCHAEOLOGY, O.M. Dalton. Still most thorough work in English on Byzantine art forms throughout ancient and medieval world. Analyzes hundreds of pieces, covers sculpture, painting, mosaic, jewelry, textiles, architecture, etc. Historical development; specific examples; iconology and ideas; symbolism. A treasure trove of material about one of most important art traditions, will supplement and expand any other book in area. Bibliography of over 2500 items. 457 illustrations. 747pp. 6⅛ x 9¼.   T776 Clothbound $8.50

THE HUMAN FIGURE, J. H. Vanderpoel. Not just a picture book, but a complete course by a famous figure artist. Extensive text, illustrated by 430 pencil and charcoal drawings of both male and female anatomy. 2nd enlarged edition. Foreword. 430 illus. 143pp. 6⅛ x 9¼.   T432 Paperbound $1.50

THE FOUR BOOKS OF ARCHITECTURE, Andrea Palladio.
A compendium of the art of Andrea Palladio, one of the most
celebrated architects of the Renaissance, including 250 mag-
nificently-engraved plates showing edifices either of Palladio's
design or reconstructed (in these drawings) by him from classical ruins and contemporary accounts. 257 plates. xxiv + 119pp.
9½ x 12¾. T1308 Clothbound $10.00

150 MASTERPIECES OF DRAWING, A. Toney. Selected by a
gifted artist and teacher, these are some of the finest drawings
produced by Western artists from the early 15th to the end of
the 18th centuries. Excellent reproductions of drawings by Rembrandt, Bruegel, Raphael, Watteau, and other familiar masters,
as well as works by lesser known but brilliant artists. 150 plates.
xviii + 150pp. 5⅜ x 11¼. T1032 Paperbound $2.00

MORE DRAWINGS BY HEINRICH KLEY. Another collection
of the graphic, vivid sketches of Heinrich Kley, one of the most
diabolically talented cartoonists of our century. The sketches
take in every aspect of human life: nothing is too sacred for him
to ridicule, no one too eminent for him to satirize. 158 drawings
you will not easily forget. iv + 104pp. 7⅜ x 10¾.
T41 Paperbound $1.85

*THE TRIUMPH OF MAXIMILIAN I, 137 Woodcuts by Hans
Burgkmair and Others.* This is one of the world's great art
monuments, a series of magnificent woodcuts executed by the
most important artists in the German realms as part of an
elaborate plan by Maximilian I, ruler of the Holy Roman Empire,
to commemorate his own name, dynasty, and achievements. 137
plates. New translation of descriptive text, notes, and bibliography prepared by Stanley Appelbaum. Special section of 10pp.
containing a reduced version of the entire Triumph. x + 169pp.
11⅛ x 9¼. T1207 Paperbound $3.00

PAINTING IN ISLAM, Sir Thomas W. Arnold. This scholarly
study puts Islamic painting in its social and religious context
and examines its relation to Islamic civilization in general. 65
full-page plates illustrate the text and give outstanding examples
of Islamic art. 4 appendices. Index of mss. referred to. General
Index. xxiv + 159pp. 6⅝ x 9¼. T1310 Paperbound $2.50

*THE MATERIALS AND TECHNIQUES OF MEDIEVAL
PAINTING, D. V. Thompson.* An invaluable study of carriers
and grounds, binding media, pigments, metals used in painting,
al fresco and al secco techniques, burnishing, etc. used by the
medieval masters. Preface by Bernard Berenson. 239pp. 5⅜ x 8.
T327 Paperbound $1.85

*THE HISTORY AND TECHNIQUE OF LETTERING, A.
Nesbitt.* A thorough history of lettering from the ancient Egyp-
tians to the present, and a 65-page course in lettering for artists.
Every major development in lettering history is illustrated by a
complete aphabet. Fully analyzes such masters as Caslon, Koch,
Garamont, Jenson, and many more. 89 alphabets, 165 other specimens. 317pp. 7½ x 10½. T427 Paperbound $2.00

Dover Books on Art

LANDSCAPE GARDENING IN JAPAN, Josiah Conder. A detailed picture of Japanese gardening techniques and ideas, the artistic principles incorporated in the Japanese garden, and the religious and ethical concepts at the heart of those principles. Preface. 92 illustrations, plus all 40 full-page plates from the Supplement. Index. xv + 299pp. 8⅜ x 11¼.

T1216 Paperbound $2.75

DESIGN AND FIGURE CARVING, E. J. Tangerman. "Anyone who can peel a potato can carve," states the author, and in this unusual book he shows you how, covering every stage in detail from very simple exercises working up to museum-quality pieces. Terrific aid for hobbyists, arts and crafts counselors, teachers, those who wish to make reproductions for the commercial market. Appendix: How to Enlarge a Design. Brief bibliography. Index. 1298 figures. x + 289pp. 5⅜ x 8½.

T1209 Paperbound $1.85

THE STANDARD BOOK OF QUILT MAKING AND COLLECTING, M. Ickis. Even if you are a beginner, you will soon find yourself quilting like an expert, by following these clearly drawn patterns, photographs, and step-by-step instructions. Learn how to plan the quilt, to select the pattern to harmonize with the design and color of the room, to choose materials. Over 40 full-size patterns. Index. 483 illustrations. One color plate. xi + 276pp. 6¾ x 9½.

T582 Paperbound $2.00

LOST EXAMPLES OF COLONIAL ARCHITECTURE, J. M. Howells. This book offers a unique guided tour through America's architectural past, all of which is either no longer in existence or so changed that its original beauty has been destroyed. More than 275 clear photos of old churches, dwelling houses, public buildings, business structures, etc. 245 plates, containing 281 photos and 9 drawings, floorplans, etc. New Index. xvii + 248pp. 7⅞ x 10¾.

T1143 Paperbound $2.75

A HISTORY OF COSTUME, Carl Köhler. The most reliable and authentic account of the development of dress from ancient times through the 19th century. Based on actual pieces of clothing that have survived, using paintings, statues and other reproductions only where originals no longer exist. Hundreds of illustrations, including detailed patterns for many articles. Highly useful for theatre and movie directors, fashion designers, illustrators, teachers. Edited and augmented by Emma von Sichart. Translated by Alexander K. Dallas. 594 illustrations. 464pp. 5⅛ x 7⅛.

T1030 Paperbound $2.75

Dover publishes books on commercial art, art history, crafts, design, art classics; also books on music, literature, science, mathematics, puzzles and entertainments, chess, engineering, biology, philosophy, psychology, languages, history, and other fields. For free circulars write to Dept. DA, Dover Publications, Inc., 180 Varick St., New York, N.Y. 10014.